MASTERING VIRTUAL TEAMS

MASTERING VIRTUAL TEAMS

Strategies, Tools, and Techniques That Succeed

THIRD EDITION

Deborah L. Duarte
Nancy Tennant Snyder

JOSSEY-BASS
A Wiley Imprint
www.josseybass.com

Published by Jossey-Bass
A Wiley Imprint
One Montgomery Street, Suite 1200, San Francisco, CA 94104-4594   www.josseybass.com

Jossey-Bass books and products are available through most bookstores. To contact Jossey-Bass directly call our Customer Care Department within the U.S. at 800-956-7739, outside the U.S. at 317-572-3986, or fax 317-572-4002.

Jossey-Bass also publishes its books in a variety of electronic formats. Some content that appears in print may not be available in electronic books.

Library of Congress Cataloging-in-Publication Data
Duarte, Deborah L., 1956-
  Mastering virtual teams : strategies, tools, and techniques that succeed / Deborah L. Duarte, Nancy Tennant Snyder.—3rd ed.
      p. cm.—(The Jossey-Bass business & management series)
  Includes bibliographical references and index.
  ISBN-13: 978-0-7879-8280-5 (cloth/cd)
  ISBN-10: 0-7879-8280-6 (cloth/cd)
  1. Virtual work teams. I. Snyder, Nancy Tennant, 1957- II. Title. III. Series.
  HD66.D8 2006
  658.4'022—dc22
                              2006000528

Printed in the United States of America

THIRD EDITION
HB Printing   10 9 8 7 6 5 4 3

To Ralphine and Donald:
We remember the laughter, love, and song of you.

CONTENTS

THE AUTHORS

DEBORAH L. DUARTE assists leaders, teams, and organizations in creating environments that promote superior performance. She works with a wide range of clients from Fortune 500 companies that span a number of industries, including entertainment and media, financial services, high technology, telecommunications, durable goods, pharmaceuticals, and industrial products, and from leading government and not-for-profit agencies, such as the National Aeronautics and Space Administration (NASA), the Environmental Protection Agency (EPA), and the United Nations (UN). Her work with virtual teams integrates approaches from a broad range of disciplines, including organizational behavior, social psychology, computer-supported collaborative work, and anthropology. Duarte holds a doctorate in organizational behavior from the George Washington University. She is coauthor, with Nancy Tennant Snyder, of *Strategic Innovation: Embedding Innovation as a Core Competency in Your Organization* (Jossey-Bass, 2003). She has written or cowritten numerous articles on virtual teams and is a frequent speaker on the topics of virtual teams, project management competencies, and change in organizational culture. She is assistant professor at the George Washington University in the Human Resource Development Program in Washington, D.C. She lives with her husband, Clay Durr, in Incline Village, Nevada, and in Arlington, Virginia.

NANCY TENNANT SNYDER has two decades of experience in organizational and leadership development. She is currently the corporate vice president for leadership and core competencies for Whirlpool Corporation. In this capacity, she is responsible for creating and implementing corporate strategies that facilitate globalization and leveraged learning, shared culture, leadership, and operational and core competencies. She also heads the David R. Whitwam Center for Leadership and Lifelong Learning, Whirlpool's Corporate University. She is a faculty member of the Business School of University of Notre Dame, teaching courses in business strategy and vision. She has held executive-level positions at Kaiser Aluminum and has consulted in the areas of globalization and organizational culture change with a number of private and public organizations. She is the author of numerous articles and the coauthor of the best-selling book *Strategic Innovation: Embedding Innovation as a Core Competency in Your Organization* (Jossey-Bass, 2003). She holds a doctorate in organizational behavior from the George Washington University. She and her husband, Robert, live in Benton Harbor, Michigan, and Morgantown, West Virginia.

MASTERING VIRTUAL TEAMS

PREFACE

When we wrote the first edition of *Mastering Virtual Teams* in 1999, we had no idea that our timing for the book would coincide with the start of an era of geopolitical and economic factors that would "flatten" the world. It was only in reading Thomas Friedman's book *The World Is Flat* (Farrar, Straus & Giroux, 2005) that we realized the scope of the convergence of megatrends that shaped a workplace where virtual collaboration had become the norm, not the exception. Consequently, *Mastering Virtual Teams* has had exposure in numerous countries and companies and among countless academics, students, and practitioners who operate in the virtual world that Friedman describes. His triple convergence of workers, workplace, and work processes necessitated multiple forms of communication and collaboration and the escalation of tools and methods for virtual teams. In the handful of years since our book was first published, we have moved from a few of us working on virtual teams once or twice a year to most of us spending some part of every day in a virtual experience. Surely, the next generation of workers will not use the term *virtual* and will be amused by the "olden days" when work was accomplished each and every day between people face-to-face and when the newest miracle of communication in the workplace was the fax machine.

With that said, communication and collaboration are still the two most important factors in team success. The virtual environment fundamentally continues to transform the ways in which teams operate. Technology introduces a critical variable that radically changes the choices for, and the effectiveness of, communication and collaboration. For example, many of us have struggled through at least one boring and nonproductive videoconference in which the images lagged behind the audio to the point of distraction, and many of us have sent an e-mail or voice mail message in an emotional moment and had it misinterpreted by the recipient.

Crossing geographical boundaries also affects the ways in which virtual teams communicate and collaborate. The preference in some cultures to consider the individual first and then the team may make someone who has grown up in a more collective or group-oriented society feel uncomfortable with the independence of teammates. The practice of "saving face" in some cultures can make a slightly negative e-mail message about a team member's work a terribly embarrassing experience. Significant differences in time zones often make virtual team meetings inconvenient for some team members.

Although we have the technological capability to work across time and distance and we dream of teams that leverage technology into competitive advantage, the fact is that we still need new competencies and practices to do these things. Leading and working in virtual teams require much more than computers and technology. Success or failure depends on the attainment of competence in and implementation of practices that facilitate working effectively virtually. It is no longer enough to just understand that technology or national culture affects teamwork; successful team leaders and members need tools, techniques, and decision-making strategies that work in a virtual environment.

Who Will Benefit from This Book

This book was created to provide the how-to for people who work in or lead virtual teams. It is targeted at people from large and small organizations as well as at individuals who work independently and need straightforward and down-to-earth advice to make their virtual teams successful. Readers from all cultures and all types of organizations can benefit from this book.

This book offers theoretical and conceptual information about working in and leading virtual teams as the foundation for more practical strategies. It contains many practical tools, including checklists, tables, and worksheets. It also answers some basic questions and offers strategies and techniques that are especially important for people who are new to virtual teams, for example:

- What types of virtual teams are there, and how does the type of team I work on affect how I work?
- How does a virtual team differ from a traditional team?
- How do I start a virtual team; what are the steps and important considerations?

- What are the technological options open to me, and how do I select the most appropriate ones?
- How do I select a technology that matches my team's task, organizational culture, and team member experience?
- How do the various aspects of national, organizational, and functional cultures affect virtual team performance, and what can I do about them?
- How do I manage the interaction of culture with selecting and using technology, building trust, and team dynamics?
- What are the competencies I need to develop in order to work in or lead a virtual team?
- What is my role as a virtual team leader?
- What is my role as a virtual team member?
- How do I build and maintain trust among team members when we can't see one another?

This book also provides more advanced information in the areas of team dynamics, virtual meeting facilitation, and working adaptively. It answers questions such as these:

- How do I plan for and facilitate a virtual team meeting?
- How do I leverage technology to make virtual meetings more effective than face-to-face ones?
- How do the dynamics of virtual teams differ from those of traditional teams?
- What are the other team variables, and how can I influence them?
- How can I design team interventions?
- What styles and leadership practices work in an adaptive and virtual environment?

Both of us work in or consult to bottom-line and results-oriented organizations in the public and private sectors. This affects the ways in which we view leadership and the roles of leaders and team members. Although it is likely that our biases will emerge at times and that our North American cultural perspective will show, we have tried to maintain broad and balanced cultural and organizational perspectives.

How to Use This Book

Mastering Virtual Teams has three parts. In Part One, "Understanding Virtual Teams," we define and explore the complexities of virtual teams. We present the important factors that make a virtual team different from a traditional one. In Chapter One, we describe different types of virtual teams and present a set of critical success factors.

We offer team leaders and members recommendations for action to ensure that these success factors are in place. In Chapter Two, we sort through the myriad of information about technology, integrate it, and offer practical guidance about the different technological options available to virtual teams. We provide guidance about what works best in different situations and present criteria to evaluate the usefulness of each technology for a particular team. In Chapter Three, we examine the ways in which national, organizational, and functional cultures affect the performance of virtual teams. We also investigate how culture can be used to leverage performance and, on the darker side, how it can be used as an excuse for nonperformance. Part One provides a foundation for understanding the pragmatic advice in the remainder of the book.

In Part Two, "Creating Virtual Teams," we present the nuts and bolts and the intricacies of starting a virtual team. This part provides straightforward suggestions, checklists, and worksheets about startup strategies that make virtual teams work. In Chapter Four, we introduce a set of myths and realities about leading virtual teams. We translate these into seven areas of competence that are critical for virtual team leaders. Each type of competence is accompanied by recommendations for developmental activities. A competence assessment is also offered as an individual development planning tool. In Chapter Five, we present a step-by-step process for starting a virtual team. This includes directions, checklists, agendas, worksheets, and techniques for obtaining sponsors, chartering the team, conducting team orientation meetings, team building with different cultural groups, developing team norms, using technology, and planning communication. In Chapter Six, we present two critical roles for virtual team members: autonomy and collaboration. We build a set of team member skills around these two roles and offer competence assessment tools and recommendations for personal development. In Chapter Seven, we cover the critical element of building trust in a virtual team environment. We also describe how trust can be affected by national culture and by the use of technology. This chapter presents a variety of tools, checklists, and exercises that are useful in building and maintaining trust.

In Part Three, "Mastering Virtual Teams," we offer more advanced information for virtual team leaders and members. In Chapter Eight, we give recommendations for facilitating virtual team meetings. This includes methods for planning and running virtual meetings and for using technology so that the virtual meeting has the potential to surpass a face-to-face meeting. In Chapter Nine, we present a model of team development and team dynamics for virtual teams. We recommend strategies for tracking and diagnosing a virtual team's effectiveness and provide interventions for dealing with typical problems of virtual teams. In Chapter Ten, we present a model for working and leading in adaptive and unpredictable situations. We also present eight practices that are factors in the success of virtual teams.

New to the Third Edition

The third edition has a number of new components. Given the reality of Moore's law, we updated the technology section to include instant messaging and personal computing devices. We have added more worksheets and checklists and updated some of the existing ones based on our experience. We have also deleted the specific references to particular companies and their practices and now focus more on ideas, concepts, tools, and methods. This is a reflection of that fact that many companies that were lauded in the 1990s are no longer on top or no longer exist. It is also a reflection of feedback that readers found the checklists and tools much more useful than the examples. Finally, we added a new section in most of the chapters, "Near Virtual Disaster." These stories of lessons learned are based on firsthand knowledge of problems that occur in a virtual world that did not occur in the real world. The rapid maturing of virtual teams has created a new and different set of problems and opportunities for digitized disasters.

Acknowledgments

Part of what made writing this book so enjoyable was the wonderful support of colleagues, family members, and friends who believed in us and provided ongoing encouragement throughout the writing process. Our husbands, Clay Durr and Robert Snyder, helped proofread and critique many drafts of the manuscript. Clay was also responsible for much of the research and content in Chapter Two.

Blythe Handy contributed countless acts of thoughtfulness and assistance. Jan Moore, Dale Crossman, Debbie Morris, Nikki Adams, Mark Linaugh, Lorence Harmer, Tammy Patrick, Kristan Murphy, and the many colleagues at Whirlpool have been a source of support and caring throughout all three editions of this book. Special thanks go to Dave Whitwam, chairman and CEO of Whirlpool, who offered motivation, interest, and support. We also want to thank Robert Quinn, of the University of Michigan, for his encouragement and advice and Dan O'Neil, John Mankins, and John Newberg for information on NASA's Virtual Research Center.

Both of us are blessed with wonderful families. Thanks go to Deborah's mother, Jackie Klotz, who has expressed nothing but pride in our accomplishments, and our brothers and sisters, Susan Peacock, Mike Klotz, Steve Klotz, Janet Dunn, Linda Tennant, and Diane Rudash, and their families, who provided laughter and fun when we needed it most.

The people at Jossey-Bass define true virtual teamwork. In particular, we thank our editor, Neal Maillet, who helped us get this third edition up and running.

We would also like to thank the people who reviewed the manuscript and contributed their valuable comments and recommendations: Sam Garnett, Danny Mittleman, and Gail Greenstein, among many others.

Please feel free to contact us at dduarte2@ix.netcom.com and Nancy_T_Snyder@ whirlpool.com.

February 2006   DEBORAH L. DUARTE
                                                                    Arlington, Virginia
                                                                    NANCY TENNANT SNYDER
                                                                    Benton Harbor, Michigan

CHECKLISTS

CHECKLISTS AND TABLES ON THE CD-ROM

PART ONE

UNDERSTANDING VIRTUAL TEAMS

CHAPTER ONE

CRITICAL SUCCESS FACTORS
FOR VIRTUAL TEAMS

In today's business environment, organizations must adapt quickly or die. Gaining competitive advantage in a global environment means continually reshaping the organization to maximize strengths, address threats, and increase speed.[1] The use of virtual teams has become a common way of doing this.[2] The formation of virtual teams allows organizations to draw talent quickly from different functions, locations, and organizations. The goal is to leverage intellectual capital and apply it as quickly as possible. The methods that organizations use to manage this process can mean the difference between success and failure.

Consider the example of a team in a global consumer products firm. This product development team, with members from around the world, had just completed the development of a new product. When the team unveiled the product to the senior staff of the organization, it included a description of the way the team worked. The presentation showed an icon of an airplane, with the entire team of twenty-two people traveling from country to country. The team members had continually moved from site to site for activities such as status reviews, design meetings, and prototyping sessions. The cost of the travel was tremendous, not only for hotels and airline tickets but also in terms of the human costs of being away from home and lost work time and productivity. In addition, talent from other parts of the organization was not leveraged in this effort—if you were not "on the plane," your ideas were not heard.

Contrast this with most other organizations that form world-class teams, with membership from many different locations and functions, to quickly address customer problems, develop products, and deliver services. These teams often operate virtually, without the physical limitations of distance, time, and organizational boundaries. They use electronic collaboration technology and other techniques to leverage the best talent where they might reside, lower travel and facility costs, reduce project schedules, and improve decision-making time and communication.

Organizations that do not use virtual teams effectively may be fighting an uphill battle in a global, competitive, and rapidly changing environment. Organizations that will succeed in today's business environment have found new ways of working across boundaries through systems, processes, technology, and people. They will make technology a valued partner in developing and delivering competitive solutions.

Understanding how to work in or lead a virtual team is now a fundamental requirement for people in many organizations. Many who began their career leading teams in a face-to-face environment find themselves leading teams virtually, sometimes not seeing team members face to face more than once or twice a year. This presents the challenge of translating what worked in an in-person environment to a virtual one.

It is also now increasingly common to encounter people who lead or work on virtual teams who do not have a great deal of experience working on teams face to face. Most of today's large consulting firms do a large majority of their work virtually. Consultants who join these firms may never have the opportunity to work on or lead a traditional team in a face-to-face environment. They are immediately placed in situations that are more virtual than traditional. In this case, these individuals may not even have baseline experience to draw from—and on the other hand, they also may not have bad habits to unlearn.

The fact is that leading a virtual team is not like leading a traditional team. People who lead and work on virtual teams need to have special skills, including an understanding of human dynamics and performance without the benefit of normal social cues, knowledge of how to manage across functional areas and national cultures, skill in managing their careers and others without the benefit of face-to-face interaction, and the ability to use leverage and electronic communication technology as their primary means of communicating and collaborating.

Types of Virtual Teams

There are many different configurations of virtual teams. One of the central themes of this book is that the task affects how a virtual team is managed. Although virtual teams can undertake almost any kind of assignment, team leaders and members need to have a solid understanding of the type of virtual team they work on and the special challenges each type presents. What these teams have in common with all teams is that team members must communicate and collaborate to get work done or to produce a product. Virtual teams, unlike traditional ones, however, must accomplish this by working across distance, time, and organizational boundaries and by using technology to facilitate as their primary means of communication and collaboration. There are seven basic types of virtual teams.[3]

- Networked teams
- Parallel teams
- Project or product development teams
- Work, functional, or production teams
- Service teams
- Management teams
- Action teams

Networked Teams

A networked virtual team consists of individuals who collaborate to achieve a common goal or purpose. Such teams frequently cross time, distance, and organizational boundaries. Typically, there is a lack of clear definition between a network team and the organization, in that membership is frequently diffuse and fluid, with team members rotating on and off the team as their expertise is needed. Team members may not even be aware of all the individuals, work teams, or organizations in the network.

Examples of this type of virtual team are often found in consulting firms and in high-technology organizations. For example, one virtual team received a request from a client to quickly research and identify a set of best practices for managing the implementation of a large supply chain project. Although the consultants did not have all the answers themselves, they were able to tap into their network of external partners and internal and external databases and provide a set of best practices for the client within a few days.

Organizations that develop technological products can also use networked virtual teams. Many research and development organizations use networked teams for many activities because the specialized expertise to solve new problems or engage in complex discovery processes usually never resides in a single organization or location. Team members for these types of teams are often drawn from many different nations, think tanks, universities, corporations, and nonprofit organizations. Team members from different organizations come in and out of the network as their expertise is needed to make recommendations.

Parallel Teams

Parallel virtual teams carry out special assignments, tasks, or functions that the regular organization does not want to or is not equipped to perform. Parallel teams are also used when expertise does not reside in one location or in one organization. Such teams frequently cross time, distance, and organizational boundaries. A parallel team is different from a networked team in that it has a distinct membership that sets it apart from the rest of the organization. It is clear who is on the team and who is not. The members of a parallel team typically work together on a short-term basis to make recommendations for improvements in organizational processes or to address specific business issues. Virtual parallel teams are becoming a fairly common way for multinational and global organizations to make recommendations about worldwide processes and systems that take a global perspective.

One consumer goods company used a virtual parallel team to make specific recommendations for a global customer loyalty system. Team members came from around the world and were supplemented by participants from an external consulting organization. After its recommendations were made to the CEO, the team dissolved. Much of the work of this team involved data collection and analysis by individual team members. The collaborative work was often accomplished in audioconferences at 7:00 A.M. Eastern Standard Time (to accommodate people from all time zones) by using e-mail to communicate and pass on "static" information, a team Web site for documenting progress, and instant messaging for real-time communication. Like many people who work on parallel teams, the team members had other projects and accountabilities.

Project or Product Development Teams

Virtual project teams and product development teams can also cross time, distance, and organizational boundaries. Team members conduct projects for users or customers for a defined but extended period of time. A typical result is a new product, information system, or organizational process. The difference between a project team and a parallel team is that a project team usually exists for a longer period of time and has a charter to make decisions, not just recommendations. A project team is similar to a networked team in that team members may move on and off the project as their expertise is needed. It is different from a networked team in that membership is more clearly delineated from the rest of the organization, and a final product is clearly defined.

Most product-focused technology and scientific organizations are well versed in the use of project or product development teams. The use of virtual teams expands the opportunities to leverage expertise from wherever it resides to develop products and services that have competitive advantage.

Work, Functional, or Production Teams

Virtual work, functional, and production teams perform regular and ongoing work. Such teams usually exist in one function, such as accounting, finance, training, or research and development. They have clearly defined membership and can be distinguished from other parts of the organization. Many work or production teams are now beginning to operate virtually and to cross time and distance boundaries. Many organizations now have business centers that operate globally around the clock, and work teams that service customers may exist in most time zones around the world.

It is has become commonplace for people on virtual work teams to telecommute from home. They have access to workflow processes over the firm's intranet, which allows them to work as a group on development activities. Team members usually meet face to face once or twice each year for a conference.

Service Teams

Service and technical help teams are now usually distributed across distance and time. Network and technical support are usually continuous operations, with technicians and call center personnel located around the world taking turns dealing with network problems and upgrades. The staff "follow the sun" and are situated so that one team is operational at all times. Each team works during its members' daylight hours and transitions work and problems to the next designated time zone at the end of the day.

Management Teams

Management teams can be separated by distance and time. Today, many management teams are dispersed across a country or around the world but work collaboratively on a daily basis. Many companies have executive team members who hold a number of different passports and live in many parts of the world and collaborate on a regular basis by means of audioconferences or videoconferences focused on the achievement of corporate goals and objectives. The United States Army's chief of staff operates his staff as a virtual team. Staff members communicate regularly via e-mail and use a chat room on an Internet Web-based network to discuss important issues as they arise.

Action Teams

Action teams can also work virtually. Such teams offer immediate responses, often to emergency situations. They cross distance and organizational boundaries. A weather team at a television station is a good example of a virtual action team. During a weather emergency, action team members are distributed in the field. The meteorologist at the television station uses radar and satellite information to tell where tornadoes may be forming and directs field crew movement toward those locations. The meteorologist analyzes the data that the crews send back and communicates the results and possible implications immediately to viewers.

The way in which NASA works during a mission is an excellent example of a virtual action team. During a flight, mission operations, usually located in Houston, collaborates with the astronauts, with tracking stations around the globe, and with experts, such as engineers and scientists, in different locations, in order to ensure that the mission proceeds as planned.

The Complexity of the Virtual Environment

It is easy to characterize virtual teams using the same categories as traditional teams. However, virtual teams can be much more complex. There are two primary reasons why virtual teams are more complex: (1) they cross boundaries related to time, distance (geography), and organization, and (2) they use electronic technological means to communicate (share information) and collaborate (work together to produce a product).

As the longitudinal distance between team members increases, so do differences in time zones. This makes communicating and collaborating at the same time problematic. Working across national boundaries complicates the situation because differences in language, culture, and access to technology impede effective communication and collaboration.

As members from different organizations join a virtual team, integration of work methods, organizational cultures, technology, and goals make communication and collaboration more difficult. Partners and suppliers often have conflicting goals and organizational cultures. This holds true even when team members come from different functional areas within the same organization. For example, people from marketing and human resources frequently use a different set of work processes than those from more technical areas such as engineering and information systems.

Finally, complexity is increased by the number of different choices for team interaction. Traditional teams typically interact face to face, at least some of the time. Virtual team interactions, however, are almost always mediated by electronic communication and collaboration technology. Interactions fall into four categories: (1) same time, same place (like face-to-face meetings); (2) same time, different place (such as an audioconference or videoconference); (3) different time, same place (such as using a chat room or a shared file on a network); and (4) different time, different place (such as exchanges of e-mail or voice mail messages and podcasting). The selection of technology and choice of interaction vary according to factors such as the type of team, the nature of its task, and the members' access to technology.

Checklist 1.1 provides a way to categorize your virtual team and to determine the number of factors that affect complexity. Understanding the type of team you work on and its complexity will help you get the most out of the remaining chapters of this book.

CHECKLIST 1.1. TYPE OF VIRTUAL TEAM.

Part 1. Team Description
Instructions: Check the description that best matches your team.

Type of Team	Description
☐ Network	Team membership is diffuse and fluid; members come and go as needed. Team lacks clear boundaries with the organization.
☐ Parallel	Team has clear boundaries and distinct membership. Team works in short term to develop recommendations for an improvement in a process or system.
☐ Project or Product Development	Team has fluid membership, clear boundaries, and a defined customer, technical requirement, and output. Longer-term team task is nonroutine, and team has decision-making authority.
☐ Work, Functional, or Production	Team has distinct membership and clear boundaries. Members perform regular and ongoing work, usually in one functional area.
☐ Service	Team has distinct membership and supports ongoing customer, network activity.
☐ Management	Team has distinct membership and works on a regular basis to lead corporate activities.
☐ Action	Team deals with immediate action, usually in an emergency situation. Membership may be fluid or distinct.

Part 2. Team Complexity
Instructions: Check as many as apply.

My team . . .

1. Has members from more than one organization	☐
2. Has members from more than one function	☐
3. Has members who transition on and off the team	☐
4. Is geographically dispersed over more than three contiguous time zones	☐
5. Is geographically dispersed so that some team members are 8–12 hours apart	☐
6. Has members from more than two national cultures	☐
7. Has members whose native language is different from the majority of other team members	☐
8. Has members who do not have equal access to electronic communication and collaboration technology	☐
9. Has members who are not formally assigned to the team.	☐
Total number of categories checked:	☐

Complexity Index: 1–2 = some complexity; 3–5 = moderate complexity; 6–8 = high complexity

Critical Success Factors for Virtual Teams

The business justification for virtual teams is strong. They increase speed and agility and leverage expertise and vertical integration between organizations to make resources readily available. Virtual teams also lessen the disruption of people's lives because the people do not have to travel to meet. Team members can broaden their careers and perspectives by working across organizations and cultures and on a variety of projects and tasks.

Although the effective use of electronic communication and collaboration technology is fundamental to the success of a virtual team, virtual teams entail much more than technology and computers. When virtual teams and their leaders are asked about successes and failures, they rarely mention technology as a primary reason for either. Bill Davidow, a former executive with Intel and Hewlett-Packard, comments: "Information and communication technology provides an infrastructure for the corporation to communicate with customers and deliver information necessary for decision making. . . . If management insists on maintaining a purely functional organization or does not empower workers, information systems will add little value."[4]

There are seven critical success factors for virtual teams, of which technology is only one. The others are human resource policies, training and development for team leaders and team members, standard organizational and team processes, organizational culture, leadership, and leader and member competencies. These are discussed in more detail later in this chapter.

Of course, all the critical success factors do not have to be in place for virtual teams to succeed. The mere implementation of virtual teams can actually put an organization on the road toward success. Because successful virtual teams require certain conditions, the existence of the teams will, over time, help bring about the infrastructure conditions that make them work.

Teams usually recognize that they need certain things to succeed, such as high levels of autonomy to do their jobs, standard team initiation processes, structured communication plans, and appropriate electronic communication and collaboration technology for all team members. Organizations that are most successful recognize that while all the factors do not need to be in place at once, there needs to be a plan to ensure that factors are systematically addressed. Many of the processes that organizations formally institutionalize get their start through the "bootstrap" approach of their first virtual teams.

This book is not specifically about preparing the organization for virtual teams. Its focus is on tools and techniques for team leaders and team members. However, team leaders and members influence the implementation of critical success factors that are associated with team success.

Let's take a look at the critical success factors for organizations. First, complete the diagnostic tool in Checklist 1.2. Your results can direct your attention to the categories of success factors that affect your situation. Although you may not be able to influence all of them, the results can serve to direct your actions when it is possible or help you develop a case to present to management for virtual team resources.

Seven factors affect the probability of a virtual team's success:

- Human resource policies
- Training and on-the-job education and development
- Standard organizational and team processes
- Use of electronic collaboration and communication technology
- Organizational culture
- Leadership support of virtual teams
- Team leader and team member competencies

Human Resource Policies

Human resource policies should support working virtually. Systems must be integrated and aligned to recognize, support, and reward the people who work on and lead virtual teams.

Career Development Systems. Team leaders can help support virtual team members by providing career opportunities and assignments that are comparable to those in traditional team settings. Applying promotion and career development policies and actions fairly to people who work in virtual settings helps reinforce the perception that working virtually is an accepted career option. Virtual team members often mention the fear that they will be overlooked for promotional opportunities because they are not seen every day. This fear is not unfounded. Managers who lose visual and verbal proximity to their employees often put up the strongest resistance to alternative work and team arrangements.[5] Virtual team leaders must ensure that the members of virtual teams have the same career development opportunities as the members of traditional teams.

Rewarding Cross-Boundary Work and Results. Organizational reward and recognition systems often favor individual and functional work. Virtual team members, however, frequently operate in a cross-functional or cross-organizational environment. Changes must be made in the ways in which people are recognized and rewarded. Leaders must develop performance objectives for team members that include working across boundaries and sharing information to support virtual teamwork.

In addition, performance measures must be adapted to reward results. In a traditional office environment, where people are seen putting in effort every day, it is relatively

CHECKLIST 1.2. ASSESSING CRITICAL SUCCESS FACTORS.

Instructions: Check the response that best matches your organization on each item.

Section One: Human Resource Policies	Strongly Disagree 1	Disagree 2	Neither Agree nor Disagree 3	Agree 4	Strongly Agree 5
1. Career development systems address the needs of virtual team members.					
2. Reward systems reward/recognize working across boundaries and working virtually.					
3. Results are what is rewarded.					
4. Nontraditional work arrangements, such as telecommuting, are actively supported.					
Section Two: **Training and Development**	Strongly Disagree 1	Disagree 2	Neither Agree nor Disagree 3	Agree 4	Strongly Agree 5
5. There is good access to technical training.					
6. There is access to training in working across cultures.					
7. There are methods available for continual and just-in-time learning, such as Web-based training.					
8. There are mechanisms, such as lessons-learned databases, for sharing across boundaries.					

(continued)

CHECKLIST 1.2. (CONTINUED).

Section Three: Standard Organizational Processes	Strongly Disagree 1	Disagree 2	Neither Agree nor Disagree 3	Agree 4	Strongly Agree 5
9. There are standard and agreed-on technical team processes used throughout the organization and with partners.					
10. There are standard and agreed-on "soft" team processes used throughout the organization and with partners.					
11. Adaptation of processes is encouraged when necessary.					
12. The culture supports shared ways of doing business across teams and partners.					
Section Four: Electronic Communication and Collaboration Technology	Strongly Disagree 1	Disagree 2	Neither Agree nor Disagree 3	Agree 4	Strongly Agree 5
13. There are consistent standards for electronic communication and collaboration tools across the organization.					
14. There are ample resources to buy and support state-of-the-art electronic communication and collaboration technology.					
15. People from all functional areas have equal access to, and are skilled in using, electronic communication and collaboration technology.					
16. People from all geographic areas have equal access to, and are skilled in using, electronic communication and collaboration technology.					

(continued)

CHECKLIST 1.2. (CONTINUED).

Section Five: Organizational Culture	Strongly Disagree 1	Disagree 2	Neither Agree nor Disagree 3	Agree 4	Strongly Agree 5
17. The culture can be described as "high trust."					
18. There is high trust between this organization and its suppliers and partners.					
19. Teamwork and collaboration are the norm.					
20. People from different cultures are valued here.					
Section Six: Leadership	Strongly Disagree 1	Disagree 2	Neither Agree nor Disagree 3	Agree 4	Strongly Agree 5
21. Leaders set high expectations for virtual team performance.					
22. Leaders help gain the support of customers and other stakeholders.					
23. Leaders allocate resources for the training and technology associated with virtual teams.					
24. Leaders model behaviors such as working across boundaries and using technology effectively.					

(continued)

CHECKLIST 1.2. (CONTINUED).

Section Seven: Competence	Strongly Disagree 1	Disagree 2	Neither Agree nor Disagree 3	Agree 4	Strongly Agree 5
25. Team leaders are experienced in working in virtual environments.					
26. Team members are experienced in working in virtual environments.					
27. Team leaders are experienced in working across organizational and cultural boundaries.					
28. Team members are experienced in working across organizational and cultural boundaries.					

Analyzing Your Results

Average your scores in each of the seven areas:

Critical Success Category	Average Score in this category (add total and divide by 4):
Human Resource Policies	
Training and Development	
Standard Organizational Processes	
Electronic Communication and Collaboration Technology	
Organizational Culture	
Leadership	
Competence	
Overall average (total divided by 28):	

An overall score of 4.0 to 5.0 in any one category and as an average of all categories is excellent.

Moderate scores are in the 2.5 to 3.99 range, and low scores fall between 0 and 2.49.

Low scores in specific areas may indicate some of the challenges you face as a virtual team leader. Scoring low in technology, for example, may tell you that all your team members may not have equal access to electronic collaboration technology. In this case, you may need to make a case for funding for groupware. The text provides an explanation of each category and actions to attain success criteria.

easy to at least partially reward people for effort as well as for results. In a virtual environment, effort is more difficult to discern. When IBM went to a virtual environment, a shift to a reward structure that was based more on results than on effort was a major part of the transition.[6] Translating measures of performance from a face-to-face environment into ones that work in a virtual environment involves working to make all performance measures focused on outcomes. It is important to note that when measures are changed for virtual team members, they must also be changed for in-house team members.

The use of formal and informal recognition of virtual teamwork through "on the spot" awards, bonuses, and other mechanisms can also reinforce the perception that working virtually is valued. You can use Web-based technology, such as setting up a site for virtual team "best practices" and advertising team successes and performance, as a way to publicly recognize people in a virtual setting. You also can use examples of your virtual team's success in speeches, presentations, and discussions with other team leaders and with management.

Providing Resources and Support for Working Virtually. Create and support policies that provide your team with technical support for working remotely. All team members should have equal and immediate access to electronic communication and collaboration technology, training, and technical support. Many virtual team leaders set a standard for technology and make certain that everyone has access to the same hardware, intranet and Internet connections, and applications. They ask the information systems group to assist in the implementation. Many organizations now have "virtual SWAT teams" that help virtual team members set up their systems to ensure that they have access to the best and latest technology.

Training and On-the-Job Education and Development

Formal training in using technology is vital for success. For example, team leaders at the World Bank believed that underfunded technological training for team leaders and team members was one reason that their efforts to implement groupware did not fully succeed the first time. Money was spent on the technology—machines, applications, and compatibility—but not on teaching people how to effectively use it.[7]

Learning how to use technology is not enough to guarantee success. Team leaders should make certain that they get the training and support they need to be adept at facilitating meetings using technical and nontechnical methods. Training in facilitation skills should also be an integral part of a development curriculum for team leaders and team members.

In addition to a formal training curriculum in using technology and facilitation, make certain that the team members have access to continual online training and technical support on other relevant topics such as working collaboratively and working across organizational boundaries. Ask your training department about the feasibility of creating and implementing these types programs for virtual team members. Most organizations who use virtual teams effectively now provide many of their technical and leadership classes through their intranet, so people can select when and where they want to learn. In addition, training, tools, and support are upgraded on a regular basis to ensure that they are state-of-the-art.

Create and implement systems for sharing knowledge across functions, projects, and organizations. Shared lessons, databases, knowledge repositories, and chat rooms are used in organizations that embrace virtual teamwork. Some company Web sites contain places where "lessons learned" are stored. They also have bulletin boards where team leaders can ask questions and receive suggestions from other team leads.

Standard Organizational and Team Processes

Consider developing and implementing standard team processes. The use of standard processes reduces the time needed for team startup and may eliminate the need for unnecessary reinvention of operating practices each time a team is chartered. Practices need to be flexible, however, to promote adaptation to a particular virtual team's situation. Common standard technical processes, especially for parallel, project, or network teams, might include the following:

- Definitions of requirements
- Estimates of costs
- Procurement
- Team charters
- Project planning
- Documentation and document sharing
- Reporting
- Controlling

It also is a good idea to define the preferred software for each of these major processes. Many organizations use standard project management software packages so that any team, virtual or face-to-face, is familiar with and trained in using that package.

All successful virtual teams have agreed team processes in "soft" areas such as the establishment of team norms, conflict resolution procedures, and communication protocols. Experienced virtual teams also prepare team charters that delineate suggested team norms and communication standards. They use these as starting points to come up with processes suitable for their unique situations. Reinforce and expect the use of both technical and soft processes from the team.

Electronic Collaboration and Communication Technology

As a virtual team leader, you will need to select electronic collaboration and communication technology that meets the needs of your team and the situation. You also will need to ensure that the organization is ready to support your technical needs. Introducing the electronic communication and collaboration technology needed for virtual teamwork, such as desktop videoconferencing, team Web sites, or groupware, requires that four primary organizational conditions be in place:[8]

1. The organization has a well-funded, respected, and established information systems staff whose members are experienced in installing and supporting electronic collaboration technology in many different locations.
2. There is commitment by the organization to keep personal computer systems as up-to-date as possible, regardless of a person's title or duties. When systems fall behind, the costs of upgrades and the time to introduce them mounts quickly. Productivity may also fall as people spend time attempting to fix their equipment or work around it.
3. The organization has a well-maintained corporate network that has room to expand to meet the needs of more complex systems and users.
4. The organization has a set of leaders who are willing to model the use of advanced forms of electronic collaboration and communication technology.

If your organization is lacking in any of these four areas, you might consider adopting a less complex technology suite. In either case, it is important to select a reasonable set of standards for your team in electronic communication and collaboration technology. Standards should meet the business needs of the team and match its mission and strategy.[9] A team that needs to communicate and work collaboratively, for example, must have a minimum set of standards for technology. For communication, this includes phones, audioconferencing equipment, voice mail, fax capability, and access to a common e-mail system that allows people to send messages and exchange files and access to the company's intranet or the Internet. Videoconferencing, calendar scheduling, real-time data conferencing, electronic meeting systems, collaborative writing tools, personal computing devices, team Web sites, instant messaging, and whiteboards can be added if the strategy calls for intensive collaborative work or if sufficient information systems resources exist to make the technology work reliably. Make certain that external partners and suppliers have access to compatible communication and collaboration technology if they are considered part of the team.

Ensure that skill in using the electronic communication and collaboration technology is equally distributed among team members from different functional areas, geographical locations, and partner organizations. Often skill and use of electronic communication and collaboration technology is more prevalent in technical functions, such as engineering and information systems, than in less technical areas, such as marketing, human resources, and finance. If this is the case, there is a risk that team members from less technical areas may be perceived by other teammates as having less status.

Ensure that the technology used by each virtual team is available to all team members, wherever they are located. One team leader ran into trouble when some of her team members in a partner organization in a developing country did not have access to the same type and level of technology as the team leader. Some organizations and national cultures use technology to signify status or just have trouble affording new technology. Of course, this puts the team members at a disadvantage relative to their teammates and decreases productivity.

Finally, factor electronic collaboration hardware and software directly into the team's budget. It is important to recognize that the benefits of technology grow over time. Virtual teams do reduce costs, but often there is an up-front and long-term investment for technology and training to make them work effectively. The more people and teams work virtually, the more quickly these business practices will translate into savings.

Organizational Culture

Organizational culture includes norms regarding the free flow of information, shared leadership, and cross-boundary collaboration. Help create organizational norms and values that focus on collaboration, respecting and working with people from all cultures, keeping criticism constructive, and sharing information. The organization's culture sets the standard for how virtual team members work together. An adaptive, technologically advanced, and nonhierarchical organization is more likely to succeed with virtual teams than a highly structured, control-oriented organization.[10]

The success of virtual teams is related to how the organization fosters or impedes trust between itself and its external partners. Treating partners as less than equal, hoarding information, forgetting to share data or results in a timely manner, and using competitive or proprietary information inappropriately can erode trust quickly.

If the organization is multinational or global, norms must honor different ways of doing business if they are to be effective. Devise policies for doing business in different cultures. Be aware that legal issues, such as who owns the copyrights on designs, can become murky when teams are working across national boundaries.[11]

Many virtual team leaders cannot affect organizational culture with the same clout as senior managers can. It is possible, however, to create a "microclimate" that supports effective norms and values. Team leaders who act in a conscious manner to build trust across boundaries and to share information and power create environments in which this type of culture can grow from the ground up.

Leadership

For virtual teams to succeed, the organization's leadership must establish a culture that values teamwork, communication, learning, outcome-based performance, and capitalizing on diversity. The key to establishing an organizational culture that promotes virtual teamwork is that managers and virtual team leaders at all levels must be open to change and must support virtual teamwork (see Table 1.1).

Virtual team leaders and members can help managers develop supportive behaviors. They can offer specific suggestions to management regarding the four categories of leadership behaviors that encourage virtual team performance: communicating, establishing expectations, allocating resources, and modeling desired behaviors.

First, it is critically important to communicate throughout the organization that working across time and distance and with organizational partners is not just a temporary fad but a new way of doing business, one that leverages knowledge and skills and capitalizes on diversity. This includes assigning virtual teams important and high-visibility tasks and projects and reporting the benefits and results of their work so that virtual teamwork is respected in the organization.

TABLE 1.1. LEADERSHIP BEHAVIORS THAT SUPPORT VIRTUAL TEAM SUCCESS.

Communicating	Establishing Expectations	Allocating Resources	Modeling Behaviors
• Communicate the business necessity of virtual teams. • Communicate that virtual teamwork is respected. • Discuss the value of diversity and of leveraging skills. • Communicate the benefits and results of working virtually.	• Define how virtual teams work and set clear procedures and goals. • Set high standards for virtual team performance. • Establish expectations of customers and other important stakeholders. • Factor in startup costs and times.	• Allocate time and money for training for virtual team leaders and members. • Allocate time and money for travel for team leaders for face-to-face meetings. • Dedicate resources for technology.	• Align cross-functional and regional goals and objectives. • Work together on management team across geographic and cultural boundaries. • Solicit input from and display trust in team members. • Show flexibility.

Second, it is important to establish clear expectations about how virtual teams work. Procedures and goals must be clear so that virtual team members know how they are to work and what their objectives are. With all the new things they must learn about operating in a virtual team, the team members need clear guidelines and objectives to steer by. The other members of the organization also need to understand how virtual teams operate and that the teams' end goals are aligned with organizational objectives and are in effect the same as those of traditional teams. Setting high expectations for performance also strengthens the perception that virtual teams deliver results.

It also is important to gain the support of customers and other major stakeholders by helping them see the benefits of virtual teamwork. This includes establishing expectations about the virtual work environment and how virtual teamwork is going to affect their contacts with team members. Leaders must stress the benefits, such as lower costs and what the stakeholders have to gain, and find ways to make customers part of the change. One best practice is to invite external customers who work with virtual teams to team kickoff sessions in which norms and communication plans are discussed. Customers and other stakeholders can also be offered training in team technology. Customers can be provided with software to "sit in" on team meetings. This helps customers who are unsure of the virtual team approach become more comfortable with it.

Leaders can also work with stakeholders such as leaders and managers from other functions or suppliers who interface with the teams, to help them understand and support the virtual team concept. They can make it clear to peers and to other managers in the organization that virtual teams work as hard and as productively as traditional teams. Leaders can become adept at providing evidence, including schedule and cost data, to sway more skeptical stakeholders. Finally, they can help establish reasonable expectations about the time it takes to realize a return on the investment. The paradox is that the complexities of working across time and distance can, in the short run, lead to increased costs and longer cycle times because of difficulties with operating procedures and startup issues.[12]

Third, leaders who allocate resources for training, technology, and travel send strong signals that bolster the message that virtual teams are important. Chartering virtual teams to work in an underfunded environment is a prescription for failure. Time and money must be allocated for training for virtual team members in areas such as cross-cultural work, project management, and technology. Time and money must be allocated for team leaders to travel for face-to-face meetings with team members at the beginning of the team's life and whenever necessary thereafter. Resources must also be dedicated to acquiring and maintaining the technology needed to facilitate the team's work.

Fourth and most important, effective leaders model the behaviors they expect. They align cross-functional and regional goals and objectives. They work with other managers across geographical and cultural boundaries. They solicit team members' input and demonstrate trust in their judgment, particularly in the members' functional areas of expertise. Effective team leaders show flexibility, changing as business conditions dictate. They do not expect behaviors from others that they do not engage in themselves.

Team Leader Competencies

The challenges that virtual team leaders face are immense. Many report that they feel as if they are the "glue" that holds their teams together. They have to establish trust in an environment with little or no face-to-face contact or feedback. These challenges necessitate the development of an additional set of competencies that complement the skills for leading traditional teams. These competencies are as follows:

1. Coaching and managing performance without traditional forms of feedback
2. Selecting and appropriately using electronic communication and collaboration technology
3. Leading in a cross-cultural environment
4. Managing the performance, development, and career development of team members
5. Building and maintaining trust
6. Networking across hierarchical and organizational boundaries
7. Developing and adapting organizational processes to meet the demands of the team

Team leaders can champion their own development by deliberately undertaking training and on-the-job assignments that build competence in these areas. Each area of competence is covered thoroughly in Chapter Four.

Team Member Competencies

The people who work as virtual team members have to develop their own competencies. First, virtual teamwork is not for everyone. Serving on a virtual team may seem too transitory for some individuals who need face-to-face interaction and stability in a work environment. Without the structure of a real-world setting and day-to-day contact with team members, they may feel alone or adrift.

All members of traditional and virtual teams need solid grounding in their respective disciplines. However, virtual team members need new competencies. Team leaders can help facilitate competency development by working with team members to devise learning plans that use training and on-the-job assignments. The definitions of team member competencies will vary, depending on the team's type, mission, and composition. There is, however, a relatively stable set of six critical competencies:

1. Project management techniques
2. Networking across functional, hierarchical, and organizational boundaries
3. Using electronic communication and collaboration technology effectively
4. Setting personal boundaries and being assertive about being included
5. Managing one's time and one's career
6. Working across cultural and functional boundaries
7. A high level of interpersonal awareness

Over time, most people can develop the competencies that are needed to work virtually. Adequate training, education, and leadership support and feedback can speed development. More detail about team member competencies is provided in Chapter Six.

Points to Remember

1. Virtual teams are more complex than traditional teams because of factors associated with working across time, distance, and organizational boundaries and the need to use technology to communicate and collaborate. Many employees now and in the future will never obtain the baseline set of skills associated with working on or leading a real-world team but will instead jump right into leading virtual teams.
2. There are many different types of virtual teams. In fact, most organizations use some aspects of virtual teaming—specifically, using electronic communication and collaboration technology to communicate even when team members work in the same building.
3. There are seven critical success factors associated with success, and organizational leaders, virtual team leaders, and members have an influence on them.

CHAPTER TWO

CROSSING TECHNICAL BOUNDARIES

The role of technology in virtual teamwork is one of overcoming the complexities of time and distance in communication and collaboration. Virtual teams and their leaders need up-to-date knowledge about technology and its role in facilitating performance. However, as this book emphasizes, the successful use of technology involves more than that. It includes understanding the technological needs of the task and the team, matching the technology available to the task, and facilitating the technology to maximize team performance. This chapter surveys the rapidly changing and frequently confusing arena of electronic communication and collaboration technology and the various tools available to the virtual team. Its goals are to simplify this topic and make it relevant. The first part explains considerations that can be used to guide technological selection. The second focuses on the technological alternatives and the strengths and weaknesses of each. Readers who are not familiar with electronic communication and collaboration technology can survey this part now and use it as a detailed reference later. The third part presents cases that illustrate some of the real-life consequences of selecting various technological solutions.

Other issues regarding the use and impact of technology are distributed throughout the other chapters of this book. For example, Chapter Eight covers concepts and techniques in facilitating virtual meetings.

Factors That Affect the Use of Technology

The starting point in enabling effective communication and collaboration over time and distance is selecting the technology that matches the requirements of the team's task. Complicated and ambiguous situations require different choices than straightforward and simple ones do. The selection process is also linked to a number of other variables, such as whether or not the team requires a permanent record of its interactions and decisions, the need for symbolic meaning in communication, team members' experience in working virtually, the team's schedule, the team's functional and organizational cultural makeup, and the team members' access to technological support and training.[1]

Two Primary Factors

There are two primary factors that can help virtual teams evaluate the effectiveness of one technological approach over another in different situations: the amount of social presence required and the amount of information richness required.[2]

Social Presence. Social presence is the degree to which the approach facilitates a personal connection with others.[3] A face-to-face discussion has one of the highest levels of social presence; an e-mail message or a form business letter has far less. Interactions with high social presence are described as more lively, social, warm, and intimate than those with little social presence. Synchronous (same-time) communications, such as face-to-face meetings, audioconferences, and videoconferences, have more social presence than asynchronous (different-time) communications, such as e-mail and voice mail, mostly because the former enable the spontaneous, back-and-forth exchanges that we associate with normal conversation. When new members are introduced to the team, when the team interacts for the first time with a customer, when the team addresses a touchy or interpersonal issue or solves a new problem, the use of techniques with more social presence may be perceived as better. Situations that are ambiguous or ill defined or that require the expression of emotions call for technology with high social presence.

However, it is not safe to assume that more social presence is always better.[4, 5] Less social presence can sometimes be better because it reduces interpersonal distractions, such as appearance, mannerisms, and being reminded of previous negative interactions with the person or group. All these have the potential of interfering with logical or analytical abilities.

The reality is that social presence is not inherently good or bad. Its usefulness depends on what the group is trying to accomplish in a given situation. Routine situations, such as the regular exchange of information between team members, may benefit from technology with less social presence. Nonroutine situations that contain high interpersonal or emotional components or ambiguity and uncertainty usually require technology with higher social presence.[6]

Information Richness. Information richness has to do with the amount and variety of information flowing through a specific communication medium. High information richness helps in the accurate transfer of clues to the meaning of the communication, thereby reducing confusion and misunderstanding. For example, the information richness in a videoconference with text and graphic capabilities is high because there is a large amount of information available, including spoken words, facial expressions, body language, and environmental information about each attendee's surroundings. Much of this information is not present in other forms of communication, such as audioconferences, voice mail, and e-mail.

Using the Factors

Social presence and information richness provide bases for a team to make choices about technology.[7] The two factors can be used as key variables to predict the effectiveness of different technological options in different situations. Implicit in this approach are two concepts: (1) that the ideal technology will be different from one type of task to another and (2) that more social presence and information richness is not always better.

In selecting appropriate technology, the types of tasks that teams work on can be divided into four broad categories:

1. Generating ideas and plans about the team's work, including collecting data to make decisions about plans
2. Solving routine problems where answers already exist
3. Solving ambiguous or complex problems where routine answers may not exist
4. Negotiating interpersonal or complicated technical conflicts between individual team members or organizations

Each category of work can be arrayed against three general types of communication technology: (1) data-only systems (such as e-mail, text messaging, or instant messaging), (2) audio-only systems (such as audio conferences and voice mail), and (3) video systems. The result is a matrix, like the one shown in Table 2.1, that rates the effectiveness of each general type of technology to facilitate achievement of each of the

TABLE 2.1. TASK VERSUS COMMUNICATION MODE.

	Types of Tasks			
Communication Modes	**Generating Ideas and Plans and Collecting Data**	**Problems with Answers**	**Problems Without Answers**	**Negotiating Technical or Interpersonal Conflicts**
Audio only	Marginal fit	Good fit	Good fit	Poor fit
Video only	Poor fit	Good fit	Good fit	Marginal fit
Data only (e.g., e-mail, bulletin boards)	Good fit	Marginal fit	Poor fit	Poor fit

Source: Adapted from J. E. McGrath and A. B. Hollingshead, "Putting the 'Group' Back in Group Support Systems: Some Theoretical Issues About Dynamic Process in Groups with Technological Enhancements." In L. M. Jessup and J. S. Valacich (Eds.), *Group Support Systems: New Perspectives.* Old Tappan, N.J.: Macmillan, 1993. Used with permission.

three main types of team tasks. Using the matrix, team members can assign a rating of "good fit," "marginal fit," or "poor fit" by evaluating the amount of social presence and information richness delivered by the technology versus what is needed to perform the task.

A rating of "poor fit" may indicate too much or too little social presence or information richness. Too much social presence or information richness is called "surplus meaning."[8] Surplus meaning, over and above what the task demands, may create a distraction from performance. For example, even though a videoconference provides relatively high information richness, team members often experience the video as distracting, especially if they know one another and are discussing routine information. Detailed information about meeting attendees' environments, such as seeing team members coming in and out of the videoconference room or watching them eat lunch, probably adds little value to the meeting.

Too little information richness or social presence can also affect team performance and decision making. The potential impact of too little social presence or information richness is illustrated by an example of a decision-making process in the United States regarding parole from prison.

Officials in a midwestern state were considering converting its prison parole board to a virtual team, using closed-circuit television as the medium for interviewing prisoners. Board members were scattered across the state and had to travel to the various correctional facilities, which were widely separated. In a pilot test, the board split into two groups for a parole interview with prisoners, with four members operating face to face and four operating remotely over closed-circuit television. The voting results for two of the prisoners were striking, with the remote members unanimously voting for parole and the face-to-face members united against parole. Subsequent interviews revealed that the board members who met face to face with the prisoners had received cues through facial expressions and body language that led them to believe that two of the prisoners were lying. These cues had not been detected by the board members in the less information-rich environment of closed-circuit television.

Other Factors in Technology Selection

In addition to social presence and information richness, a number of other factors should influence the team's selection of technology. These are permanence, symbolic meaning, experience and familiarity with virtual operations, time constraints, organizational and functional cultures, and access to technological training and support.

Permanence. Permanence is the degree to which the technology is capable of creating a historical record of team interactions or decisions.[9] A discussion by e-mail has permanence because all team members' inputs can be saved on what are called e-mail threads. An audioconference often does not have permanence unless the conversation is recorded or someone takes detailed notes. More, of course, is not always better. Many teams end up with reams of data that are never referred to again or can be used in ways never intended by the team members.

Symbolic Meaning. Symbolic meaning refers to context (meaning) over and above the message that is implied by the technology, such as receiving a handwritten thank-you letter rather than a typed one.[10] With symbolic meaning, the act of selecting one type of technology rather than another, such as voice mail versus an interactive telephone call, adds meaning to the message. Even though the words are the same, the handwritten thank-you note means something different from the typed note, and the real telephone conversation means more than the voice mail message. For example, team leaders who use voice mail to express concern about team performance send a different message than those who schedule face-to-face meetings or videoconferences to discuss problems. The first choice implies that the problem is not important and that the leader is not actively involved in the solution. The second relays the message that the problem is serious and important to the team leader.

Experience and Familiarity with Virtual Operations. Team members who are familiar with working virtually become accustomed to performing work without seeing one another daily—or at all. Such individuals sometimes prefer, and can actually perform work effectively with, less rich technology. Experienced virtual team members often find high social presence or information-rich environments distracting and call them a waste of time. Many elect not to attend a face-to-face team orientation meeting because of the demands of travel and the time it takes for detailed discussion! However, most teams report that a face-to-face meeting or other environment with social presence and information richness is necessary for effective team interaction at the beginning of the team's life cycle. The point is that the more experienced we become in working virtually, the better we become at—and the more we can begin to prefer—using technology with less social presence and information richness.

Time Constraints. Often there is not sufficient time to select and procure the optimal technology and to train people to use it. In such a case, the team needs to make the best possible decision regarding technology, given the schedule and the resources available. Unless all team members are trained, more is not necessarily better. Many virtual team members have spent valuable time in urgent situations trying to get new technology to work. Teams with short time spans and little experience with sophisticated electronic communication and information technology might be better served using the simplest possible solution. Even if one or two people on the team are familiar with advanced technology, the time, frustration, and cost of installing a new system and training people to use it might not be worth the benefit.

Organizational and Functional Cultures. Virtual teams that have varied membership require special consideration because of the differences in functional or organizational norms among members regarding group work and technology. For example, one individual moved from a telecommunications company in which e-mail was the preferred mode of communication to a consulting firm in which voice mail was favored. She learned quickly that people did not answer e-mail messages for weeks (if ever) but would respond to voice mail the same day. The use of videoconferencing and the use of groupware or other methods like instant messaging also vary greatly from one organization to another. In some organizations, all global management meetings are conducted by means of biweekly videoconferences; in others, quarterly face-to-face meetings are held. In some organizations, almost all communication is via instant messaging. In others, people don't use IM at all.

Access to Technological Training and Support. Some technologies may not be available to all team members, or there may be issues regarding the compatibility of systems or the availability of hardware and software in certain parts of the organization or in partner organizations. It is not uncommon for one part of an organization or partner organizations to be ahead or behind in hardware or software capability (or both). One virtual team leader, in California's Silicon Valley, was shocked to discover that one of her partner organizations, a biotechnology firm, did not have access to a groupware system for team meetings. She offered to buy the system for the partner organization but then discovered that it did not have money allocated for training. Even if there is money to buy and distribute technology for all team members, they need access to training and practice.

In grappling with these variables, the virtual team faces challenges and opportunities. The challenges are to overcome the deficiencies that result from working across time and distance with little of what we consider normal, face-to-face feedback. The opportunity is that the thoughtful use of technology can overcome some of the traditional problems encountered in face-to-face environments. By planning for the challenges and taking advantage of the opportunities, virtual team leaders may be able to achieve performance levels that approach—and possibly even exceed—traditional, face-to-face work.

The following section explores the complicated world of technology. It categorizes the major technological options currently available to virtual teams and rates them on some of the factors outlined in this section, such as social presence, information richness, and permanence. We suggest that team leaders and members use it to develop a working knowledge of different options and their uses and benefits.

Technology: Electronic Options

We use the term *groupware* to describe the entire category of electronic options available to a virtual team. It is a broad term that refers to electronic systems that integrate software and hardware to enable communication and collaborative work.[11] The most commonly used groupware today is e-mail and instant messaging. Most other groupware, such as desktop data conferencing, either has not been available to most people in most organizations or is not yet in widespread use.[12]

In recent years, groupware has evolved as individual products have increased in functionality and usability and people have become more familiar with their use and use of the Internet. This evolution, along with rapidly increasing data transfer capacity (bandwidth), is ushering in a totally new era of practical and user-friendly groupware products. Soon most groupware will be available to and used by the typical virtual team. The question then will be, is it appropriate to use all the power of groupware, or might it be best to go "lower-tech"?

In the development of this chapter, we researched an extensive literature base and talked with groupware vendors and users in large and small organizations. Our task was to identify and focus on those technological families that have the potential to improve the performance of virtual teams. We avoid identifying specific vendor products by name because many of these are rapidly evolving in both function and technology access (for example, through user licenses or "by the yard" off the Internet).

The following section describes the most commonly used groupware applications.[13] It describes each category and then rates it on a number of factors, such as its ability to produce social presence, information richness, and permanence. We have separated groupware into two general categories: synchronous (products that allow team members to interact at the same time) and asynchronous (products that facilitate delayed interaction).

Synchronous Groupware

Synchronous groupware includes the following:

- Desktop and real-time data conferencing
- Electronic meeting systems (EMS)
- Electronic display
- Videoconferencing
- Audioconferencing
- Instant messaging

Desktop and Real-Time Data Conferencing. Team members who use desktop and real-time data conferencing engage in synchronous interaction with one or more team members from their individual computer workstations. Individual team members have up-to-date computer, video, and audio capabilities (this may include a separate telephone or data line for conference call or video linkups) and specialized groupware software. Such systems allow team members to store common documents and to use a number of separate functions, including electronic chat, whiteboards, and desktop audio and video links.

Electronic chat (also called *instant messaging* or *instant messenger*) allows team members to have typed conversations with other team members or with anyone with a similar system. The questions, responses, and comments of all participants are visible in a "chat window" on each participant's desktop monitor. Unlike e-mail, an electronic chat is a conversation that occurs in real time. A feature that many team members like is that a record of the discussion is immediately available so that the development of ideas can be traced. However, because comments from everyone appear as they are typed, the more people who are participating in a chat session, the more chance there is for confusion regarding who said what when. Also, participating in chat conversations can be difficult for team members who have poor typing skills or who are participating in a language that is not their native one.

Chat or instant message applications are gaining popularity as office communication media for all types of teams as a way to circumvent clogged e-mail.[14] Some software packages make it possible to instantly create a private chat room (metaphorically, on the computer) so that two team members can have a private conversation at any time.

Instant messaging is also an effective way to "find" other people and for team members to have quick one-on-one conversations without the delay of e-mail or the pressure of a long telephone conversation. Instant messaging allows people to find out if others are at their desk and open for a quick chat session or phone call. In addition, most provide a busy or out-of-office message so that people will know if someone is open to hearing from them. Instant messaging has the informality of a quick hallway conversation. The drawback is that it can be intrusive. Many team members view it as yet another way of having their work interrupted or people tracking where they are and what they are doing.

Desktop and real-time data conferencing frequently combines electronic chat with an electronic whiteboard that can display shared documents and allow the sketching of thoughts or ideas. A whiteboard allows team members to view a shared document, to diagram ideas on their computers, and to see the notations and comments of other participants. Some desktop and real-time data conferencing tools include audio links that allow real-time voice discussion, in addition to chat, about the shared work.

The most advanced form of desktop and real-time data conferencing, known as "multipoint multimedia" technology, includes full-motion video in addition to the chat, whiteboard, and audio links. This integrated capability allows team members to see and hear one another and to create and edit still-frame documents or images. Each participant can view other team members on the screen through the video capability; talk with them; and see, manipulate, and annotate the same images. For team members who want to talk one on one or in breakout groups, there is the capability of creating private chat rooms for small group discussions.

The multipoint multimedia solution, due to its information-rich, multichannel capability, is ideal for team tasks that require a high amount of information richness and social presence. Still, team members report that it often does not have enough social presence or information richness for tasks that involve quick and lively interactions about highly contested technical issues or interpersonal conflicts. In addition, it does require a high-speed Internet or corporate network (intranet) link, and it requires all team members to have specialized desktop software and hardware with audio and video capabilities.

Tables 2.2 and 2.3 summarize the strengths and weaknesses of two types of desktop and real-time data conferencing. The text in each table summarizes the strengths and weaknesses on factors such as social presence, information richness, and permanence. In general, desktop and real-time data conferencing—in particular, multipoint multimedia—provides high social presence, information richness, and permanence.

TABLE 2.2. DESKTOP AND REAL-TIME DATA CONFERENCING (ELECTRONIC CHAT).

	Generating Ideas and Plans and Collecting Data	Problems with Answers	Problems Without Answers	Negotiating Technical or Interpersonal Conflicts	Other Factors
Usefulness for Virtual Teams	◕ (useful)	◕ (useful)	○ (least useful)	○ (least useful)	
Good for	Brainstorming and generating ideas for plans, ideas about products, comments	Collecting data, discussing trends	Listing options, discussing options	Stating opinions	Low cost, easy to use, permanence, minimum technical support needed
Not so good for	Voting on ideas, prioritizing ideas, outlining	Organizing data, prioritizing data, displaying data	Debating options, voting on options, prioritizing options, making decisions	Discussing opinions, reaching compromises, deciding among optional approaches, settling interpersonal disputes	Not suited for large groups; may require facilitation to maintain focus; low social presence

● = most useful ◕ = useful ○ = least useful

The cost of the system can be high, and all team members must have access to compatible systems. These systems are good for teams that have complex and long-term projects and those that have tasks that require high levels of interaction.

Electronic Meeting Systems (EMS). Electronic meeting systems have been used in face-to-face settings for a number of years to increase the productivity of group deliberation and decision making.[15] Face-to-face electronic meeting systems range in complexity from simple voting or polling systems, with wireless data entry keypads that each participant uses to cast a ballot (and a projection system to process and display the results), to computer-aided systems in which each participant uses a laptop computer to provide input to a central display screen. As the effectiveness of electronic meeting systems has grown, they have been adapted to a distributed environment to

TABLE 2.3. MULTIPOINT MULTIMEDIA REAL-TIME DATA CONFERENCING (CHAT, WHITEBOARD, VIDEO, VOICE).

	Generating Ideas and Plans and Collecting Data	Problems with Answers	Problems Without Answers	Negotiating Technical or Interpersonal Conflicts	Other Factors
Usefulness for Virtual Teams	◖ (useful)	● (most useful)	● (most useful)	◖ (useful)	
Good for	Sketching ideas, drawing concepts, gaining agreement on concepts	Listing data, displaying data, analyzing data, discussing trends, working on documents	Listing options, debating options, prioritizing options, making decisions, making judgments, working on documents	Stating opinions, discussing opinions, reaching compromises, deciding among optional approaches	Multi-technology collaboration, permanence, social presence, information richness
Not so good for	Brainstorming, voting on ideas			Settling interpersonal disagreements	Moderate-to-high cost, requires skill and facilitation, requires high bandwidth connection, video quality may be low

● = most useful   ◖ = useful   ○ = least useful

enable same-time but different-place collaboration. EMS technology is now based on wide-area networks or intranets and are becoming suitable for the Internet. The use of EMS typically requires every team member to have a computer loaded with special electronic meeting software. A professional facilitator is also needed to structure the agenda, lead the meeting, and work with the electronic meeting software.

EMS has traditionally been used to facilitate certain types of tasks:

- Tasks that tend to be sidetracked with excess discussion
- Tasks that require everyone to get a chance to express an opinion
- Tasks that require anonymity for a freer flow of ideas

EMS provide a number of useful functions that address these types of tasks,[16] including the following:

1. *Idea generation and brainstorming.* For this function, EMS resembles a chat application. Virtual team members enter ideas about a topic from their desktop computers simultaneously and are able to see the ideas from all other team members immediately on their monitors. Participants are also able to annotate or add comments anonymously about other people's items or ideas so that there is a documented and free-flowing commentary. In this way, everyone has a chance to submit ideas. Input can also be anonymous, thereby reducing the social pressure to conform or pressure to avoid stating opinions that differ from those of the majority.

2. *Idea grouping and issue analysis.* This function allows the virtual team to collectively move ideas into different categories. After team members brainstorm and comment on ideas or topics, they can identify those that merit further discussion and then agree to categorize them into smaller lists. Again, because EMS can be used anonymously, there is no social pressure to agree or disagree with a categorization.

3. *Voting.* Teams can use this function to gauge the degree of consensus about ideas and decisions without team members feeling pressure to respond one way or another. Virtual team members can prioritize and vote on ideas or decisions anonymously without the pressure to conform to the majority in the group or to the most powerful people on the team. The use of rank ordering, rating scales, and other prioritizing methods is also possible. Results are displayed in graphic or tabular form.

4. *Outlining.* This function allows team members to translate ideas and concepts into the beginnings of work products through the use of outlining features. Team members can jointly organize ideas into product or document outlines that the whole group can view and comment on. Individual team members can take the outlines and associated comments away to work on them.

5. *Annotating.* Individuals can respond to an identified set of topics in any order, making comments and suggestions at their own pace. It is up to the team leader and facilitator to decide whether comments and annotations are to be anonymous or ascribed to specific individuals. Some team leaders and members use the annotating function to begin a meeting, using the participants' comments on a group of ideas or concepts as the basis for the remainder of the session.

Electronic meeting systems are becoming more compatible with other applications, such as word processing, spreadsheet, presentation, and project management software. Team members can move back and forth from the work application to the EMS software as the situation requires. If they need information to help them make a decision, they can import it from the other application so that all team members can view it, discuss it, vote on it, and revise it. After a decision is made, the new data can be transported back.

EMS can also be integrated with other systems, such as desktop video, so that the interpersonal dynamics of a meeting can be captured. Participants can view other team members on their desktop screens at the same time as they view the information generated from the meeting. In this way, gestures, facial expressions, and other cues that provide a feeling of being there add to information richness. Chat capabilities also can be added so that participants can break off into small groups to focus on specific items or decisions.

In their current versions, many electronic meeting systems require a significant economic investment by the organization, as well as an organizational culture that will support their use.[17] Cost are becoming less of an issue as software vendors make such applications available on their Web sites on a charge-per-use basis. There are, however, significant training costs associated with the use of some of these systems, and many perform best with a trained facilitator.

In summary, electronic meeting systems are good for teams that require a lot of meeting time in which ideas can be generated and issues can be categorized and prioritized (see Table 2.4). EMS technology also is appropriate when large power differences exist between team members and when a team wants to facilitate differing opinions. EMS technology has high permanence and moderate social presence and information richness. Currently, the cost of such a system is a factor, and there is a need for a skilled facilitator.

Electronic Display. Like the blackboard, flipchart, and overhead projector, a family of technologies has evolved to aid in the presentation, communication, and discussion of ideas and concepts. These tools have recently been adapted to virtual environments. Computer-based whiteboards bring the utility and versatility of the office whiteboard to virtual teams. They allow team members to display the shared whiteboard on their computer monitors. Virtual meeting participants, seated at their workstations, can watch teammates write or draw ideas and can add their own thoughts and drawings. Whiteboards are most effective with added communication links, such as audio, video, and chat windows. Computer whiteboards usually do not require special computer equipment and are frequently bundled with other software features into integrated groupware products.

Although computer whiteboards are designed for fully distributed virtual teams, with each member at his or her own workstation, electronic whiteboards can also be used by virtual teams that are distributed into small groups. Electronic whiteboards that participants work with in small groups facilitate the joint preparation, discussion, and editing of information that is simultaneously displayed to all participants at all locations. These systems are optimized for conference rooms that are equipped with compatible hardware and software and are electronically linked. They also incorporate audio, video, and computer conferencing to simulate a face-to-face environment.

TABLE 2.4. ELECTRONIC MEETING SYSTEM (EMS) WITH VOICE LINK.

	Generating Ideas and Plans and Collecting Data	Problems with Answers	Problems Without Answers	Negotiating Technical or Interpersonal Conflicts	Other Factors
Usefulness for Virtual Teams	●	◐	◐	◐	
Good for	Brainstorming, prioritizing, outlining, voting on ideas, reaching consensus	Defining problems, reaching consensus	Listing options, prioritizing options, making decisions	Stating opinions, discussing opinions, deciding among optional approaches, reaching compromises	Permanence; compatible with other applications, such as project-management software; available on Internet and can be purchased as needed or "by the yard" for specific meetings; moderate social presence and information richness
Not so good for	Depicting complex concepts, process flows, scenarios, or sketches	Displaying and diagraming data, performing in-depth and complex analysis	Debating options, making judgments about ambiguous topics	Resolving interpersonal conflict	High cost, requires special training and facilitation

● = most useful   = useful   ○ = least useful

Advantages and disadvantages are displayed in Table 2.5. The primary advantage of using these display tools is that they build on the team members' existing skills and meeting behaviors and provide some sense of social presence.[18] The primary disadvantages are that the team members must have access to specially equipped conference rooms and must disrupt their work to physically go to these rooms. Desktop systems provide the advantage of permanence. These systems are good for teams that need to share ideas and concepts graphically.

Videoconferencing. Videoconferencing is one of the most commonly used tools for virtual teams. Although it can provide high information richness and social presence, it is often not the tool of choice of experienced virtual team members. The quality of the video picture, in terms of motion quality (jerkiness) and the crispness or resolution of the image, is dependent on the bandwidth of the data link. Bandwidth is determined by variables such as the speed of the computer modem, the type of network (Internet or intranet), and the capacity of the cables or wires attached to the team member's desktop computer. Virtual team members who have low-bandwidth connections can experience low-quality images. Team members who use the Internet can encounter traffic congestion that degrades the video transmission. Video transmission and reception problems such as these can restrict the usefulness of desktop video, so that the video image distracts from, rather than enhances, the collaborative experience.[19]

There are two primary types of video applications: desktop video and specialized video facilities. Desktop video is almost always accompanied by audio communication and frequently by document-sharing capabilities. As most computers are equipped with the necessary hardware for desktop video, virtual teams that have recently purchased desktop equipment and a data link to an intranet or the Internet probably have video capabilities. A team member who has older desktop equipment may have to augment the hardware by purchasing a video card, microphone, speakers, and a video camera.

A second option that may be available to virtual team members in larger organizations is the use of specialized video rooms. Video rooms employ video equipment and high-bandwidth networks that transmit full-motion video. They may also contain whiteboard or other presentation software that allows the sharing of and collaboration on documents. Video rooms can augment desktop systems by providing higher-quality video images than some desktop systems. Unfortunately, however, like desktop systems, these video images can degrade and become distracting, especially if there are more than two locations on the same link.

Another video technology that has been experimented with in high-technology organizations such as Xerox is video walls or windows. These are shared audio and video spaces that are open all the time. People in the halls, conference rooms, and offices of one location are continually able to see and hear team members in other locations walking

TABLE 2.5. ELECTRONIC DISPLAY WITH VOICE LINK.

	Generating Ideas and Plans and Collecting Data	Problems with Answers	Problems Without Answers	Negotiating Technical or Interpersonal Conflicts	Other Factors
Usefulness for Virtual Teams	⬤	⬤	⬤	◯	
Good for	Brainstorming, sketching ideas, drawing concepts	Listing data, displaying data, discussing trends	Listing options, debating options	Stating opinions, discussing opinions	Low cost, easy to use, permanence
Not so good for	Voting on ideas, converging on complex concepts	Detailed or complex analysis	Prioritizing options, making decisions, making difficult judgments	Reaching compromises, deciding among a number of technical approaches, resolving interpersonal conflicts	Lower social presence, less information richness

⬤ = most useful   ⬤ = useful   ◯ = least useful

through halls, working in conference rooms, and sitting at their desks. In essence, it is like being in the same building with other team members.

Team members who use these types of systems over long periods of time say that they contribute to a sense of social presence and ongoing team unity, especially after people get to know one another. There have been reports of team members seeking each other out through the video wall and the forming of lasting and personal relationships.[20]

Teams that use a video wall technology find that the development of social protocols for taking turns, avoiding sudden movements, and minimizing "video rudeness," such as leaving a meeting site empty in the middle of a meeting, is important. In addition, privacy is sometimes an issue, as people are able to watch other people work without the others' awareness. To help counter this, Xerox developed a "Big Brother" system, in which a set of eyes on the computer screen opened when someone was looking at a team member. The system also created a five-second "peek" capability to allow someone to look into an office to see if the other person was there.[21]

As shown in Table 2.6, most teams can benefit from the use of video technology. When used appropriately, it provides a high level of social presence and information richness. Overuse in situations that do not have these requirements is a mistake, as is attempting to link too many parties into one conference.

Asynchronous Groupware

Asynchronous groupware includes the following:

- E-mail
- Personal computing devices
- Group calendars and schedules
- Bulletin boards
- Team Web sites
- Non-real-time database sharing and conferencing
- Workflow applications

E-Mail. E-mail is the most common and best-understood computer-mediated technology for distance collaboration. It is the electronic version of postal mail. The message, usually a written one that can have a computer file attached, is sent over a network from one computer to another. The features of e-mail as a collaborative tool are frequently compared to postal mail and to voice mail. Like voice mail, e-mail is easy to use, provides people with time to reflect and consider their responses, can reach people in a short time, and can broadcast the same message to a number of different people. E-mail is more effective than voice mail when extensive information, such as a text or video file, needs to be included with the message or when the message or the response to it is complicated and requires a written explanation. E-mail also makes it easy to forward messages or to send copies or blind copies to others.

Unlike the telephone or voice mail, some e-mail systems will notify the receiver that a message was opened by a recipient (although not whether it was read and understood). Most e-mail systems also provide a means of visually tracking the original message, as the original is restated in the reply and in replies to replies. This concept of "message threads" is analogous to documenting or recording a face-to-face or telephone dialogue. A major advantage of e-mail over the telephone or voice mail, however, is that e-mail provides a permanent, written record of the discussion with no extra effort. Attorneys and police departments are even starting to use e-mail threads as evidence.

TABLE 2.6. VIDEO WITH VOICE.

	Generating Ideas and Plans and Collecting Data	Problems with Answers	Problems Without Answers	Negotiating Technical or Interpersonal Conflicts	Other Factors
Usefulness for Virtual Teams	○ (least useful)	● (useful)	● (useful)	● (useful)	
Good for		Defining problems, prioritizing options, making straight-forward decisions	Listing options, debating options	Stating opinions, discussing opinions, deciding among straightforward optional approaches, reaching simple compromises	Available on Internet, low cost (desktop), transmits some information for social presence
Not so good for	Brainstorming, prioritizing, outlining, reaching consensus about complicated topics	Displaying and diagraming complex data, performing analyses	Making complex judgments	Resolving interpersonal conflicts	High cost (video room), needs high bandwidth, small or poor-quality picture limits utility, low permanence

● = most useful   ● = useful   ○ = least useful

For teams that are working on highly proprietary product ideas or other activities that require confidentiality, e-mail security services can ensure that messages have not been altered or modified and can even identify the origin of a message. We used e-mail to administer a 360-degree feedback instrument to over ten thousand people globally. The e-mail system not only allowed us to track responses but also provided security features that were especially valuable in ensuring managers who were not used to using an electronic process that their feedback had not been tampered with and that it was confidential.

More advanced, "smart" e-mail systems are able to filter and prioritize incoming messages.[22] Using filters and "if-then rules" (for example, "*If* it is from my boss or customer, *then* I want to see it first"), team members can designate which messages they want to see immediately, based on the content or the sender. A team member also can designate the location to which a message should be forwarded, based on the topic, date, or names of team members. This feature facilitates quick responses to action items.

As with other groupware, e-mail is being merged with other technologies, such as voice and video. It is now possible to leave voice mail messages in e-mail mailboxes and to have e-mail messages read by voice-synthesizing computers over the telephone. This provides more social presence and information richness to e-mail systems but still falls short of video, audio, and other synchronous interactions.

E-mail is a necessity for virtual teams. It is an excellent way to communicate about simple and straightforward issues and to share information. It is inexpensive and easy to learn to use. The drawback is its low information richness and social presence. The other drawback is that it is most probably the most overused technology. E-mail is not a substitute for real-time conversations that need high social presence. Many people spend most of their time on e-mail, even if they are not working on a true virtual team. E-mail is good for information-rich tasks but not so good for tasks that require high social presence. Table 2.7 shows a summary of e-mail's strengths and drawbacks.

Personal Computing Devices. Personal computing devices are electronic devices that allow people to access the Web, send and receive e-mail, and in some cases make phone calls and receive voice mail. These devices are heralded as time savers, especially for virtual team leaders who travel extensively. They enable real-time access to team Web sites and in some cases instant messaging, real-time communication with other team members for problem solving, and enable non-real-time access to other team members for organizing and sharing data via e-mail and Web sites.

The upside of personal computing devices is that they are easy to use and keep team members in touch with one another on a real-time or almost real-time basis. They also allow team members to share information easily. The downside is that they are often described as intrusive in that some team and functional leaders expect team members to be "on call" all the time. This emphasis on real-time accessibility can hamper the time team members have for other tasks, such as production of deliverables and real-time interactions with team members.

Group Calendars and Schedules. The importance of time and coordination to a virtual team makes calendaring and scheduling software a high-priority tool. Calendaring involves the manipulation of information on an individual's calendar; scheduling involves the communication and negotiation of information, meetings, and other items that need to be coordinated between individual calendars.[23] Such programs are widely available, and the software is included with many groupware applications.

Calendaring and scheduling systems range from individual schedule managers to enterprisewide systems based on client servers. Enterprisewide systems permit

TABLE 2.7. E-MAIL.

	Generating Ideas and Plans and Collecting Data	Problems with Answers	Problems Without Answers	Negotiating Technical or Interpersonal Conflicts	Other Factors
Usefulness for Virtual Teams	●	●	○	○	
Good for	Discussion of ideas and plans, exchanging comments, revising plans and documents	Defining problems, discussing problems, transmitting data	Identifying options, discussing options and approaches	Stating opinions, discussing opinions	Low cost, easy to use, widely available, fits with the culture of most organizations, cross-platform compatible, high permanence
Not so good for	Brainstorming, prioritizing, outlining, voting on ideas, reaching consensus	Reaching consensus on problems, performing analysis	Debating options, prioritizing options, making decisions, making judgments	Deciding among optional approaches, reaching compromises, resolving conflicts	Subject to misuse for messages requiring higher symbolism, low social presence and information richness

● = most useful ● = useful ○ = least useful

coordination of schedules between team members from any location or function. They are most useful to virtual teams, especially if team members are located across a number of different time zones, because they coordinate differences in time zones. Depending on the size and complexity of the team, scheduling may also necessitate coordination across organizational lines with vendors, customers, and venture partners. If multiple organizations are involved, the team needs to establish rules that determine the priority of scheduled events that originate outside the team or in the parent organization. In other words, decisions must be made about what takes precedence, the needs of the team or the parent organization.

Teams also need to determine who has the authority to schedule whom and when. Some teams make their systems available to anyone in the organization, even individuals with whom they would not normally be in touch. Calendaring systems can be combined with databases that provide others with information about people who have specialized expertise that might be of interest to a team member. Virtual team members can tap into the database, identify others with the expertise they are interested in, and then use the system to make appointments to talk with those experts.

Virtual teams also are able to link to project management software, such as scheduling and reporting applications, to integrate personal and team calendars with project or work schedules.

As these systems become as ubiquitous as e-mail, the tendency to overuse them may parallel the overuse of e-mail. For example, the scheduling of team activities on a global basis will have to be carefully monitored to combat "time-zone creep"—the tendency to routinely commit team members to activities outside their local working hours. Calendaring and scheduling tools are meant to be used for team coordination; they have no social presence and little information richness, and they are not appropriate for resolving technical or interpersonal issues.

Bulletin Boards and Web Pages. Electronic bulletin boards and Internet or intranet Web pages provide shared work spaces for the posting of messages and ideas, the display and editing of documents, and for non-real-time discussions about questions that do not require immediate answers. Many teams set up their own team bulletin boards or Web sites. The bulletin board and Web site are accessible to all team members (and to other stakeholders if the team wants this) and have a degree of permanence similar to that found in chat rooms and e-mail. Bulletin boards are useful for gathering large amounts of information about specific topics from diverse groups of people outside the team. A bulletin board feature is often included as a standard part of a large corporate e-mail system and can be accessed by desktop or laptop computers.

Because bulletin boards and Web sites allow many conversations to occur simultaneously, these technologies are time savers. People do not have to meet face to face or talk on the telephone in order to offer input in a topical area or read a document. Bulletin boards and Web sites also allow people to deliberate what others have said before composing their own input. In addition to the generalized ability to build on and comment on the ideas of others, these programs allow for the creation of specialized topical databases that can be used in team collaboration and in the joint writing of products.

Bulletin boards also can lead to disasters when not properly used. One company's team, focused on gathering input about the organization's strategy, set up a public bulletin board and posted "questions of the week" about specific employee issues. The idea was that instead of holding a face-to-face focus group session every week to gather employee feedback, the team would do it remotely. Many responses were very constructive, but others were cutting and directed at specific managers in the organization. Still others were off topic completely and were just used as a way for people in the organization to "meet virtually." Although the team learned a lot about what some people were feeling, it was not able to judge how representative the sentiments were or to control the damage to people's reputations. It might have been better to hold this type of no-holds-barred discussion in a face-to-face and less public setting.

Although these tools are relatively inexpensive and easy to use and they facilitate permanence, they have low information richness and low social presence. Table 2.8 summarizes the benefits of bulletin boards and Web pages for virtual teams.

Non-Real-Time Database Sharing and Conferencing. For virtual teams that are part of a larger organizational effort or whose work will be used as a basis for future work by other teams or organization units, the management of large amounts of information and knowledge is critical. Shared database systems were among the first

TABLE 2.8. BULLETIN BOARDS AND WEB PAGES.

	Generating Ideas and Plans and Collecting Data	Problems with Answers	Problems Without Answers	Negotiating Technical or Interpersonal Conflicts	Other Factors
Usefulness for Virtual Teams	◓ (useful)	◓ (useful)	◯ (least useful)	◯ (least useful)	
Good for	Brainstorming, generating ideas for plans and ideas about products, commenting on products	Collecting data, discussing trends	Listing options, discussing options	Stating opinions	Low cost, easy to use, high permanence
Not so good for	Voting on ideas, prioritizing ideas, outlining complex topics, in-depth feedback on products	Organizing data, prioritizing data, displaying data	Debating options, voting on options, prioritizing options, making decisions	Discussing opinions, reaching compromises, deciding among optional approaches	Low social presence, low information richness

● = most useful   ◓ = useful   ◯ = least useful

groupware applications on the market, and they perform a number of information management functions, such as these:

- Providing the team access to reference materials and stored knowledge from other teams or from the results of other organizational activities such as studies
- Providing a place to store the work of individual team members
- Ensuring that all work in progress is updated to the latest edition and available to all team members
- Providing a place to store the team's experiences, lessons, and products for future use

Shared database systems usually accept a wide range of data, including multimedia information. Often information is distributed on servers throughout the organization, and individual team members have extensive freedom to search the database and to transfer the information to personalized databases and tailor it for their own use. Most systems require the purchase of special software and a desktop system to download, view, manipulate, and store the information.

Another application for non-real-time data conferencing is collaborative note-books.[24] Notebooks are built on distributed databases and employ a user interface that simulates real notebooks. The interface, usually on a desktop or laptop, features pairs of pages separated by a binder. Often the right page, like a commercial organizer, contains space to make notes or add comments and provides hyperlink capabilities to other notebook pages. The left page contains flexible space in which any document or team product can be embedded. Notebooks can be created for specialized team topics and are designed so that each team member can contribute to the others' notebooks on the topic. Individual team members control the writing and editorial access to the notebook in accordance with their task responsibilities and can in this way facilitate and manage collaborative writing, document sharing, and editorial review by multiple users.

As shown in Table 2.9, non-real-time databases contribute to permanence but have little social presence or information richness. Their use is heavily dependent on team member access to software and training and on whether or not the culture of the organization supports their use. In addition, there is evidence that most team members will interpret non-real-time information as having the least priority. If you want someone's attention, non-real-time data conferencing is probably not the way to go.

Workflow Applications. Workflow applications are used to design and operate repetitive business processes that involve sequential steps, such as the electronic processing of forms in a loan application and a new-hire request. The adaptation of workflow software to organizational intranets and the Internet enables repetitive work to be done virtually. Workflow software has a rather specialized application to virtual teams that are engaged in assembly-line work, service, or production and those engaged in operational or reengineering tasks.

TABLE 2.9. NON-REAL-TIME DATA CONFERENCING.

	Generating Ideas and Plans and Collecting Data	Problems with Answers	Problems Without Answers	Negotiating Technical or Interpersonal Conflicts	Other Factors
Usefulness for Virtual Teams	⬤ (useful)	⬤ (useful)	◯ (least useful)	◯ (least useful)	
Good for	Brainstorming, generating ideas for plans and ideas about products, commenting on products, collaborative authoring	Collecting data, discussing trends	Listing options	Stating opinions	Low cost, easy to use, permanence
Not so good for	Voting on ideas, prioritizing ideas	Organizing complex data, discussing and prioritizing data	Discussing or debating options, voting on options, prioritizing options, making decisions	Discussing opinions, reaching compromises, deciding among optional approaches	Little social presence, little information richness, requires cultural change to implement, may require training on special software

⬤ = most useful   ⬤ = useful   ◯ = least useful

Near Virtual Disaster

The "leadership development Web site" team consisted of two sets of Web developers located in two different locations (about 1,000 miles apart). Each had a specific task in the update of the Web site's look and feel and in the development and integration of new content into the Web site. Because each team felt that it was "Web-savvy," it was decided that communication would primarily be through a beta Web site where each team could see the other's work. E-mail updates, real-time data conferences with the active Web site, and a project management schedule would keep each team informed of the other's progress. As the timeline progressed, tensions began to rise. It seemed as if both teams were doing overlapping work, and the products were not meshing together. Although some people suggested a face-to-face meeting or regular teleconferences, team members felt that the more advanced technology was a better solution. One week before the project was due, they realized they had both produced the same products and that certain deliverables had not been worked on at all. It was decided that one team would finish the task, since the teams "obviously could not work together."

Clearly, this team needed to spend more time understanding how to align the needs of the task with the technology used on the team. Even though all were experienced virtual team members, this task required much more real-time high-social-presence technology than was used.

The template in Exhibit 2.1 provides a means for virtual teams to avoid "near virtual disasters" by aligning the needs of the team in terms of social presence and information richness to each major team task. The idea is that the team should spend time listing all major tasks (staff meeting, reviews, joint writing, and so on) and then describe the needs of each task in terms of social presence and information richness. Next the team should align the technology with the needs of the task. This process should be repeated on a regular basis to ensure that an appropriate mix of technological techniques are being used that are appropriate for each task and to ensure that the team is not overusing or becoming too reliant on one particular type of technology.

Cases in Virtual Collaboration

The following brief case studies are based on the experiences of real virtual teams in real organizations. They have been selected to illustrate some of the factors discussed earlier and for their varied approaches to the use of technology. In the first example, a government research team applies a technology-intensive approach; in the second, a team is in a technological environment coping with a task that is complex and politically charged. The third example describes a research team that is operating from ten remote locations.

The Government Research Team

The advanced launch vehicle (ALV) virtual team's task was to identify and assess the most promising new technologies to lower the cost of launching satellites into space. The team was the first user of the organization's new virtual research center (VRC), a groupware suite designed to bring together, virtually, the best technical specialists available, regardless of where they were located in the United States or elsewhere in the world.

The team's virtual home was a wing in the VRC, a make-believe facility located on the surface of the moon. Each team member checked in by e-mail to get a badge

EXHIBIT 2.1. ALIGNING SOCIAL PRESENCE AND INFORMATION RICHNESS TO THE TECHNOLOGY.

Technology planning depends on two variables:

Social presence   ⇨   The extent to which technology mimics face-to-face interactions

Information richness   ⇨   The amount of information the message can convey

First, list technology options available to your team:

1. _____
2. _____
3. _____
4. _____
5. _____
6. _____
7. _____
8. _____

Then use the following table to determine what types of tasks the team will be performing, esti-mate the need for social presence and information richness, and finally, match technologies to the team's tasks, given the need for social presence and information richness.

Team Activity	Requirements for Social Presence and Information Richness	Technological Solution Selected

that permitted access to different rooms of the facility, including the library, where project-related data were stored; the laboratory, where engineering simulations and analyses were performed; and the conference room, which accommodated real-time team meetings.

The team's first task was to discuss a preliminary listing of state-of-the-art space propulsion technologies that were to be examined by the team. This discussion was the first use of the real-time meeting technologies in the virtual conference room. The available technology options were desktop video, audio, and a shared electronic whiteboard. The VRC had been designed as an Internet-based capability in order to accommodate scientists who were not on the government's high-speed data network.

Early tests conducted during the development of the VRC groupware suite raised questions about the suitability of the Internet to support multimedia multipoint real-time data conferencing. During these tests, low-modem-speed connections and Internet congestion combined to limit communications. It was decided to let the first team try the system before making any final decisions about modifying it.

The team's leader started the meeting with an introductory presentation using the whiteboard. The presentation started out with the full system, which included—in addition to the whiteboard—an Internet telephone and slow-scan video. When several participants complained that the audio was breaking up, the team switched to a separate conference call link (a normal telephone line) that was available as a backup. This cleared up the audio problem, but now the audio was out of synchronization with the whiteboard because Internet congestion was slowing down and sometimes freezing the whiteboard images. Meanwhile, the video image was cycling in speed (frames per second) from very slow to stop and was a distraction to the participants. Once the video was turned off, the whiteboard speeded up, and the meeting proceeded with good results.

The pilot test had served its purpose. It had demonstrated that the Internet (on a bad day) was not yet robust enough to support bandwidth-heavy multimedia usage.

Lessons Learned. As the ALV team discovered, use of the Internet is still more of an art than a science. The current Internet protocol (TCPIP) was designed in the 1960s, and upgrades are on the way. But in the meantime, virtual team leaders should become familiar with the limitations of Internet use. Lessons learned include the following:

- Plan carefully for the use of untested technology.
- For synchronous communication using the Internet or low-bandwidth organizational networks, make the most of traditional technology options, such as conference calls, augmented with single-function groupware, such as a whiteboard.

- Encourage virtual team members to get the latest in computer modem technology and the highest-speed (bandwidth) Internet access available.
- Carefully assess the quality and benefits of desktop video in relation to the task at hand, especially for larger team sessions.

The Certification Process Team

A large international organization implemented a virtual team to design and pilot a professional certification process for a significant population of managers. The team consisted of fourteen members in North America and Europe. Eleven members were considered a technical advisory group. There was one project manager and two individuals from an external consulting organization. The project was strategically important to the organization and had high management visibility. It was also unique in that a formal certification process for nontechnical work had never been developed or implemented in the organization.

The external group and the project manager did most of the development of the certification process documentation, with the other team members acting in review and advisory capacities. Upper management granted final approval of the process. Because travel money was tight and the organization had a long history of working virtually, it was decided that there would be no large, face-to-face meetings. The technology selected was traditional and consisted of the following components:

- E-mail for the coordination of schedules and for sending messages and small, attached files
- Regular conference calls for team meetings
- A Web page for posting the draft certification process

After several meetings, the process began to bog down. Because the laser printers in the different locations created different page breaks in the sixty-page e-mail files, it was difficult to discuss the documents during the conference call meetings. In addition, the meetings became repetitive, covering the same materials as previous sessions. Even bringing in a meeting facilitator, who prepared objectives and detailed agendas, did not seem to help. To make matters worse, some team members appeared to lose interest and stopped attending the regular reviews. When they did attend, their input was increasingly negative rather than constructive. Some even began to question their investments of time. Meanwhile, the authors were making so many changes to the documents that it was hard to track them all.

Finally, the first team product was placed on a team Web page for open review and comment. Although the product was not complete, it was considered a good way to get feedback from the broader organization. The comments were less than positive in some areas, and it was hard to know which comments to take seriously. The team overcompensated by taking them all seriously. Making changes to the Web page, however, was a complicated process that involved coordinating with the corporate organization responsible for Web page development. Working through a third-party organization not only made it difficult to make changes but also made it almost impossible to check them in a timely manner.

Lessons Learned. The certification process team learned that it needed to select its technology more wisely for such a complex project. In some parts of the project, technology was underused and in others, it was overused or misused.

- The team had underestimated the degree of complexity involved in the coordination and review of team products. More information-rich technologies, such as desktop video with audio and shared text and graphic support, could have avoided the page-break problem and made reviews more efficient.
- The team had underestimated what it took to collaboratively write this type of document. Collaborative notebooks or composition software would have helped greatly.
- Because the team kept going over the same information in its review meetings, it could have benefited from using an electronic meeting system to generate ideas, prioritize them, vote on them, and make decisions.
- One or two face-to-face sessions might have helped eliminate confusion and address the more complicated and politically charged parts of the task.
- Placing unfinished products on a Web page for anyone to review is dangerous. It was difficult to know who to take seriously and when to change the document. Also, once a product is on a Web page, it is much more difficult to modify.

The Leadership Research Team

A government research team was formed to collect information for a study of leadership skills. Team members came from across the United States. Only two team members were from the same location. Part of the team's task was to collect data through interviews and focus groups about leadership knowledge, skills, and experience from over eight hundred people in ten different locations.

The government organization had extensive experience in using EMS. As a result, the team members decided to leverage their experience with that technology and to use the electronic meeting system to collect and manage the interview data. After an initial face-to-face meeting that included training in the use of EMS, all team members gathered information using EMS at their locations and then downloaded their data into a central database. All team members used a prescribed data collection and input format and a protocol that was agreed on in the orientation session. Following each team member's input, the system automatically updated the database with the latest information. Technical support in using EMS and the central database was available to all team members if they needed it.

During the data collection phase, the team members kept in touch by e-mail and voice mail. Regular updates about the progress of the data collection were provided by all team members to the team leader and then distributed to the team members. Any problems that were encountered were shared in these communications.

Because the nature of leadership is a complex phenomenon, a face-to-face session was held to discuss the results of the interviews, conduct detailed data analysis, and reach agreement on the final leadership model. Information from the database was downloaded during the meeting and was used in analyzing results and in discussing and agreeing on the final model. A face-to-face electronic meeting system was also available in the meeting to help the members brainstorm ideas, vote on final results, and prioritize areas that were ambiguous.

At the end of the project, many team members said that the project had been productive as a result of the use of the central database and the use of EMS to collect and analyze the data. They also said that they felt a sense of team unity and camaraderie.

Lessons Learned. The leadership research team selected its technology wisely. It leveraged existing experience with a specific technology that was already well accepted in the organizational culture. The team leader also called for face-to-face meetings when they were necessary: at the beginning of the project, to gain agreement on the task, process, and method, and at the end of the project, when detailed discussion and debate were required. In addition, the team was provided training in the use of EMS and the central database, and team members had adequate technical support and updates on progress and problems.

Points to Remember

1. All teams benefit from face-to-face discussion, especially in the beginning. Experienced teams can be effective with less.
2. There is no ideal technology set for all teams. Most teams continue to benefit from basic, computer-mediated capabilities, including e-mail, calendaring and scheduling systems, whiteboards, and document sharing. Many teams—even experienced teams in high-technology organizations—rely on non-computer-mediated technologies (such as the telephone and facsimile) and single-function technologies (such as e-mail).

3. A virtual team needs to have a clear strategy for matching technology to the task. It should consider the needs for social presence, information richness, and permanence. Other factors, such as time constraints, the experience levels of team members, and the availability of technological solutions, also need to be considered.

4. High levels of social presence and information richness are not always desirable. For example, some team activities, such as standard review meetings, can be performed better without the distractions of face-to-face interaction.

5. Complicated or unproven technology is not always a good choice. For example, many people find videoconferencing, in its current state of maturity (characterized by poor picture quality and inconvenient facilities), far inferior to well-run audioconferencing.

6. Bandwidth, cost, and compatibility issues can affect a team's performance.

7. Underestimating the complexity and scope of the job can lead to a number of other problems, including the wrong choice of technology.

CHAPTER THREE

CROSSING CULTURAL BOUNDARIES

Culture is one of a virtual team's most significant boundaries. Culture can be national, organizational, or functional. This chapter describes all three types of culture and how each can affect the performance of virtual teams.

Defining Culture

The word *culture* comes from the same root as *cultivate,* a Latin verb meaning "to till the soil." It describes the way in which people act on nature. For humans, culture is a set of learned mores, values, attitudes, and meanings that are shared by the members of a group. Culture often is one of the primary ways in which one group differentiates itself from another.

Culture can be viewed as the collective programming that separates one group of people from another.[1] One way to look at culture is as the hidden "scripts" that people use to guide their behaviors. These scripts are created by repeated interactions between members of a group. They are often not even visible to the members of the group that created them. Over time, they become second nature and serve as short-cuts for guiding actions and making decisions. Like an iceberg (see Figure 3.1), culture is often partly or totally hidden. It can, however, affect people's assumptions, behaviors, and expectations about leadership practices, work habits, and team norms.

FIGURE 3.1. THE HIDDEN DIMENSIONS OF THE CULTURE ICEBERG.

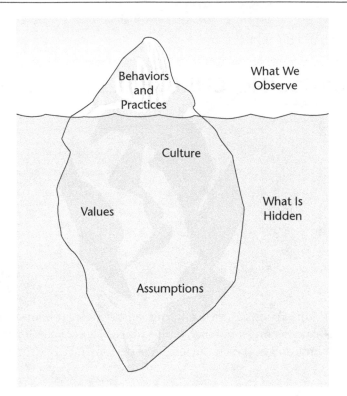

Three Categories of Culture

There are three types of culture that can affect a virtual team: national, organizational, and functional. Each team member brings his or her culture, and as the team evolves, the unique blend of team members' national, functional, and organizational cultures create a unique team culture.

National Culture

With the escalation of the globalization of organizations, more virtual teams are multinational. Even in domestic teams, cultural differences may influence the team members' ways of working. For example, in the United States, there are many different cultural groups that could be represented on a team. It is possible that a domestic virtual team could have as much diversity as an international team—or even more.

The patterns associated with national culture are often established in childhood and are the most deeply embedded. These, coupled with life experiences, create the differences in behavior and thinking that exist when we talk about a person's cultural background. It is a long-term identity that most of us cannot remove or replace. It becomes such an identifier that it represents who we are as much as anything in our lives except perhaps our names. This was evident in the resistance to the merger of European economies and currencies in many member countries of the European Union. People in the European community have described the resistance at least in part as an expression of national pride; people from the different European countries identify with their cultural histories, practices, boundaries, and currencies.

In 1967, Geert Hofstede began looking at employees of IBM Corporation to discern patterns of national behavior. He studied responses to employee surveys administered in many countries around the world. From this research, he derived four dimensions of culture: power distance, uncertainty avoidance, individualism–collectivism, and masculinity–femininity.[2] Later, with the help of Michael Bond, Hofstede added a fifth dimension, long term–short term.[3] A sixth dimension is based on the work of Edward Hall, who presents a contextual dimension of communication.[4]

Power Distance. Power distance refers to the degree of inequity among people that the population expects and accepts. Organizations in low-power-distance countries tend to be more participative, with managers seeking input from their staff members. Different levels in the organization freely challenge one another. In high-power-distance countries, employees expect and accept that managers make decisions with little or no consultation with their staff members. In a virtual team, this may affect team members' expectations about leadership styles and the role of the team leader.

For example, one virtual team in a durable goods firm with a global presence created a set of shared values for the team. One value encouraged employees to challenge the team leader openly in order to reach the best solutions. The Chinese members of the team could not agree to challenge the team leader, no matter what the circumstance. China is a high-power-distance country in which there is great respect for one's superiors, so questioning a superior is not appropriate behavior in the Chinese culture. As a result, this value was not adopted because it directly clashed with the values held by the Chinese team members.

High-power-distance countries include Brazil, Venezuela, Indonesia, India, Singapore, France, Hong Kong, Mexico, and Arab countries. Lower-power-distance countries include Great Britain, Germany, Switzerland, Finland, Norway, Denmark, Austria, and the United States.

Uncertainty Avoidance. Uncertainty avoidance is the extent to which members of a culture are uncomfortable with uncertainty. Individuals from cultures that have high uncertainty avoidance seek details about plans, desire closure, and prefer more predictable routines. People from such countries may exhibit more anxiety in ambiguous situations or when there are no right or wrong answers. People from cultures that have low uncertainty avoidance tend to be more comfortable with ambiguous situations and tend not to have as strong a need for defined rules, procedures, and processes. Differences in uncertainty avoidance create differences in team members' preferences for detailed team plans, formalization of team members' roles and responsibilities, defined schedules, and review processes.

Countries where uncertainty avoidance is high include Belgium, Japan, Peru, France, South Korea, Brazil, and Italy. Countries that have lower uncertainty avoidance include most of Great Britain, Hong Kong, Singapore, Ireland, Canada, the United States, and India.

Individualism–Collectivism. Individualism is the degree to which people prefer to act as individuals rather than as members of groups. A culture with high individualism is one in which there are loose ties between people, and individuals are expected to look after themselves. People from countries with high individualism value personal time and the freedom to take individual approaches to their jobs. Countries with high individualism include the United States, Australia, Great Britain, Italy, France, and Germany.

In a collective society, people integrate into strong, cohesive groups—often for life. People from countries with high collectivism value a strong identity with the group and tend to put the needs of the group before their own. They prefer not to be singled out for praise or reward. Countries in most of Asia and Central America have higher collectivism.

Implications for virtual teams include differences in team members' expectations about team unity, differences in closeness to other team members, and the ways in which rewards and recognition are handled. Members from collective cultures, for example, may prefer team-based rewards to individual recognition.

Masculinity–Femininity. The title of this dimension dates Hofstede's work. The masculinity–femininity dimension describes the extent to which a "masculine" orientation—concerned with things such as earnings, signs of visible success, and possessions—has priority over a more "caring" (that is, feminine) orientation, which includes nurturing, cooperation, and sharing. Countries rated higher on the masculinity dimension include Japan, Austria, Italy, Mexico, Germany, and the United States. Countries rated higher on the femininity dimension include Thailand, Norway, Sweden, and East African nations.

Long Term–Short Term. Long-term cultures value persistence and thrift. They are oriented toward the future. Short-term cultures value more immediate physical and financial returns. Asian countries score highest in long-term cultural behaviors. European countries occupy the low-to-middle range, and the English-speaking countries have a shorter-term orientation. This dimension has implications for what motivates virtual team members. Team members from long-term cultures may be motivated by long-term success. Team members from short-term cultures may be more impatient and need more immediate reinforcement.

Context. The cultural variable Hall identified is context.[5] Context may be one of the most important cultural variables for virtual teams. It refers to how people perceive the importance of different cues in communication. In high-context cultures, messages have little meaning without an understanding of the surrounding context. People from high-context cultures prefer more historical information and more subjective personal opinions. This may include information about the backgrounds of the people involved, previous decisions, and the history of the relationship. People from low-context cultures prefer more objective and "fact-based" information. The message itself is sufficient. This has a significant implication for the way in which team members communicate. Members from high-context cultures may prefer communications that are able to carry a great deal of contextual information. This implies that information-rich technologies that convey a number of clues regarding meaning may be more suited to a team with a number of members from high-context cultures.

High-context cultures include Japan, China, Greece, Mexico, Brazil, and Spain. Moderate-context cultures include Italy, France, French Canada, and Britain. Low-context cultures include English Canada, the United States, Scandinavia, and Germany.

Table 3.1 summarizes Hofstede's and Hall's dimensions of culture and the implications for virtual teams.

Culture also may have an impact on the way in which technology is used by a team. Table 3.2 offers several considerations to be used when selecting technology for teams with members from different cultures.

Organizational Culture

The organizational cultures of team members may also influence their performance and consequently the performance of the team. Members of virtual teams are drawn from various organizations, including customers, suppliers, associations, communities, and other stakeholder groups. Each member brings his or her organization's culture to the team, increasing complexity and the time needed to complete team tasks.

Edgar Schein defines organizational culture as "a pattern of shared basic assumptions that the group learned as it solved its problems of external adaptation and internal integration, that has worked well enough to be considered valid and, therefore, to be taught to new members as the correct way to perceive, think, and feel in relation to those problems."[6]

TABLE 3.1. CULTURAL DIMENSIONS AND BEHAVIORS FOR TEAM MEMBERS.

Cultural Dimensions	Definition	Advice for Team Members
Power Distance	Extent to which the less powerful members expect and accept that power is distributed equally	Expect that team members from high-power-distance cultures will want to make decisions and take charge. Team members from low-power-distance cultures will prefer more consultation. Set very clear expectations about the leader's management style and what it implies for team members' behaviors.
Uncertainty Avoidance	Degree of structure required for a task	With members who require more structure, spend more time detailing the task. With members who require less structure, detailing the task will cause them to feel micromanaged.
Individualism–Collectivism	Preference to act as individuals rather than as members of groups	In collectivist cultures, tasks will be completed by members together, bringing along the slower members. In individualist cultures, assign tasks to individuals but make sure they realize that they are part of the larger team and cannot work alone.
Masculinity–Femininity	Extent to which masculine values are given priority over more "caring" values	With members from feminine-nurturing cultures, be careful not to overdo the "kill the competition theme."
Long Term–Short Term	Degree of parsimony, family orientation, virtuous behavior, and acquisition of skills and knowledge	For members from long-term cultures (such as Asian cultures), providing opportunities to contribute to long-term goals and to learn and acquire skills can be very motivating.
Context	Amount of sensing and extra information needed to make decisions versus "just the facts"	With members from high-context cultures, spend more time reviewing the histories and backgrounds of situations. Use more information-rich technologies. With members from low-context cultures, more information than "just the facts" will appear nonessential and be frustrating.

TABLE 3.2. TECHNOLOGY AND CULTURE.

Cultural Factor	Technological Considerations
Power Distance	Members from high-power-distance cultures may participate more freely with technologies that are asynchronous and allow anonymous input. These cultures sometimes use technology to indicate status differences between team members.
Uncertainty Avoidance	People from cultures with high uncertainty avoidance may be slower adopters of technology. They may also prefer technology that is able to produce more permanent records of discussions and decisions.
Individualism–Collectivism	Members from highly collectivistic cultures may prefer face-to-face interactions.
Masculinity–Femininity	People from cultures with more "feminine" orientations are more prone to use technology in a nurturing way, especially during team startups.
Context	People from high-context cultures may prefer more information-rich technologies, as well as those that offer opportunities for the feeling of social presence. They may resist using technologies with low social presence to communicate with people they have never met. People from low-context cultures may prefer more asynchronous communications.

These basic assumptions cover many complex areas. For example, different organizational cultures carry different perceptions of the importance and nature of time (regarding schedules and timetables), the organization's relationship to its competitive environment (leading it or reacting to it), and theories about human nature (good or evil). It is a challenge to identify shared basic assumptions in an organization.

Organizational culture is a determinant of performance because it deals with basic assumptions that people are not aware of until the culture is challenged or organizational performance deteriorates. When properly managed, cultural differences can lead to innovative solutions. However, failure to address differences in organizational cultures can derail even teams with experienced members.

For example, a multinational organization formed a virtual team to develop an executive education course for senior leaders. The members of the team included three directors who were located in three different parts of the world and two university faculty members who were based in Europe. The directors had global positions and consulted with cross-cultural leaders within the organization. The faculty members also worked almost exclusively in global settings.

A university culture has a different concept of time than that of most companies. Faculty members tend to think in terms of academic cycles, semesters, and trimesters and generally have longer task-to-completion time spans. They also tend to schedule calendars in yearly increments and have higher degrees of certainty about their commitments. In business organizations, however, most calendars do not exceed one fiscal quarter, and priorities shift continually.

As the task progressed, tension built. The organization pushed for a final design. The faculty members said that they needed longer lead times. They wanted to wait until they had breaks in their course schedules to work on the program. This frustrated the organization's directors, who needed to show ongoing action to their supervisors.

Over time, because of these and other culturally rooted assumptions, the relationships in the team deteriorated. Weeks slipped by without a single telephone call or e-mail message. The distance between the team members made it difficult to communicate, and the team members eventually used distance as an excuse and stopped communicating.

The high-technology industry has long been known for cultures that are fast-paced. Their notion of time is based on the quick nature of the Internet industry, with new technologies and businesses emerging all the time. Contrast this to some older-line companies whose product development cycles might be years, not weeks or months. It is easy to see how a virtual team with members from both types of organizations could have misunderstanding and even conflict around the meaning of time.

The Competing Values Model is based on the premise that every group has shared and competing values and assumptions. These reflect the group members' preferences for certain things over others. When two virtual team members who have different values and assumptions come together, their values and assumptions may compete and create tension. The tension is the result of two sets of polar opposites, resulting in four types of cultures: clan, market, hierarchy, and adhocracy.[7]

• *Clan Versus Market Culture.* The first pairing is clan versus market cultures. The clan culture views the organization as an extended family and its leaders as parent figures. Clan members are highly committed. Teamwork and participation are paramount. The market culture is results-oriented, with competitive members and aggressive leaders. There is a penchant for winning.

• *Hierarchy Versus Adhocracy Culture.* The second pairing is hierarchy versus adhocracy cultures. The hierarchy culture is very formal and is governed by procedures, with a focus on stability and control. Low risk and "no surprises" characterize success. The adhocracy culture is dynamic and adaptive, with a great deal of risk taking and innovation. There is a penchant for trying new things.

Using the Competing Values Model, one can map the degree to which each of the four cultures is represented on a given team. The resulting score can be plotted on a kitelike graph, with the four cultures forming the four quadrants, as shown in Figure 3.2. The strength of each culture is expressed on a scale from 0 to 50. The culture" depicted in Figure 3.2 ("Present Culture") has a strong clan and hierarchy focus.

FIGURE 3.2. THE COMPETING VALUES MODEL.

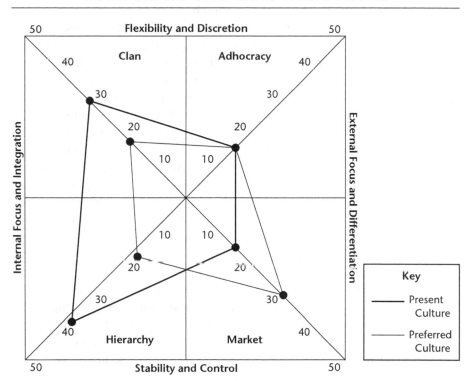

Source: Used by permission of K. S. Cameron and R. E. Quinn, Copyright © 1998 by K. S. Cameron and R. E. Quinn.

The Competing Values Model facilitates examination of a team's present organizational culture, and it can be used to determine whether that culture is aligned with the team's task. If there is a mismatch between the existing culture and the demands of the task, the team may decide to develop new norms or to add new members who represent the culture it is trying to create. In Figure 3.2, for example, the thin lines ("Preferred Culture") show that the team is trying to become more market-focused and less clan- and hierarchy-focused.

Functional Culture

Most specialists in organizations work in functional groups, such as engineering, marketing, finance, production, and human resources. People who work in the same functional area often share a common background in terms of education, professional goals, and skills. Functional experts develop their own practices and ways of doing business, so when members of a virtual team come from different functional areas, they bring different assumptions and practices that may affect the team. Engineers, for example, learn a slightly different set of techniques for managing projects than software designers do. On a virtual project team, these two groups may disagree about which approach is most appropriate.

The cultural dimension of context also affects functional perspectives.[8] In general, people who are in functional areas such as human resources, marketing, and sales tend to prefer more contextual information in communication than people from information systems, engineering, and finance. Team leaders need to take these preferences into account when sending messages and establishing agendas for meetings. Members who come from high-context functions may prefer and expect more information-laden communications. They may be frustrated by agendas that are developed by low-context team members. Conversely, the low-context team members may be frustrated if they feel that they have to provide "extraneous" information to the high-context members.

In organizations that have traditions of cross-functional teamwork, a virtual team leader will likely have an easier job in managing functional differences. Team members from such organizations have experience in subordinating their functional biases to achieve the broader, integrated goals of their teams. They also know how to bring needed functional expertise to their teams and how to leverage differences and maintain balance. Table 3.3 provides examples of selected functional areas and suggested actions to manage functional integration.

Functional teams that mostly work within their own functional area should be careful not to get too caught up in their own identity and practices. One of the benefits of virtual teaming is that team members get access to different perspectives and ways of doing business and so use virtual teaming as an opportunity to try out new behaviors

TABLE 3.3. EXAMPLES OF BEHAVIORS THAT AFFECT FUNCTIONAL CULTURES.

Engineering	Prefer to lay out plans in a rational fashion and work with logical detail.
Software Development	Prefer to lay out plans in a rational fashion. Have a horizontal process orientation to work versus a vertical orientation within functions.
Research and Development	Prefer structure and detail within a research or scientific context. May not appreciate rush schedules, cost limitations, and a short-term business focus.
Accounting and Finance	Prefer to organize, plan, and quantify. Add structure to tasks.
Sales and Marketing	Operate with a sense of urgency. Can conceptualize and create quickly. Prefer high-context communications.
Production and Manufacturing	Manage projects, processes, and problem solving. Operate with a sense of schedule and urgency.

and practices. Team leaders of any functional team would be wise to make their biases transparent and keep team members open to others' perspectives and ways of doing business.

Using Culture as a Competitive Advantage

Cultural diversity in a virtual team can provide a competitive advantage. Hofstede recognized decades ago that "the presence of a dominant national culture is an asset rather than a liability for the functioning of an organization, and it should be fostered carefully."[9] Virtual teams that leverage the power of differences can outperform teams that have members who are more similar in background and culture. Many innovations come from people who are outside the prevailing schools of thought.

One question that perplexes virtual team leaders is, "To what extent should I try to change functional, national, or organizational cultures to fit the team culture?" It is next to impossible for a virtual team to change organizational and functional cultures. And it is not the purview of a team or an organization to try to change national culture, even if it could. A more appropriate question is, "What of these different cultures can be adopted into the team culture to create an advantage?"

In managing cultural diversity within a virtual team, being aware of built-in biases and resisting or countering them is one of the biggest challenges. Harry Triandis and Richard Brislin found that when a supervisor from one culture appraises the performance of a subordinate from another culture, the accuracy of the appraisal is likely to be lower than if both individuals come from the same culture.[10] Triandis and Brislin concluded that people from different national cultures have different ideas about what constitutes good performance. Virtual team leaders should be mindful of this and understand their own cultural biases and how these biases may affect their judgments.

Virtual team members should engage in cultural training at the beginning of the team's life. Training about national, organizational, and functional cultures is a useful component of team orientation, no matter how experienced the team members. Training creates a shared experience and language that the team members can draw on in working together. Checklist 3.1 provides suggested topics for cultural training.

CHECKLIST 3.1. SUGGESTED TOPICS FOR CULTURAL TRAINING.

1. Present basic cultural dimensions (such as the work of Hofstede, Hall, or another researcher). Make sure that the presentation is based on research. If possible, let subgroups of team members from different cultures present these to one another.   _____

2. Discuss how these dimensions might affect team interactions and performance. Let members from the different cultural groups speak for their own cultures at this point.   _____

3. Discuss business practices and ethics that might affect team performance and interactions, including:

   - Differences in time zones   _____
   - Holidays   _____
   - Availability of technology   _____
   - Work hours   _____
   - How decisions are made (off-line, in meetings, and so on)   _____
   - Facilitation payments and bribes   _____
   - Entertainment   _____

4. Discuss when and how such differences will be discussed on an ongoing basis within the team.   _____

5. Discuss how these differences might affect team norms and practices, including the exchange of information, decision making, and communications.   _____

Understanding that culture consists of values and shared assumptions is critical to helping a team succeed. Bringing cultural differences to the surface in a productive way can help create a virtual team culture that builds on differences. Rather than trying to circumvent differences that members bring to the team or to attempt to make everyone the same, teams can leverage the differences to create a team culture that is the basis for team development, growth, and success.

There are several considerations to ensure that culture is used to the team's advantage. Checklist 3.2 offers a way for team members to begin to open up to cultural differences. Checklist 3.3 presents some guidelines for using cultural differences to the best advantage.

Business Practices

Business practices (work hours, holiday schedules, and the like) vary significantly in different parts of the world. In many Latin countries, people tend to work from 9:00 A.M. to 7:00 P.M. and to work late on Friday evenings so that they can take the weekends off.

CHECKLIST 3.2. TEAM CULTURE PROFILE.

Instructions: Each member of the team should complete the questionnaire individually. The team should discuss the areas that members respond to differently.

	Yes/No
1. I am aware of each team member's nationality.	_____
2. I am aware of the team leader's nationality.	_____
3. I feel capable of discussing the key similarities and differences of each member's national culture.	_____
4. It feels natural to discuss whether problems are task-related or culturally based.	_____
5. I know the functional background of each team member and of the team's leader.	_____
6. I understand the similarities and differences that exist in the organizational cultures that are represented on the team.	_____
7. I feel comfortable in addressing cultural issues by means of electronic communication.	_____
8. The team has set up ground rules to address cultural issues before they become problems.	_____
9. The cultural differences on the team can be used to help the team to be more successful.	_____

CHECKLIST 3.3. TEAM LEADER CONSIDERATIONS TO ENSURE THAT CULTURE IS USED TO THE TEAM'S ADVANTAGE.

1. Be aware of your own biases and talk about them openly with other team members. Ask for their help in overcoming the biases that could hurt the team or its work.   _____

2. Adopt ways other than your own. Ask other team members to teach you different ways of doing things and then practice them. Be open to different ways to solve problems and do things.   _____

3. Participate in cultural training for the team. This will serve as a foundation that the team can refer to when problems arise. It will also be the first step in creating an appropriate team culture.   _____

4. Conduct the Competing Values Model organizational culture analysis. Openly discuss the effects that culture is having on the team. Determine whether these effects can be used to the team's advantage.   _____

5. Don't hide behind, or let members hide behind, culture as an excuse for poor performance.   _____

6. Trust your instincts to know what is right and wrong and when to intervene.   _____

Business dinners in Latin America, especially in Argentina or Spain, rarely begin before 9:00 P.M. and can last until midnight. On the other hand, dinner in the United States can begin as early as 5:30 P.M. and be finished by 7:00. Many Latins wonder why Americans eat dinner "in the middle of the day."

Differences in time zones can derail tasks. Even sophisticated executives may count on their fingers when trying to figure out what time it is somewhere else in the world. Even differences in time zones within one country can cause problems.

One effective practice is to distribute a guide to team members, with the time zones in each team member's location beside the member's name. Include not just the name of the time zone but the difference in hours—for example, "If it's 1:00 P.M. at the corporate headquarters, it's 7:00 P.M. in Italy and 1:00 A.M. the next day in Hong Kong."

Holidays also create dilemmas for global virtual teams. The process of selecting dates for meetings and conferences can be hampered significantly by trying to work around all the holidays that are celebrated around the world. One team started by having each team member list the holidays he or she observed and indicate which were absolutely essential and which were not (meaning that the members could work on those days). This was a culturally sensitive way to solve the problem. Care was taken to ensure that members from any one culture were not unduly inconvenienced.

Business Ethics

Work schedules, time zones, and holidays are relatively simple problems to solve compared to the more significant issues related to business ethics. Problems related to bribes and facilitation payments plague teams that have members in certain countries. It is essential to be very clear about the organization's and the team's positions on these issues and the ramifications and consequences if team members do not comply.

Organizations often appear hypocritical about what is allowed. One global company set clear ethical standards prohibiting facilitation payments in India or Indonesia. When questioned as to why a salesperson in the United States could take a customer on a cruise ship without that being considered a bribe, the company could not answer the question satisfactorily.

In terms of bribes and facilitation payments, there are shades of gray that the organizational leaders and team leader need to resolve. In some countries, it is often impossible to get a business telephone without making a facilitation payment. Most organizations have decided that this is the price of doing business in those countries. On the other hand, giving under-the-table money to customers or suppliers is still frowned on by many Western companies.

Near Virtual Disaster

Cultural sensitivity can be taken too far. There are many stories about organizations or teams that did not act fast enough because they were being overly sensitive to the local culture. Bad performance is bad performance in any culture. Cultural traits should not be used to cover poor performance or as excuses for such performance.

To help make the issues described in this book come to life, we present a series of vignettes with Sara, a virtual team leader, as the main character. We base the stories on real examples that we have experienced. In the first vignette, Sara is having trouble with one of her virtual team members, who is hiding behind cultural differences to cover up performance problems.

Sara worked with her virtual team for several months. As the team leader, she structured the team in an exemplary way. She even conducted a cultural workshop during the team's orientation. She assigned each member tasks and is now in the process of checking to see how each member is progressing.

Sara had not heard from the member from Italy and decided to e-mail her. After two e-mails, there still was no response. Not wanting to seem too pushy, Sara waited longer than her instincts told her was appropriate—much longer than she would have waited if this member were Canadian, like Sara. She finally reached the Italian team member by telephone and asked how she was progressing. Sara was told that there had been several Italian holidays and a transportation strike in the team member's part of the country that had prevented her from traveling. The message was that Sara needed to understand that Italy is very different from Canada. Sara listened and asked when she could expect the first output, which had been due the previous week. She was told that it would come in a few days. Sara waited and then e-mailed the member on the agreed-on date. Meanwhile, other things were being held up, waiting for the input from the team member from Italy.

When there was still no communication, Sara called the team member and was told that the task was much more difficult than Sara realized when she assigned it. She also was told that the information systems in Italy are much more rudimentary than those in Canada. The Italian member said that she had to do much of the information systems work manually, which took more time. Again, there was the implication that Sara was insensitive to the team member's culture.

Days passed, and Sara still did not receive the input she needed. Finally, she called the team member to discuss the situation. The team member said that she had sent her work to Sara and was surprised that Sara had not received it, implying that Sara's office was less than efficient. Sara waited two more days. Finally, the e-mail arrived, and Sara reviewed it. It was a dismal attempt at the task. Sara did not want to go through another round of inter-actions with the Italian team member. Instead of sending the work back, Sara decided that it would be easier to finish the task herself.

Sara wrote in the journal she had been keeping that on reflection, she should have listened to her instincts in her first encounter with the team member. After all the back-and-forth communication, Sara realized that she faced a performance problem, not a cultural one.

Problems like Sara's arise regularly in virtual teams. Although national culture figures in Sara's story, it could be retold using functional or organizational culture. No matter what the type of culture, when problems arise, sorting out whether they are performance-based or culturally based is difficult. In similar situations, team leaders and members need ask only two questions: (1) If this person were from the same culture as I am, would I still think that there was a problem? and (2) Is this person violating agreed-on team norms regarding performance? The answers to these questions can help team leaders and members decide whether a problem is culturally based or performance-based. However, making such a determination still can be difficult for virtual teams because of distance and the limits of technology.

Keeping a journal can help a virtual team member reflect on his or her actions and consider new approaches to cultural issues. Keeping a journal can also help a team member identify patterns in behavior that may help in determining whether problems are culturally based or performance-based. Checklist 3.4 is a format that can be used to create a journal in which to reflect on cultural issues.

CHECKLIST 3.4. KEEPING A PERSONAL JOURNAL.

At times, especially in new situations in which there is little time to reflect on your experiences, keeping a journal allows you to keep track of your feelings, reactions, and learnings. A leader of a virtual team, especially, can benefit from keeping a journal.

Instructions: To begin, answer the following questions. Do this after each major or important interaction with your team members.

1. What was this interaction about? What was its focus?

2. What were the personal and work challenges you faced?

3. Describe your feelings during and after this event.

4. Which cultural dimensions apply to this situation?

5. What did you learn about yourself? About culture?

6. What will you do the same and/or differently the next time?

Points to Remember

1. There are national cultures, organizational cultures, functional cultures, and team cultures. They can be sources of competitive advantages for virtual teams that know how to use cultural differences to create synergy. Team leaders and members who understand and are sensitive to cultural differences can create more robust outcomes than members of homogeneous teams with members who think and act alike. Cultural differences can provide distinctive advantages for teams if they are understood and used in positive ways.

2. The most important aspect of understanding and working with cultural differences is to create a team culture in which problems can be surfaced and differences can be discussed in a productive, respectful manner.

3. It is essential to distinguish between problems that result from cultural differences and problems that are performance-based.
4. Business practices and ethics vary in different parts of the world. Virtual teams need to clearly articulate approaches to these that every member understands and abides by.

PART TWO

CREATING VIRTUAL TEAMS

CHAPTER FOUR

MYTHS AND REALITIES OF LEADING VIRTUAL TEAMS

This is the age of the virtual team leader. It seems at times that it is actually rare to lead a team that is located all in one place. Sometimes a reorganization propels someone into the leadership of a virtual work team, service, or production team. When organizations merge or form alliances, partnerships, or joint ventures, especially internationally, it is not uncommon for people who have been leading functional areas to find that they are virtual team leaders or on virtual management teams. These days, team members who work in different buildings across a city or large campus might work virtually.

Very quickly, most virtual team leaders discover that leading a virtual team requires a special set of skills. Although many traditional leadership principles apply to virtual teams, virtual team leaders experience unique challenges. First, they have to rely on electronic communication technology to send and receive information. As a result, they need to modify the ways in which they provide feedback and gather data. In most instances, the team leader cannot walk down the hall to ask a question, work out an issue over lunch, or call the team together for a meeting in the conference room. Some virtual teams struggle to find a common language. If the team is located across time zones, the team leader must be available in all time zones while balancing heavy work demands with home life. An audioconference at 6:30 A.M. in the United States or 8:30 P.M. in Asia may be the only way to talk a problem through. When virtual team leaders are asked about the biggest challenge in leading a virtual team, they usually mention the increased sense of burden and responsibility it places on them. Perhaps because of geographical dispersion and the potential for team member isolation as a result of cultural and language differences or functional specialty, the team leader usually feels as if he or she is the "glue" that holds the team together.

More often than not, organizations and team leaders pay little systematic attention, beyond cross-cultural awareness training, standard team leader training, or e-mail etiquette, to developing the skills that team leaders need in a virtual environment. This is a mistake. Virtual team leaders need to find ways to develop competence in areas that are specific to virtual teams, even if the organization does not formally support their development.

The first step in developing competence is to understand (1) what it is really like to lead a virtual team and how it is different from leading an in-house team and (2) the areas in which competence is needed for success. Once people have experienced leading virtual teams, they quickly identify mistaken ideas that they held prior to their virtual team experiences, and they begin to recognize the areas in which they need to develop.

Myths Regarding Virtual Teams

There are several common myths about virtual team leadership. The skills necessary for leading a virtual team effectively can be aligned with the myths, and developmental activities can be recommended for each area of competence.

Myth 1: Virtual Team Members Don't Need Attention

The knowledge that this is a myth distinguishes successful virtual team leaders from unsuccessful ones. Successful virtual team leaders understand the fundamental principles of team output, accountability, and team members' need for direction and feedback and do not let time and space alter these precepts. The team leader, whether virtual or in-house, is accountable for the team's output and team member performance. Management, customers, and peers all hold the virtual team leader accountable for the performance of the team. Even when the team's task calls for a high level of team member autonomy, the leader is still accountable for the final output of the team and for team member performance.

Some virtual team leaders believe that each member should be able to produce without direction, feedback, or coordinating with the leader and other team members. It seems awkward for a team member in Bangkok to have to check with the team leader in London on key decisions. For this reason, successful virtual team leaders are very explicit with their team members concerning the issues about which they have to be informed, when they need to be involved, and on what level decisions will be made. Virtual leaders need to work with team members to develop a shared understanding of the level of detail the leader needs to know before and after a decision is made. Virtual team leaders also need to be effective in coaching and in managing performance in virtual environments. A team leader should never assume that team members will "figure out what to do" without clear direction.

Competence 1: Performance Management and Coaching

Effective virtual team leaders actively balance the tension between business and people. Although team member autonomy, empowerment, and participation are important concepts in making a virtual team successful, there is a task that needs to be completed. An effective virtual team leader is the team's leader, performance manager, and coach. Effective team leaders understand that they can provide some autonomy within a structure that facilitates results. Managing performance occurs at the team level and at the individual level.

Managing Team Performance. At the team level, the leader is accountable for completing the task within certain technical requirements. Activities at the team level that can make this happen include the following:

- Developing the team's vision, mission, and strategy with input from team members and stakeholders. In a virtual setting, clarity and shared understanding of vision, mission, and strategy direct the actions of team members in ambiguous situations.
- Negotiating the accountabilities of the team members in relation to one another. In a virtual setting, because team members cannot see one another's work, it is very important that there is shared understanding about roles and accountabilities. This leverages expertise, facilitates coordination, and avoids redundancy and duplication of work.
- Identifying results-oriented performance measures for the team and for each team member.[1] Although all team leaders should identify performance measures, performance measures for virtual teams may have to be more concrete and results-oriented than they do for in-person teams. Because there is no day-to-day feedback about the efforts of individual team members, results-oriented measures provide an objective and reliable way to determine whether action is needed to get the team back on track.
- Developing methods to review progress and results. Working virtually does not allow the give-and-take of normal, day-to-day feedback on progress and problems. As a result, successful virtual team members don't take anything for granted and create formal mechanisms to accomplish this. Weekly audioconference updates and templates for reporting remotely are often critical parts of a strategy to provide visibility in team performance.
- Sharing best practices with other teams in the organization. Virtual team leaders often develop or provide input into "lessons learned" databases, electronic bulletin

boards, and other mechanisms by which to share intellectual capital. Most large consulting firms have "sharing knowledge and best practices" as a job requirement for their team leaders.[2]

Effective virtual team leaders, even if they are not leading project teams, often borrow practices from the discipline of project management to help them accomplish team-level performance management activities. Some of the first virtual teams were project teams, and many of their management methods can be used with most virtual teams, especially in the areas of team startup and chartering and in the development of ongoing status and review mechanisms.

Managing Individual Performance and Coaching. There are a myriad of activities in the area of managing performance and coaching that virtual team leaders need to undertake with individual team members. Leaders must provide members with timely feedback about their performance. In virtual teams, this often requires soliciting informal input from various people, such as customers and remote stakeholders, who interact with team members. It can also include formal communication with invested parties about the performance of team members. Often—especially in parallel, project, or product teams—negotiating a performance rating for a team member includes gathering input from such sources as functional leads, customers, matrix managers, and the team's sponsor.

A successful virtual team leader uses this input and acts as a performance coach for team members. It is dangerous to assume that anyone can perform effectively without timely feedback. Virtual team leaders need to interact with team members on a regular basis regarding their performance. Virtual team leaders in cross-cultural environments must also adapt their coaching styles to accommodate team members from different cultures. For example, team members from high-power-distance cultures may expect more direct coaching than members from low-power-distance cultures may expect.

Managing Compensation. A virtual team leader may have accountability for the compensation of team members. Most organizations use the same compensation and benefits system for virtual teams as they use for the rest of the organization. A virtual team leader should determine whether special circumstances must be acknowledged for the virtual team's unique nature. For example, some virtual teams count vacation accrual in terms of hours rather than days. This is to account for the unusual work schedule that some virtual teams have.

The real difficulty, especially with ongoing work, service, and production teams, arises when compensation systems do not flow across boundaries and the organization does not have one compensation structure for all businesses. If virtual team members are pulled out of disparate places, with different compensation structures, the compensation and benefits schedule for virtual team members is impossible for the team leader to manage. When this is the case, the team leader must address the issue with top management and push for an organizationwide solution.

Developmental Actions

Development activities in this area of competence include the following:

1. Participating in organization-sponsored courses in performance management and coaching
2. Developing a performance plan for the team and a performance, coaching, and feedback plan for each individual team member
3. Participating in organization-sponsored or external courses in project management or reading about project management and applying its principles to the virtual team
4. Meeting with compensation specialists within the organization to understand what is possible and what is not
5. Leading or working in as many virtual teams as possible

Myth 2: The Added Complexity of Using Technology to Mediate Communication and Collaboration over Time, Distance, and Organizations Is Greatly Exaggerated

The complexity of communicating over time, distance, and organizations causes unique problems that are not easy to solve. Practical experience and research show that when not managed properly, virtual teams can be less effective than traditional teams. For example, virtual teams often take longer to get started in meetings and to produce results than many traditional teams do.[3] Even the use of very advanced technology, such as groupware, is no guarantee of success. In fact, at times, overreliance on or inappropriate uses of technology can interfere with the output of the team.

One virtual team that was tasked with developing recommendations to increase customer satisfaction for a lagging product line used a distributed EMS to help generate ideas to increase sales. Although the system was well suited to assist in the task, hardware and software compatibility issues made it difficult for people in Europe to participate. As a result, their input was not well represented in the final product, although it should have been, because the product was lagging in sales more in eastern Europe than in any other part of the world. The team no longer uses the system, but the European team members still have negative feelings about the team.

Another team used an electronic bulletin board to collect team members' input about a set of activities. Team members had strong opinions about the topics and felt that the bulletin board could not possibly capture their thoughts with enough social presence to display the passion they felt. As a result, few used the bulletin board.

Competence 2: Appropriate Use of Information Technology

Virtual team leaders must select and use appropriate methods of communication and collaboration. A leader cannot rely exclusively on technology to satisfy all of a team's communication, information-sharing, and productivity needs, but technology provides the critical link. A team leader must be able to match the appropriate technology to the team's task, the current stage of the project, the type of team, and the level of technological sophistication of the team members. The leader also needs to keep up with new technology to evaluate its usefulness for the team.

Matching Technology to the Task and the Type of Team. Effective virtual team leaders have a number of technology-based strategies for communication and collaboration. They understand that the nature of a team's task will to some extent dictate which technology is selected. Tasks that are ambiguous often require a communication and collaboration technology that is media-rich and provides a wide bandwidth that mimics the give-and-take of normal conversation. For example, using audioconferences and e-mail to design a complex technical system may not be as effective as using a combination of video, audio, whiteboard, data conferencing, and face-to-face interaction.

The team leader also needs to match the use of technology to the type of team. Work and production teams, for example, are more likely than parallel or action teams to need workflow software. A parallel team that is working on a complex organizational problem is more likely than a virtual management team to have an ongoing need for groupware that can import project management software.

Virtual team leaders must also consider whether to use synchronous or asynchronous methods. Synchronous methods are better for complex and ambiguous subjects, for brainstorming and reaching consensus, and for collaborative writing sessions. Asynchronous methods, such as scheduling software, e-mail, and voice mail, can be used for updates and information exchanges and for collaborating on schedules. They are very appropriate for workflow processes. Team leaders need to be competent in developing agendas for and facilitating both synchronous and asynchronous meetings.

Matching Technology to the Team's Life Cycle. Another critical skill is aligning the use of technology and face-to-face interaction with the team's life cycle. Typically—and especially with a team whose members have not worked together virtually—information-rich technologies, such as videoconferencing, desktop videoconferencing, and face-to-face interaction, are necessary at the beginning of the team's life so that the team members can get to know one another.[4] Leaders of project and parallel teams may select these types of technologies and face-to-face interaction at the beginning of the project and in the middle, in order to maximize team dynamics.

Matching Technology to the Team Members' Situations. In many large and complex organizations that operate on a global basis, there are sometimes wide discrepancies between employees' levels of technological sophistication. People who work in information systems or engineering functions may be very comfortable working with groupware, whiteboards, and e-mail as their primary means of communication. People in other functions, however, may not have much experience in using these technologies. In addition, the team leader should match the use of technology to the overall environment. Team leads who are "first out of the gate" with new technology might meet more resistance than they expect. Matching the sophistication of the technology to the organization while pushing limits is a delicate balance.

Discrepancies can also exist between a team and its external partner organizations. The virtual team leader needs to select a set of technologies that matches the skill levels of all team members or provide training and backup resources in the technologies selected. The team leader also needs to address hardware and software compatibility issues and ensure that all team members' systems work well. If necessary, the team leader should provide technical support at each team member's location.

Humility and Skepticism. Finally, virtual team leaders must know what they don't know about technology. Virtual team leaders who are not technical experts need to seek help in evaluating the use of technology and in facilitating distributed meetings using technology that they are not familiar with. They must be aware of new systems and technologies that might be of use to their teams, and they should remain skeptical enough not to use an untested system without trying it out first. Team leaders can also attend conferences on and demonstrations of new technologies and ask to "pilot-test" technologies that might help their teams.

Developmental Actions

Development activities in this area of competence include the following:

1. Developing a technology use plan that takes into account the appropriateness of the technology for the team's task and the type of team and how the selection of technology may change over the team's life cycle
2. Participating in organization-sponsored or external courses in selecting and using information technology
3. Attending technology conferences and demonstrations and asking to have one's team serve as a pilot team for new technology

4. Keeping a log of and noting which technologies work well and which do not in different situations

Myth 3: The Leader of a Cross-Cultural Virtual Team Needs to Speak Several Languages, Have Lived in Other Countries, or Have Worked in Different Functions

People who are new to working virtually or globally often overrate the need to speak several languages or to have lived in different cultures in order to be effective in a cross-cultural environment. Conversely, team leaders often underrate these attributes, believing that the language of the headquarters country is what is widely accepted. In fact, what is required more than linguistic knowledge or international experience is a sensitivity to other cultures and an attempt to learn how to communicate on more than a "menu" level with team members.

Competence 3: Managing Across Cultures

Managing across cultures entails understanding more than the obvious differences in backgrounds and languages. There are what Mary O'Hara-Devereaux and Robert Johansen call a multitude of subtle and less obvious ways in which culture affects the ways in which people work.[5] The challenge for the virtual team leader is to understand the differences among team members and to leverage them to create an advantage. Virtual team leaders need to develop multicultural as well as multidisciplined perspectives. In doing this, they need to become aware of their own cultural biases and how those affect personal assumptions and behaviors toward team members. Furthermore, they need to understand the many ways in which each team member's culture affects his or her biases and his or her expectations of other team members and the team leader.

Team leader competence goes beyond knowledge of surface similarities and differences; the leader must proactively create what O'Hara-Devereaux and Johansen call "third ways of working."[6] Third ways of working are techniques for working or interaction that do not elevate one cultural bias over another. For example, one team leader from North America made the mistake of taking a typically North American management custom—publicly lauding a particular team member for his work—and applying it to a multicultural setting. To make matters worse, he singled out, complimented, and gave a generous performance reward to a team member from Japan in front of the entire team (most members of which were from Japan and China). For a North American, this "honor" might have been slightly embarrassing. For this Japanese team member, however, to be singled out for high performance in front of other team members who had also contributed to the team's performance was not honorable or rewarding at all. After discussing the matter with more experienced team leaders, the leader in question said that the next time he led a multicultural team, he would ask the team members individually how they would like to be recognized before taking any action.

This advice is also relevant for team leaders leading virtual teams with cross-functional or organizational membership. First, understanding that differences in functional or organizational cultures can be as powerful as national culture is critical. Next, applying respect to different ways of working and looking for "third ways of working" is equally important in teams with this type of composition. It is dangerous to assume that national culture is the only cultural variable that influences team performance.

Developmental Actions

Development activities in this area of competence include the following:

1. Participating in organization-sponsored courses on working cross-culturally
2. Aligning with another team leader or mentor who has worked cross-culturally
3. Keeping a log or journal of actions and biases, and tracking what works and what doesn't
4. Asking people from other cultures how they prefer to work
5. Visiting as many countries as possible and observing cultural mores
6. Working on a number of cross-cultural teams

Myth 4: When You Can't See People on a Regular Basis, It Is Difficult to Help Them with Current Assignments and Career Progression

Most of us are not used to working with people whom we don't see frequently. Some virtual team leaders think that if they can't see a team member, they can't assist in the person's career development. However, the virtual environment does not change the fact that the leader is still a primary force in planning for the team members' next assignments and career progressions. Because it is easy for virtual team members to feel isolated and unnoticed, it is even more important for the virtual team leader to actively assist them with their career planning and development. If members of virtual teams feel that they have been shortchanged in this important area, their motivation to work on such teams will diminish rapidly.

Competence 4: Aiding in Team Members' Career Development and Transition

When virtual team members are asked about the negative aspects of working on virtual teams, they almost always say that they are afraid that their careers will suffer. Their fear is that no one will keep track of their contributions and professional growth.

Many high-performing professionals have been passed over for good assignments in favor of someone who has more visibility with management.

Virtual team leaders must anticipate this concern and develop specific strategies to deal with it. This is especially true for parallel, project, and product development teams during the closeout phases of the team's work. Even if a team member is assigned formally to a local or functional manager, the team leader needs to act as an advocate for that person and provide the manager with a solid understanding of the team member's accomplishments, experiences, abilities, and interests.

On a work, production, service, functional, or management team, the team leader is responsible for the virtual team members' careers and must fulfill the role of mentor and career coach. Care must be taken not to give preference to people who are closer geographically. The team leader also needs to be diligent about being cognizant of the team members' accomplishments, goals, and objectives by actively seeking this information.

The virtual team leader is in a position to help team members obtain good assignments after a project has been completed. Team leaders can serve as advocates for team members with the team members' managers, stakeholders, and other virtual team leaders. Team members' reassignments should be planned in advance in order to minimize downtime and to optimize the use of newly acquired expertise. Virtual team leaders who show concern for the welfare of their team members after the end of their projects provide a valuable service to the organization and gain reputations as good people to work for.

Another frequently mentioned problem with virtual teams is the transition period required for new members to get up to speed on the project and the technology used. A virtual team leader needs to have competence in training and coaching new team members. The quality and timeliness of the orientation new members receive can affect the team's overall productivity. The inadequate or untimely orientation of a single member can result in wasteful downtime for the entire team. Good team leaders develop novel ways to orient members, such as using a "partner system" for the first few weeks of participation. Some create partners for the entire project.

Developmental Actions

Development activities in this area of competence include the following:

1. Participating in organization-sponsored courses on career development
2. Creating and using a process for career planning and next-assignment planning for team members
3. Holding career development discussions with team members

4. Attending to personal career needs
5. Asking team members about their next-assignment preferences and coordinating this information with other team leaders, stakeholders, and customers

Myth 5: Building Trust Is Unimportant in Virtual Teamwork

One of the biggest mistakes a virtual team leader can make is to underestimate the power of trust. Charles Handy points out that trust is one of the foundations for performance in a virtual setting.[7] He suggests that if we do not find ways to build trust and understand how technology affects it, people will feel as if they are always in a very precarious state. The fact that virtual team members might be outside what we consider to be our normal radius of trust, the immediate work group, makes the task of developing and maintaining trust even more critical for performance. Trust requires leadership to set and maintain values, boundaries, and consistency.

Competence 5: Building and Maintaining Trust

Although trust is usually thought of in the context of a long-term relationship, when people join teams for a short period of time, building and maintaining trust is more difficult and therefore more important.

In face-to-face settings, a number of familiar clues help us determine whom we should trust and whom we should not. Direct exposure to people provides us with the history and context necessary to understand their motivations and therefore to make judgments about their trustworthiness. We are able to evaluate people's nonverbal communication and observe their interactions with other team members. Part of the way in which we judge trustworthiness is through our perceptions, over time, of the other person's reliability and consistency.

On a virtual team, team members may never have the opportunity for face-to-face contact or to use other traditional sources of information that form the basis for developing trust. In a virtual team, creating trust requires a more conscious and planned effort on the part of the team leader. For example, when one of us assumed leadership of a virtual project team and took a tour to meet the team members, people in three locations voiced serious concerns about what would happen to them after the team had finished its work. These individuals had known other people who had worked on a similar project. When the project failed, nine months into the work, none of the team members were able to find new work on interesting assignments. It seems that the team leader not only did not help them find new assignments but also allegedly criticized the team to upper management. It was clear that these individuals would have a difficult time focusing on the new team's work until the issue of trust was addressed.

Developmental Actions

Development activities in this area of competence include the following:

1. Developing an explicit trust plan for the team
2. Examining the behaviors of someone you trust, noting what the person has done to build this trust, and modeling your actions after that person's
3. Asking team members what you can do to build trust and asking team members to state how they will evaluate whether or not they trust you

Myth 6: Networking Matters Less in a Virtual Environment; It Is Only About Results

Even though the use of technology is omnipresent in virtual teamwork and there is an increased emphasis on outcomes over effort, team leaders should never forget that work is accomplished through people. Networking, keeping people informed, and soliciting input from team members, stakeholders, partners, and customers will always be an integral part of a team leader's job. Because virtual teams are more dispersed than traditional teams, team leaders may find themselves spending even more time networking across boundaries.

Competence 6: Networking

If we analyze how effective virtual team leaders spend their time for the first few weeks of the project, we notice that often no "real work" is completed. Activities are focused on establishing links across boundaries and networking. These boundaries and networks are numerous. Networks include team members, managers from local and remote functional areas, customers, and people outside the organization, such as partners, customers, vendors, and suppliers. A large portion of the team leader's time needs to be spent finding ways to create shared perceptions among outsiders about the project and its goals. The network has to be broad and strong enough to withstand competing priorities and changing requirements, to obtain needed resources, and to instill a sense of trust in the team and its work.

On functional teams, networking is also critical. Becoming insular is not an option in most organizations today. Leaders of functional virtual teams need to take special care to look for new practices outside their geographical location and functional area and apply and share these lessons with the team itself. Many organizations with virtual teams hold sharing sessions within and between functions on a regular basis—often at least once a year.

The irony of crossing boundaries and networking in a virtual environment is that often much of it takes place face to face. Attending planning meetings with senior management, conducting team initiation sessions with team members, conducting sharing sessions with other functional leaders, meeting with partner organizations, and visiting customers to establish expectations are all part of the role of any team leader. After solid relationships have been established, some of the face-to-face interaction can be replaced with technology.

Developmental Actions

Development activities in this area of competence include the following:

1. Analyzing relationships with important people across different boundaries, noting patterns of good and poor relationships and what may cause them, and noting what you can do to address the poor patterns
2. Examining the behaviors of someone you respect as a good networker, noting what the person has done, and modeling your actions after that person's
3. Asking team members in what areas they believe the team is effectively networked and in what areas it is not and then working with them to develop a plan to more effectively network and to reach new and important stakeholders
4. Holding sharing sessions with team members and with people from outside the team's core area

Myth 7: Every Aspect of Virtual Teams Should Be Planned, Organized, and Controlled So That There Are No Surprises

Virtual teams exist in adaptive, changing environments. These environments can turn chaotic and can menace or destroy a team's progress. Team leaders should lead in an adaptive way, helping team members understand the uncertainty and nonroutine nature of their work. Managing a virtual team with rigid controls and plans will destroy the team's ability to experience breakthrough performance. Balancing structure with adaptability is a constant tension that virtual team leaders face.

Competence 7: Developing and Adapting Standard Team Processes

In some organizations, although standard processes are available, there may be significant functional or regional differences. The team leader must be adaptable enough to adjust these for the team's task and situation. For example, many organizations use a standard product development process and a set of product development "gates." Often, however, there are distinct differences in how these processes are applied in different product categories or different business units. An experienced virtual team leader understands that there is a need for subtle differences in implementing the process and can lead a team in doing it.

A leader who has detailed process knowledge and a practical understanding of process exceptions is able to address such issues early and provide the team with needed adaptability. Also, team leaders who are open to adaptation are more likely to find creative ways to address the complex problems that today's organizations and teams face.

Developmental Actions

Development activities in this area of competence include the following:

1. Speaking with other virtual team leaders to discover if there are common processes that are relevant to all teams
2. At the team initiation session, developing a list of standard and agreed-on practices and noting the processes that can be adapted
3. Be flexible, and listen to other options for adaptation

Evaluating Competence for Selection and Development

Checklist 4.1 is a diagnostic instrument that can be used to determine the readiness of virtual team leaders through self- or peer assessment. The instrument evaluates the seven areas of competence. The resulting scores can be used to help identify and develop virtual team leaders. To improve the accuracy of this instrument, it is recommended that other team leaders, team members, partners, and customers also complete the assessment with respect to the individual.

The results of the assessment will help identify areas for developmental action.

Developing Expertise

Development efforts should be focused on areas of strategic importance to the organization and the team and on areas that are critical to the leader's career. Virtual team

CHECKLIST 4.1. COMPETENCE AUDIT.

Instructions: Select the level in each area of competence that best characterizes the current skills and experience of the individual being assessed (your own skills and experience if this is a self-assessment).

Competence Area	Skills	Skill Level (1 = low, 2 = medium, 3 = high)	Experience	Experience Level (1 = low, 2 = medium, 3 = high)
Performance management and coaching	• Is able to develop strategy and set performance objectives • Can establish measures for team effectiveness • Is able to give and receive informal and formal performance feedback • Is able to implement strategies that make the contributions of team members visible to the organization		• Has led and managed a number of virtual teams • Has been accountable for a team output	
Appropriate use of technology	• Can plan for the use of technology, given the team's task and type, the backgrounds of team members, and the sophistication of the organization • Is skilled in planning agendas and facilitating virtual work meetings • Is aware of general technology options to support virtual work		• Has experience using a number of different electronic communication and collaboration technologies • Has planned and facilitated a number of virtual team meetings	
Cross-cultural management	• Is able to constructively discuss dimensions of cultural differences • Is able to create ways of working that not only accommodate but optimize cultural differences • Is able to plan major team activities, such as planning, communicating, reviews, and team meetings while taking into account how these activities interact with the cultures of team members		• Has worked in teams with cross-cultural membership	

(continued)

CHECKLIST 4.1. (CONTINUED).

Competence Area	Skills	Skill Level (1 = low, 2 = medium, 3 = high)	Experience	Experience Level (1 = low, 2 = medium, 3 = high)
Career development and transition of team members	• Is able to work with team members to plan careers and transition processes • Is able to act as an advocate for team members' careers and transitions to new assignments		• Has acted as a career and transition coach for team members	
Building trust	• Keeps commitments • Can state personal values • Can portray the team's work to management • Is able to build personal relationships in short periods of time		• Has worked in a virtual team or in a virtual environment	
Networking	• Can identify important stakeholders • Is able to plan and implement networking activities • Is able to exert influence over time and distance		• Has worked in a number of different locations and functions within the organization • Has worked with external partners, such as vendors and suppliers	
Developing and adapting team processes	• Is able to identify the types of standard team processes appropriate for the team's task • Is able to identify standard processes that link to team performance • Is able to adapt team process to the task, the culture of team members, and functional differences		• Has worked with major organizational processes • Has created and/or adapted team processes for other virtual teams	

Total number of 3s: _____   Total number of 3s: _____

Total number of 2s: _____   Total number of 2s: _____

Total number of 1s: _____   Total number of 1s: _____

Total: _____   Total: _____

(continued)

CHECKLIST 4.1. (CONTINUED).

Scoring

Instructions: Total the numbers in the skills and experience boxes for each competence (for example, circling 3 in all skill areas would give you a total score of 21 for skills). Interpret the numbers as follows:

Skill

7 or less: You are probably just getting started in leading a team in a virtual setting. Your challenge is to gain skill in the areas of competence in which you scored 2 or less. This can be accomplished through training, reading, working with a mentor, and working in multiple virtual teams with experienced leadership.

8 to 15: You have a solid understanding of the requirements of virtual team leadership. Your main challenge is to refine your skills for application in a number of different situations. This can best be accomplished through leading multiple virtual teams under the mentorship of experienced managers.

15 and above: You have excellent virtual-team leadership skills. You may want to work on skill areas in which you scored 2 or less and to help others acquire knowledge in this area. This can best be accomplished through working as a mentor or coach or by leading multiple virtual teams.

Experience

7 or less: You probably have not had the chance to practice team leadership in a virtual setting. Your main challenge is to gain experience. This can be accomplished through working with a mentor or by beginning to lead virtual teams under the guidance of experienced management.

8 to 15: You have solid experience in leading in a virtual team setting. Your main challenge is to broaden your experience in a number of different situations. This can best be accomplished through working with a mentor or by leading multiple virtual teams.

15 and above: You have exceptional experience in leading virtual teams. You may want to expand your experience in any areas in which you scored 2 or less and to help others to acquire skills and experience. This can be accomplished through working as a mentor or coach and through leading multiple virtual teams.

leaders can identify their needs for competence development by taking the following assessment and then asking the following four questions:

1. Given the goals of the organization and of the team, what are the important requirements for succeeding as a virtual team leader?
2. Given my results on the competence audit, what are the areas in which I need development? What are my strengths?
3. Where do gaps exist between what the organization and the team require and my personal career plans, skills, and experience?
4. What developmental actions (such as training, special assignments, reading, sharing lessons learned and best practices, mentoring, and on-the-job experiences) can I take to fill the gaps?

Checklists 4.2 and 4.3 provide a framework for analyzing competence gaps and a format for constructing an action plan for improving skills and experience in target areas.

CHECKLIST 4.2. INDIVIDUAL COMPETENCE.

Instructions: Locate the rating of each area of competence as a high, medium, or low priority for your virtual team. Note areas in which there is a mismatch between the priority for the team and your level of competence. Developmental priorities are areas in which a high team priority exists and your competence rating is medium or low.

Type of Team	Performance Management and Coaching	Appropriate Use of Technology	Cross-Cultural Management	Career Development and Transition of Team Members	Building Trust	Networking	Developing and Adapting Team Processes
Network	Medium	High	Depends on team composition	Low	High	High	High
Parallel	Medium	High	Depends on team composition	Medium	High	Medium	High
Project or Product	High	High	Depends on team composition	Medium to high	High	Medium	High
Work or Production	High	Medium to high	Depends on team composition	Medium to high	High	Medium to high	Medium to high
Action	Medium to high	Medium to high	Depends on team composition	Low to medium	High	Medium to high	Medium to high
Service	High	Medium to high	Depends on team composition	Medium to high	High	Low to medium	Medium to high
Management	Medium	Medium	Depends on team composition	Medium	High	High	Medium
Priority for development? (Yes/No)							

CHECKLIST 4.3. PLANNING DEVELOPMENTAL ACTIONS.

Instructions: Use the following worksheet to plan training, on-the-job-assignments, and other activities that can develop your skills and experience.

Area of Competence	Developmental Plans	Estimated Time Frame
Performance management and coaching		
Appropriate use of technology		
Cross-cultural management		
Career development and transition of team members		
Building trust		
Networking		
Developing and adapting team processes		

Near Virtual Disaster

Sara was pulled from her day-to-day role leading the finance team to lead a group of people to design a new funds transfer process. The team was located in ten different locations across the United States. Team members were senior in their field and knew each other but had never worked together before. Sara thought this would be easy. The task was fairly technical, and the team was from the same functional area: finance. Sara decided that she did not need to have a face-to-face kickoff. Trust was not an issue here; just the process: team members were older and savvy—they knew what to do. As work on the task proceeded, however, Sara noticed that they were making no progress at all. Although people were attending meetings and seemed to be agreeing about what needed to happen, nothing was happening. Team members disagreed about how easy or hard the task was, how much they shared information about their current processes with each other, and how hard they were willing to work.

Sara soon discovered that she needed to exercise her virtual leadership skills. She needed to set expectations for team members around performance and deliverables. She needed to make the current process transparent, as most team members could not even agree what it was, and she needed to build some trust between team members. Sara was reminded, again, that the need for leadership did not disappear just because the team members are virtual.

Points to Remember

1. Most people will lead a virtual team at some point in time.
2. Experienced virtual team leaders recognize the myths associated with leading virtual teams.
3. Leading a virtual team requires the development of additional skills that go beyond the traditional ones.
4. A virtual team leader needs to have a personal development plan that is strong in the seven areas of competence.

CHAPTER FIVE

STARTING A VIRTUAL TEAM

This chapter highlights the process involved in starting a virtual team and suggests a six-step plan for doing so. It is possible, however, to enter the process at any of the following steps:

1. Identifying team sponsors, stakeholders, and champions
2. Developing a team charter that includes the team's purpose, mission, and goals
3. Selecting team members
4. Contacting team members
5. Conducting a team orientation session that focuses on explaining the task, team norms, technological planning, communication planning, and team building
6. Developing team processes, such as status mechanisms, review points, and documentation

Certain parts of this chapter apply more to network, parallel, project, product, and action teams than to management, service, production, functional, and work teams. The latter types of teams are usually preexisting rather than starting up. Nevertheless, some of the principles covered in this chapter can be applied to management and work teams after a reorganization, a reengineering effort, or transition to a virtual work environment. In such cases, activities such as rechartering, selecting team members, developing norms, and planning for communication and technology become relevant.

Many aspects of the six steps are also appropriate for functional, work, production, service, and management teams even if they have not just undergone a transition or change. Each step has the underlying objective of providing structure and support in bridging time and distance.

Step 1: Identify Team Sponsors, Stakeholders, and Champions

Because the success of a virtual team often involves effective interaction with and the participation of constituents from a number of functions, locations, and external organizations, virtual team leaders need to ensure from the start that they have the strong support of sponsors, stakeholders, and champions. Sponsors, stakeholders, and champions link the team to the management power structure across locations and organizational boundaries.

Sponsors

A sponsor is the person (usually a member of management) who works closely with the team leader and who acts on the team's behalf to cross organizational barriers, resolve conflicts of interest, obtain resources, and provide a link with upper management. It is vitally important that every virtual team have a sponsor who is strategically positioned in the organization. The sponsor should have a broad perspective, be respected by all appropriate constituents (such as external organizations and supporting functional areas), be influential, and be able to obtain resources. Sponsors apply more to product, project, action, parallel, and networked teams.

Stakeholders

When a virtual team is created, it is also imperative that the team leader identify the stakeholders who have the greatest impact on the team's success and those who will be most affected by the team's results. Stakeholders may be individuals from different functional areas, regions of the world, levels of management, and partner organizations. The virtual team leader should take the time to map the team's inputs and outputs and relate them to appropriate stakeholders. If the team has an identified client or an existing sponsor, that person may be able to assist in this activity. Stakeholder mapping applies to all types of teams. All teams have stakeholders who may or may not be part of the team's leadership chain. It is recommended that all teams take the time to map their critical stakeholders. Don't forget stakeholders who are remote to the team.

When mapping stakeholders, remember that not all stakeholders are created equal. The following is a set of guidelines for categorizing stakeholders:

- Type 1 stakeholders: The two to four people whose opinions and sponsorship are critical to your team's success
- Type 2 stakeholders: The groups whose opinions and sponsorship are critical to your success
- Type 3 stakeholders: Everyone else

Make certain that the team focuses on type 1 stakeholders.

Champions

A champion, although further removed from team activities than sponsors and stakeholders, may be able to find resources, promote the team's activities, remove barriers, and provide advice. A champion frequently has a strong interest in the team and may be found in various functions, regions, and partner organizations. Because part of the champion's role is to assist in the attainment of resources and to create perceptions of the virtual team as successful and productive, it is best if the team's champion is a member of the organization's top management.

Checklist 5.1 provides a strategy for mapping and identifying sponsors, stakeholders, and champions. It also presents a starting point for planning communication and boundary management activities. It presents a way to map the importance of specific characteristics to each sponsor, stakeholder, and champion so as to plan communication activities more efficiently.

Step 2: Developing a Team Charter

It is necessary to have a clearly understood statement of direction and purpose for any team. The charter, succinctly setting out the team's purpose, mission, and goals, serves as a point of departure for more detailed plans and for alignment of team member effort and measurement of performance. For traditional teams, if the starting point is properly aimed, the day-to-day contact of the team members can add meaning and reinforce shared understanding between team members. The synergy that results from day-to-day interaction tends to facilitate a smooth transition from the charter to other activities. For virtual teams, the lack of physical contact may erode meaning and understanding and make the link between charter and work more tenuous. For this reason, preparation must be more thoroughly planned and reinforced.

CHECKLIST 5.1. IDENTIFICATION OF SPONSORS, STAKEHOLDERS, AND CHAMPIONS.

Part One

Instructions: Use this worksheet to identify the requirements for the sponsor, stakeholders, and a champion for your team. The top row of the table lists potential requirements for these individuals. Mark those that apply to your team. Rate each requirement as high, medium, or low for the specific category of sponsor, stakeholder, or champion.

On the second part of the worksheet, list people you know who might fit these requirements. If no one comes to mind, check with other team leaders, with your managers, or with your sponsor.

Requirements	Can Remove Roadblocks	Has Cross-Cultural Experience	Is Respected Across Functions or Organizations	His or Her Organization Has a Stake in the Outcome of the Team's Work	Can Provide Relevant Technical or Political Input into the Team's Work
Sponsor: *Importance* High Medium Low					
Stakeholder: *Importance* High Medium Low					
Champion: *Importance* High Medium Low					

(continued)

CHECKLIST 5.1. (CONTINUED).

Part Two

Names of Potential Candidates

Sponsor	
Stakeholders	
Champion	

Most virtual teams have extended membership throughout the organization and beyond. Stakeholders, even if they are not part of the everyday work team, need to be included in creating the team's charter. The task of developing the team's charter is overlaid and affected by an equally important set of tasks having to do with ensuring team members' willing participation, cooperation, and input. Eliciting this support early in the team's life cycle helps reduce the number of issues that may arise later due to conflicts of interest, shifting priorities, or loss of resources. Because virtual teams cross so many boundaries, the potential for conflicts of interest or priorities is great.

Many organizations use a standard set of elements for a team's charter. Some proj-ect management software packages also provide templates for team charters. The best format is one that is familiar to the team's stakeholders, clients, and team members.

Sometimes the team is provided with the charter's content. If so, all that remains is to validate the information with the team's sponsor, stakeholders, and clients and to make sure that all the immediate questions and concerns are answered. It is generally a good idea to plan the validation session so that all the important stakeholders can interact in real time. If the project is complicated, a face-to-face session is especially recommended. If this is not possible, desktop video with data-conferencing capabilities for reviewing documents is the next-best option.

When a virtual team has been working for some time but does not have a well-stated charter, the "new" virtual team leader must create one. This is best done in a face-to-face session with management and other stakeholders and champions. Developing the team's charter in a manner that facilitates interaction and participation from all stakeholders is best done in a face-to-face or synchronous meeting, especially if the team's task may later have to address issues regarding conflicts of interest or resource reallocation. A less preferable option is to conduct the session remotely, in real time, using a videoconference, desktop video with text and graphics, or audioconference with text and graphics. The least effective method is to use an asynchronous method, such as e-mail or voice mail, in which the virtual team develops the materials and forwards them to each stakeholder or member of management for comment and validation.

If a videoconference is the selected technology, make certain that the video system is of sufficient fidelity so as not to be a distraction for the attendees. Choppy pictures that result from outdated or inadequate technology hinder effective interaction. Especially after the introductions, many participants find that the video does not add much to ensuring task performance.

Checklist 5.2 offers a suggested agenda for a meeting to validate a team's charter.

Step 3: Selecting Team Members

Sometimes, especially in the case of work and functional teams, team members already belong to the team. The optimal situation, however, is to have the freedom to identify and select members who meet the demands of the task and who are well suited to working virtually. A good idea, if a team leader has the luxury of selecting team members, is to review their experience and competence in working virtually using the checklist in Chapter Six. Most team leaders check technical and interpersonal skills, which is a good start. The virtual environment adds the need for a third set of competencies.

Most network, parallel, project, and product virtual teams have at least three types of team members: core, extended, and ancillary (see Figure 5.1). Core team members are accountable for direct task output. Core members may include employees from distant locations, vendors, suppliers, and customers. Extended team members do not usually work with the team on a daily basis but provide expert support or advice when necessary. Extended team members may be internal and external consultants, sponsors, and stakeholders. Ancillary team members do not work on the team but review and approve the team's work and deliverables. Ancillary team members include the team's client or sponsor, major stakeholders, and certain high-level managers. It is possible, depending on the type of team, the point in its life cycle, and its structure, that team membership may be dynamic, with certain members moving from one category to another. This is especially the case with network, parallel, project, and product teams.

After identifying individuals who appear to meet the team's requirements, it may be a good idea to check the logic of the selection (and the reputation of each team member) with the sponsor and a few stakeholders or champions. Sometimes a person has a good local reputation but is not respected in other parts of the organization or in other functions. For teams that require extensive boundary management and networking, team members who are respected and productive in a number of different geographical or functional settings can help teams attain their objectives.

CHECKLIST 5.2. AGENDA FOR VALIDATING A TEAM'S CHARTER.

This agenda can be adapted by a facilitator for a distributed format.

Activity	Estimated Time
Send agenda, draft of team's charter, potential schedule, review schedule, and other relevant information to all participants at least one week before the meeting. Be certain that each person has all elements of the charter in front of him or her when the meeting begins.	N/A
Begin the session by introducing yourself, the agenda, and the outcomes (approval of team's charter, mission, purpose, and goals). Ask for feedback on the agenda. Make changes if necessary and announce them to the group.	15 minutes
Have the team's sponsor provide a short overview of the team and its history. Have stakeholders introduce themselves and their roles vis-à-vis the team.	30 minutes
Go through each element of the current charter: mission, purpose, and goals, one at a time. Have each participant rate each element on a scale of 1 to 5, with 5 as "completely agree" and 1 as "not agree" with the element. Ask if there are questions regarding each element. Keep a written log of comments and changes.	60 minutes
Work through each element one by one until you have reached agreement on it. You may have to go around a number of times. Use a consensus process.	1–2 hours
Review changes, modifications, or new actions for each element.	30 minutes
Discuss risks associated with the team's work and how they may be mitigated. Introduce the idea of potential conflicts of interest and resources. Briefly discuss how these might be addressed.	15–30 minutes
Discuss a preliminary schedule and how often work should be reviewed with each type of stakeholder or champion. Have a draft of this to present to the group, including agreement on the method of information sharing (e-mail, shared software, and so on). Select the simplest method. Understand each stakeholder's experience in using these technologies.	30–45 minutes
Set a follow-up schedule. Ask if there are any final comments. Distribute notes within 48 hours.	15 minutes

FIGURE 5.1. TEAM MEMBERSHIP.

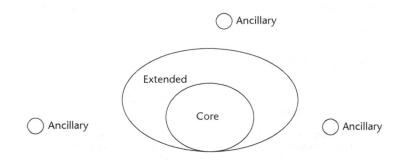

You will want to work out in advance how to make sure that extended and ancillary team members are included in team decisions, meetings, reviews, and other relevant matters. These individuals often complain that they are overlooked on traditional teams; on virtual teams, there is an even greater chance that they might be left out, most likely unintentionally, but that oversight could foster and fuel trust issues.

Step 4: Contacting Team Members

Effective virtual team leaders pay a lot of attention to the first interactions they have with their team members, either when chartering a new team or when introducing a new team member to an existing team. They carefully orchestrate how team members meet one another and how new members are introduced. There are some very simple practices that experienced virtual team leaders engage in during this step:

1. They make sure that all team members clearly understand the team's task and their own work function and role on the team.
2. They arrange for appropriate amounts of interaction among team members before the work actually begins or at the beginning of the person's tenure if this is a functional, service, or work team.
3. They make special efforts to facilitate the feeling of being part of the team.

The third item is complex. Because the focus of many virtual teams—especially action and parallel teams—is on the task, team members may feel that too much attention to togetherness is inappropriate and nonproductive. This is especially true of team members whose national cultures are low-context and individualistic and of team members who come from engineering and science backgrounds. Highly experienced virtual team members may also have less need for activities that facilitate inclusion, especially if the task is a repetition of earlier work or if the schedule is extremely tight.

Let's look at how Sara introduces team members to one another as an example of best practice in this area.

Sara prefers to have a face-to-face meeting to initiate the real work of the team. Prior to the meeting, she tries to visit each team member and major stakeholder, sponsor, and champion. At the very least, she sets up telephone calls with team members to review the fundamentals of the task or project, to introduce herself, and to find out a little about the individual team members and their backgrounds. Sara uses this opportunity to ask about each team member's communication capabilities and computer hardware and software applications. She sends each team member the team's charter and other relevant information. Sara has found from experience that meeting team members face to face or spending time with them on the telephone can solidify feelings of being part of the team.

Sara also makes a practice of asking each team member to set up a personal Web page.[1] (Presenting each team member to the others can also be accomplished using CD-ROM or video technology.) Each Web page is linked to a directory of team members and contains the following information:

1. Contact information, such as telephone number, voice mail number, e-mail address, fax number, and pager number
2. How often e-mail and voice mail are checked and how long it is until a page, e-mail message, or telephone call is answered
3. Time zone, work hours, and availability on evenings and weekends
4. Hardware and software tools and applications
5. Personal information the team member would like to share, such as areas of expertise, how that expertise relates to the team's task, and any hobbies or interests

Once the team is up and running, team members can add to the Web page information regarding what they are working on each week and their progress.

The objective for the team leader is to facilitate interaction with each team member before the team actually begins work or as a new team member enters the team. The team leader should make sure that each team member has at least one personal interaction with the team leader, feels welcome, and has chance to discuss his or her background and expertise. At this point, it is important not to go too far with activities that may be too personal or threatening for any team member. The team leader should be aware of cultural considerations and understand that people from collective cultures may want more interaction than individuals from individualistic cultures.

Here are some best practices for establishing contact with team members prior to the team's formal initiation meeting:

1. Call or visit each team member personally.
2. Provide some mechanism for team members to find information about one another.
3. Facilitate interaction in a nonthreatening way.
4. Send all team members information about the team, including its charter and if it is an existing team and information about the person's role and others' roles.
5. Make certain that a forum exists for answering team members' questions.
6. Find out whether any team members have hardware or software availability or compatibility issues.

Some leaders of functional, work, or service teams assign a new team member a "buddy" or someone other than the team leader who can orient the new team member to the team.

Step 5: Conducting a Team Orientation Session

The ideal orientation, cited as a best practice by virtual teams, is a face-to-face meeting that is attended by all team members.

Face-to-Face Meeting

Currently, no technology can provide the give-and-take, the feeling of human interaction, and the understanding that develop from a face-to-face meeting. Because the outcome of the session is the creation of a rather complex plan for team performance, which includes team norms and communication protocols, face-to-face communication can facilitate shared understanding. Such a session is especially important for team members from high-context and collective cultures who expect and respond to more personal contact. A virtual team leader should lobby diligently for the resources and time for a face-to-face meeting. Not doing so usually means that a team whose members do not know one another can take up to twice as long to understand their task as teams who meet face to face.

When should a face-to-face sessions be held?

- If team members do not know each other and the project or work is complex and requires a high degree of interaction
- If the task is new and ambiguous or the team members are new to each other.

Furthermore, the team leader should consider holding regular face-to-face meetings every two to three months with new teams until effective communication patterns have been established and every six months thereafter.

If a face-to-face orientation session is not possible, an audioconference or video-conference is the next best choice—ideally backed up by a team Web site and interactive Web tools for sharing information. Virtual teams should not be tempted to use e-mail, bulletin boards, data-only conferencing, or groupware without video capability. These tools can help in the exchange of information prior to the session or afterward, but they are not as suitable for events that require extensive interaction.

The Agenda

The agenda for the orientation session, at a minimum, should feature the following:

1. Orientation to the team's task, including an overview of the team's charter or mission, an opportunity for team members to react to and offer suggestions about the elements in the team's charter or mission, and a review of each team member's expertise and accountabilities
2. Development of team norms, technological plans, and communication plans
3. Team building

Orientation to the Team's Task. All team members should leave the orientation session with a shared understanding of the task of the team and their roles in completing it. Using the team's charter as a starting point is a good idea because most team members have had a chance to review it prior to the orientation meeting. The review of the charter should include the team's mission, purpose, goals, initial timelines, and deliverables. The purpose of reviewing the charter in detail is to ensure that team members understand each element of the charter and have an opportunity to ask questions. Team members can often make useful suggestions and add to the elements of the charter. They should also be given the chance to identify barriers to success that may be unique between specific functions, locations, or organizations.

An important part of the outcome of this part of the agenda is for every team member to develop a clear understanding of his or her task accountabilities in regard to the team's schedule and the tasks of the other team members. The roles and accountabilities of external partners must also be defined. The resulting clarity will facilitate smooth collaboration across organizational boundaries in the future.

Other things to be defined include who has the authority to change other people's work and who will approve final products. Often team leaders use a process in which team members' and partners' accountabilities and decision-making authority are mapped with respect to critical team outputs. This can be done using a responsibility matrix, borrowed from project management practices, to create a table of each team member's accountabilities in regard to important team deliverables and decisions. In this way, team members know who is responsible for what and when. The matrix can be placed on the team's Web page and can be updated as tasks are completed or when team members change.

Development of Team Norms. Establishing team norms helps clarify expectations about acceptable and unacceptable behaviors for all persons who work on or with the team. Team norms guide participation, communication, conflict management, meeting management, problem solving, and decision making. Virtual teams may require unique and more detailed process norms than traditional teams. Virtual team norms include the following:

- Telephone, audioconference, and videoconference etiquette and meeting management, such as techniques for ensuring participation from all team members, protocols for saying who one is before one speaks, using the mute button when one is not talking, giving people who are using a second language time to collect their thoughts, using a meeting agenda, taking and distributing minutes, and rotating time zones.
- Guidelines regarding acceptable time frames for returning telephone calls and e-mail messages and the uses of voice mail and pagers.
- Guidelines about using e-mail: when it should be used, when it should not be used, and how e-mail messages should be constructed—including when to flag messages as "urgent" and as "important."
- Which meetings must be attended in person, which can be attended by audioconference or videoconference, and which can be missed.
- How work will be reviewed and approved. This includes which team members will review work and which ones can approve deliverables.
- Procedures for scheduling meetings using group-scheduling systems.
- Technological applications to be used by team members and policies regarding upgrades. (Compatibility problems can result if one team member upgrades software ahead of the others.)

A sample set of norms for a virtual team is presented in Table 5.1. A worksheet for developing team norms is provided in Table 5.2.

Development of Technology Plans. Planning what types of technology the team will use is a vital part of the team's orientation session. In planning how technology will be used, the first step is to consider the type of work the team will be doing. Work on many teams can be characterized as parallel or independent, sequential, or pooled sequential or team work.[2]

Parallel work occurs when team members work independently on separate parts of a document or other product. Their outputs are then integrated into a final product.

TABLE 5.1. SAMPLE TEAM NORMS.

Voice Mail

- Check voice mail every day, and return calls within twenty-four hours.
- If you are unable to check voice mail, record a greeting that informs others of your limited access.
- When leaving messages for others
    Speak slowly and clearly
    Be clear and concise about what you need, when you need it, and how you want to receive it
    Leave your complete phone number (including country code)
- State your name and phone number at the beginning and end of each message.

E-Mail

- Check e-mail every day, and return urgent e-mails within twenty-four hours.
- If you will not be checking your e-mail for any reason, use the "out of office" alert.
- Assume that if you are sent a copy of a message (that is, if your address is listed after "Cc:" rather than after "To:"), it is for your information only, and no reply is required.
- Remember that certain comments can come across as somewhat harsh in e-mail; be as diplomatic as possible in your choice of words.
- If you write a message in an emotional or agitated state, save it for a day and review and revise it as necessary before sending it.
- Do not use e-mail to resolve interpersonal issues, communicate sensitive information, or avoid personal interaction.
- Indicate in the subject line what you need and by when.
- Use keywords in the subject line to help the recipient prioritize:
    FYI means that the e-mail is not urgent but contains something of interest.
    ACTION BY (DATE): (SUBJECT) means that a response or action is needed by the given date—notify the sender immediately if you cannot make the deadline.
    URGENT FYI means that the information must be read immediately.
    URGENT ACTION: (SUBJECT) means that the recipient must read and take action on the noted subject immediately.
- "Reply to All" should be used only when all parties need to have your information; attachments to such replies should be deleted.
- Review e-mail lists regularly to be sure they are up-to-date, and ask to be taken off old lists.
- If there are more than three e-mail threads, make a phone call to resolve issue.
- Always run spell-check before sending a message.
- Do not use ALL CAPITALS in the message body.
- Schedule meetings via a calendaring function and not by e-mail.
- When declining a meeting invitation, provide a reason and possibly an alternative time.

Instant Messaging

- Log on when you get into the office.
- Use the "I am away" and "Do not disturb" features of the application when you are away from your desk or already participating in an e-meeting.
- Turn IM off when you are in meetings or presenting.

(continued)

TABLE 5.1. (CONTINUED).

Cell Phones and Pagers

- Switch to vibrate mode during meetings.
- Answer during meetings only when the call is urgent.
- Use only when the other party has agreed that he or she wants to use this as a method of communication.

Audio- and Videoconferencing

- All participants should announce their presence at the beginning of the conference or when they arrive—don't be a stealth participant!
- Identify yourself when speaking.
- Use mute buttons when people are not speaking.
- Do not engage in side conversations during a meeting; it is very frustrating for people not in the location of the actual discussion.
- If you have a problem hearing someone, notify the speaker.
- The leader of a videoconference should arrive early and establish the conference link prior to the meeting's start time.

Meeting Management

- Be on time for videoconferences, audioconferences, and other meetings, and attend the entire meeting.
- Rotate time zones for meetings.
- Link time and date to North American Eastern Standard Time (or whatever time zone is appropriate for the team).
- Take breaks every sixty to ninety minutes during audioconferences and videoconferences.
- Do not interrupt others in any meeting.
- Respect the facilitator's attempts to foster participation from all team members.
- The agenda should be sent out via e-mail no less than forty-eight hours in advance of every meeting, and minutes are sent out via e-mail no more than forty-eight hours after each meeting. Follow the agenda, and rotate taking minutes.
- If there are participants whose native language is different from the language in which the meeting is being conducted, give them time to think and time to speak. We provide "think breaks" so that people can gather their thoughts.
- At the end of each meeting, evaluate everyone's performance against the team norms.

Decision Making and Problem Solving

- Use a common approach to problem solving and decision making.
- Keep the interests and goals of the team in the forefront of all decisions.
- Balance the local interests of team members with those of the entire team.
- If advice is needed, turn first to the team member who is considered an expert before going outside the team.
- Strive for consensus but realize that consensus takes time and is not always necessary. If consensus cannot be reached, accept the expert team member's opinion.

(continued)

TABLE 5.1. (CONTINUED).

Conflict Management

- Resolve differences in ways of doing business using the company code of conduct.
- Do not settle differences via e-mail. Call and speak directly to the person. Approach the person first, not the team leader or another team member.
- Use an established conflict management process.
- Realize that conflict is a normal part of the team's life cycle and that conflict focused on the task and not each other is healthy and productive.
- Recognize that unproductive conflict is more difficult to detect in a virtual setting, so take the pulse of the team frequently to ensure that conflict produces positive tension. Don't let tensions build.

Working Together to Produce or Review Documents

- Do not review details of long documents on group audioconferences; send them to the team leader or another person designated to integrate information and send out as notes.
- When working in an "assembly-line" fashion, move the document through the system in a timely manner. Give each other feedback when promised.
- Keep confidential documents within the team, and do not allow external team members to review them.
- Review the team's progress at the same time each week for a specific length of time via audioconference.
- Send agenda items and updates to the facilitator by the same deadline every week.
- The team leader is the only one with authority to release the documents to the client.

Sequential work occurs when one or two individuals work on a document or product and then pass it to other team members, who also work on it and then pass it on. This way of working is analogous to an assembly line, in which parts are added sequentially until a final product is created. It is a common way of working for work teams and production teams that use workflow processes and associated software.

Pooled sequential work can be likened to a library: team members check out a document (or part of one), make changes, and then turn it back in. The document or product is kept in its original place (pooled) and is updated each time a team member works on it. This way of working is well suited to virtual teams. It allows all team members to work on a product simultaneously and can replace the sequential way of working that many traditional teams use.

Each virtual team needs to determine how it wants to work and then select the most complementary and cost-effective technology. For parallel work, there are very simple solutions. E-mail (assuming that there are no major compatibility issues) is often an easy answer. Sequential work can also be accomplished using e-mail or other data

TABLE 5.2. TEAM NORMS.

Instructions: Use this worksheet to document your virtual team norms. Make certain that all team members agree to each norm and have all team members sign the document. You may choose to post this on a team Web site.

Team Name: _____

Team Norms

Category	Norms
Keeping in Touch with Other Team Members	
Meeting Management	
Decision Making and Problem Solving	
Conflict Management	
Working Together to Produce or Review Documents	
Other	

Team Member's Signature:

_____

exchange technologies. Pooled sequential work requires more sophisticated technology, such as a distributed database or an Internet document repository. Such systems store information and documents in a central electronic location, from which team members can access the latest versions of the team's work, work on it, and then replace it. Such systems are capable of automatically updating all previous versions of the team's work, including related documents and data.

Teams that collect data from many different locations find that input into a common database saves time and confusion. Many systems automatically mark data as coming from a specific location, integrate new data with existing materials, store the data, and update the database as new information is added. Many team members estimate that using a shared database saves weeks of time that would have been spent passing the database from one location to another.

Using technology to perform pooled sequential work requires some preparation. First, team members must learn how to use the requisite software. Training and practice for all team members should become a requirement for orientation. In addition, the team needs to establish very clear team norms and protocols. These include, at a minimum, all of the following:

1. Authority and security measures that enable team members to check out materials. There may be core team members or ancillary members who do not need to see the information until a certain point in the process. They might be customers or external partners whom the team does not want to see an unfinished product.
2. A statement of who has the authority to add, change, and delete which portions of the product.
3. A statement of how often the team, or a subteam, will formally discuss and review the status of the product. Although many people prefer to communicate informally, formal discussions that mark decision points are important.
4. Established time schedules for development, modifications, and revisions.
5. A statement of who has the authority for final review and approval.
6. A mandate for team members to actually use the system consistently and not to exchange information or add to documents in any other electronic or nonelectronic manner.

It is not uncommon for teams who attempt to use distributed databases, collaborative notebooks, and other, more sophisticated, computer-supported collaborative-work software for pooled work to find that implementation of these systems is not a smooth process.[3] In many cases, the systems are never used or are underused by the team. The use of such systems must be to address specific problems, not as the result of a "technology push." Four guidelines are relevant for teams in selecting technology for pooled work:[4]

1. Team members may overestimate how much time they spend in team-related or pooled work. Most work may actually be accomplished using relatively independent activities. If that is the case, the information shared by distributed databases may be perceived as irrelevant. Prior to selecting technology, ensure that the task actually requires pooled work.

2. Different styles of work are usually preferred by people in different professions. Professionals such as artists and architects tend to prefer more open work spaces in which they can peruse other people's work. Software engineers, academics, and writers tend to prefer more enclosed and private work spaces.[5] As a result, people from the latter categories of professions may prefer to wait until their products are more finished before sharing them with others.

3. The technology selected should integrate with existing systems, including messaging, calendaring, and scheduling systems, and other applications. Even if it is easy to use and portable, if it is not integrated, it will become another box on the desk.

4. Technology works best when it is integrated into the beginning of the team's work. Infiltrating a system into existing work is difficult because it disrupts existing patterns of behavior.

Checklist 5.3 will help in selecting technological strategies.

Development of Communication Plans. How team members communicate with one another and with important stakeholders throughout the team's life is a critical success factor. It is the primary way in which virtual teams manage organizational boundaries. Teams that keep to themselves or engage in low levels of communication do not perform as well as more communicative teams.[6] However, frequent communication does not in itself ensure success. External communication needs to be carefully orchestrated, with the goal of managing other people's perceptions of the team and their access to the team's progress and problems.

Managing boundaries involves three vital functions: (1) providing the team with access to the power structure (usually top management); (2) managing horizontal interfaces and dependence on other teams, organizational functions, and external partners; and (3) providing the team with access to important information.[7] Each of these functions necessitates a separate communication strategy.

Access to the power structure is achieved through communications called ambassadorial behaviors. These activities promote the team and its work, building bridges to resources and lobbying with the top management of the organization for support. Top managers who are crucial to the team's success, stakeholders, and champions must maintain positive views of the team. The communication plan and other team activities are directed at influencing these key people. The team uses its communication plan almost as an organization performs public relations.

CHECKLIST 5.3. TECHNOLOGY PLANNING.

Instructions: Use the information in this worksheet to match technology to the team's work. In the first column, list different team activities under different types of work. In the second column, list the names of team members involved in the work. In the third column, list the types of technologies that will be used.

Type of Work	Team Members Who Work This Way	Technology to Be Used	Special Notes
Parallel			
Sequential			
Pooled Sequential			

The active assistance of virtual team members is vital in performing this function. Team members are especially valuable for identifying people in their functions, organizations, and regions who should be targeted for ambassadorial behaviors. Team members can help establish a coordinated method for ensuring that the right messages are sent to these people at the right times. The answers to questions such as "What do people think of us?" "Who supports us and who doesn't?" and "What can we do about it?" should be reviewed on a regular basis. Team members are often the best ambassadors for the team because they understand the team's work and have high stakes in its successful outcome.

The second function of boundary management, managing horizontal interfaces, is accomplished by employing strategies that emphasize lateral communication and integration of work. This entails the establishment of two-way communication links about the team's activities to people in other teams, functional groups, and external partner organizations. This is done in order to align or harmonize team efforts with outside activities.

The third function of boundary management, accessing information, is facilitated by a communication activity called scouting. Scouting is aimed at obtaining information from many different customers, stakeholders, experts, and managers about their preferences, wants, and needs. Extensive scouting is most useful in the beginning stages of the team's life and during plan development. Intense scouting activity becomes less useful as the team moves forward.

In general, the most successful teams are those that either spend time engaging in ambassadorial behaviors or carry out comprehensive strategies that integrate ambassadorial, horizontal, and scouting activities.[8] Over the short run, teams that emphasize ambassadorial strategies perform well in the areas of adhering to the schedule and budgeting. Team members also report strong feelings of team unity and cohesiveness. Teams that integrate all three strategies feel lower levels of team unity but have, in the long run, higher performance in terms of scheduling and budget outcomes. Teams that integrate ambassadorial, horizontal, and scouting activities are also more likely to be perceived by management as innovative. Teams that overuse scouting or horizontal integration and teams that do not use any of the three strategies are usually perceived as performing poorly in the long run.

The implication for virtual teams is that matching boundary management objectives with detailed communication plans is a critical activity. A carefully crafted and integrated plan should identify items such as the following:

- What information scouting should target, how it should be accomplished, and when scouting should be suspended or modified
- When ambassadorial behaviors will be effective, whom they will be directed at, and what the message will be
- When horizontal integration is appropriate, with what functions or organizations, and by what communications media

An effective communication plan establishes accountabilities for data collection, data analysis, and information sharing. It also defines the specific messages that will be delivered as well as the most appropriate communications media. For example, the members of a team that has an effective boundary management and communication plan will never send e-mail messages to a top manager who prefers face-to-face briefings.

Checklist 5.4 provides a methodology for developing an external boundary-spanning and communication plan.

Team Building. A key part of the team's orientation session is a nonthreatening team-building activity that is appropriate for the team's task and the cultural composition of the group. There is usually ample opportunity to do this in a face-to-face orientation session. Possible activities include going out to dinner as a team, engaging in outdoor

CHECKLIST 5.4. EXTERNAL BOUNDARY SPANNING AND COMMUNICATION.

Part One

Instructions: In column 1, list the major stakeholders, champions, and managers involved in your team's success. Also list partner organizations, functions, and other groups that can impact your team's work or may be impacted by its results.

For each listing in column 1, have the team members rate their perceptions of the person's, group's, or organization's support of the team, with 1 being high and 5 being low. Use this information in planning what types of communication activities need to be part of the team's interactions with those persons, groups, or organizations.

Stakeholders, Champions, Managers, Organizations, Functions, Other Groups	Support of the Team? (1 = high; 5 = low)	Comments

(continued)

CHECKLIST 5.4. (CONTINUED).

Part Two

Instructions: Use the information you generated in Part One of this worksheet to plan your boundary-management and communication activities. Use the following table to plan activities. Pay particular attention to any individuals or groups rated as low supporters.

Try to anticipate communication that should occur throughout the team's life cycle. The team should check the effectiveness of communication and boundary-spanning activities on a regular basis.

Boundary-Spanning Function	To Whom?	How Often? At What Points in the Team's Life Cycle?	By What Media or Technology?
Ambassadorial			
Horizontal communication with other functions, partner organizations, groups			
Scouting and information gathering			

activities, completing personality inventories that reveal how team members prefer to communicate and work, and engaging in indoor games that point to the value of teamwork. In an audioconference or a videoconference, the options for team building are more limited. In both types of sessions, the team leader should keep two things in mind: (1) the selection and use of team-building activities may be subject to cultural bias, and (2) experienced virtual team members may perceive too much time spent on team building as inappropriate and wasteful.

Some team leaders ask team members to write and post interesting information about themselves on the team Web site. There are a number of different approaches for doing this: (1) have people post a short but interesting résumé, (2) have team members create a visual collage that communicates something about themselves, or (3) have team members create and post a radio spot or personal ad about themselves. During the orientation session, team members can share interesting information about themselves using these team-building tools.

Cultural Bias. Formal team building is conducted primarily in Western nations. In North America, Canada, and Europe, team-building exercises typically focus on sharing personal information, discussing the results of personality inventories, and participating in competitive games. People from collective or low-context cultures sometimes do not feel as comfortable when participating in many of these activities. Individuals from more collective cultures may feel that discussing personalities draws too much attention to each individual team member. People from low-context cultures may perceive personal information as irrelevant. In addition, although many personality inventories work well in North America and in many parts of Europe, some have never been validated in Asia, South America, Africa, and other parts of the world. "Adventure" activities and competitive games may be perceived by people from collective cultures as breaking down rather than building up a team. For these reasons, a team leader should be very careful in selecting team-building activities.

Table 5.3 outlines how specific cultural dimensions fit with team-building activities. Table 5.4 lists team-building activities that are appropriate in any cultural setting.

Working with Experienced Virtual Team Members. Many experienced virtual team members view team building that does not involve discussion of the work content as a waste of time. Experienced virtual team members and team members who have worked together before and are comfortable with one another often want to understand the task and get to work.

Step 6: Developing Team Processes

During the orientation meeting, the team leader should explain the processes that will be used to manage and control the team's work. These can often be reviewed or developed with the team members' assistance during the orientation meeting. Many high-performing virtual teams adopt project management practices to control their work. Even work, functional, and production teams are often able to use these tools effectively. They provide some of the additional rigor necessary to see and assess performance across time and distance boundaries. It is quite easy to find project management software packages that assist in these processes. Many can be imported into standard groupware systems.

TABLE 5.3. TEAM-BUILDING CONSIDERATIONS.

Cultural Dimensions

Individualism/ Collectivism	Uncertainty Avoidance	Power Distance	High or Low Context
If your team has a high concentration of individuals from individualistic cultures: Use team-building activities and instruments that allow individuals to talk about themselves first, then move to how the team members will work together.	If your team has a high concentration of individuals from high-uncertainty-avoidance cultures: Use team-building activities and instruments that allow individuals to discuss very concretely how the team members will work together.	If your team has a high concentration of individuals from high-power-distance cultures: Use team-building activities and instruments that allow individuals to discuss their backgrounds in relation to others in the organization. Use team-building activities that do not disrupt power differences in the team.	If your team has a high concentration of individuals from high-context cultures: Use team-building activities and instruments that allow individuals to discuss their backgrounds and preferences in great detail.
If your team has a high concentration of individuals from collective cultures: Use team-building activities and instruments that allow individuals to talk about the team first, then move to how each individual contributes. Avoid activities or instruments that call too much attention to the individual apart from the team.	If your team has a high concentration of individuals from low-uncertainty-avoidance cultures: Use team-building activities and instruments that allow individuals to discuss very generally how the team will work together; discuss specifics later.	If your team has a high concentration of individuals from low-power-distance cultures: Use team-building activities and instruments that allow individuals to discuss their backgrounds in relation to the team. Feel free to use competitive team-building activities in which any team can win. Be certain to discuss the pros and cons of competition.	If your team has a high concentration of individuals from low-context cultures: Use team-building activities and instruments that allow individuals to discuss their backgrounds and preferences in general terms.

TABLE 5.4. TEAM-BUILDING ACTIVITIES.

Team-Building Activities That Can Be Used in Any Cultural Setting

1. Team-member dinner party for a face-to-face setting.

2. Ask each individual to describe his or her expertise and background as well as his or her best practices collected from other team experiences.

3. Ask each team member to tell the team something interesting about his or her culture or function and its way of doing business that the team may want to adopt.

4. Ask each team member to explain how he or she plans to facilitate boundary-management activities with his or her function, region, or organization.

5. Ask each team member to describe how the team can best use his or her particular expertise.

6. Use a whiteboard or other presentation software to share interesting information about previous projects or best practices.

7. Examine best-practice documents from other teams and apply them to the team. Subteams of people from different cultures can work together on this activity.

8. Use groupware functions, such as anonymity, to vote or poll in the early part of the team's activities so that team members from collective or high-power-distance cultures feel comfortable stating their opinions.

9. Share resumés, picture collages, and favorite music among team members for team building.

The most common items are templates that are used for scheduling, assigning tasks to team members, reporting work status, and obtaining data on slips in the schedule and costs. Teams should also plan regular, frequent reviews by establishing agendas that address milestones, plans, problems, status vis-à-vis milestones, and costs.

An important part of this step is a discussion about the ways in which information about the team's history and progress will be documented, stored, and exchanged. Information such as reference materials, historical information, plans, scouting reports, the status of related internal or external activities, and team-generated products are valuable in orienting new team members. They are also valuable resources for future teams that are performing related tasks. Team leaders must ensure that distributed databases and other information-sharing applications provide equal access to all team members.

Many project, product, parallel, and network teams create electronic project folders that support communication and collaboration on a single project. Different types of system users—usually owners, members, and an administrator—are identified. Accounts for team members are created with passwords to ensure control over the system. Owners, perhaps of subteams, create folders and can invite other people to use, view, or modify the contents. In this way, documentation about the project is maintained by team members who "own" certain tasks or part of the project or process. Suggestions for documentation are provided in Table 5.5.

Steps for Existing Teams

Leaders of existing virtual teams may choose to undertake some of the activities described in this chapter. Many of the activities are also appropriate for use in replanning, indoctrinating new team members, redirecting work, and addressing team problems. For example, after significant team deliverables or a process-reengineering activity, the team leader may conduct a lessons-learned session to explore improvement opportunities. This lends itself well to reestablishing norms, communication plans, and technological plans. Because a number of face-to-face team sessions are common for long-term virtual teams, including work and production teams, a team leader can also use such gatherings to review the effectiveness of the team's norms, technological plan, and communication plan.

Finally, team orientation sessions are appropriate when a number of new members join the team and when new stakeholders are introduced to the team. Checklist 5.5 lists activities that should be considered critical in orienting new team members.

TABLE 5.5. DOCUMENTATION AND STORAGE GUIDELINES.

1. Templates should be available to document the following:
   - The team's charter, technology plans, and communication plans
   - Schedules
   - Cost estimates
   - Requirements from customers
   - Changes in plans
   - Weekly status reviews
   - Monthly status reviews
   - Problems
   - Lessons learned and best practices
2. All team members should exchange documents using _____ (application).
3. All team members should store current deliverables in _____ (location). Use the following security protocol: _____

_____

_____

_____

CHECKLIST 5.5. NEW TEAM MEMBER ORIENTATION.

Note that most of the orientation would be conducted over the phone following a face-to-face visit from the team leader.

1. First face-to-face or phone meeting with the team leader _____
   - Welcome to the team _____
   - Review of team mission, purpose, charter, and objectives _____
   - Review of deliverables and schedule _____
   - Review of roles and accountabilities _____
   - Development of new team member's role, accountabilities, and deliverables _____
   - Introduction of partner system _____
   - Review of status meeting schedule and access (phone, e-mail, and so on) _____
   - Determination that team member has adequate technical and other resources _____
2. Initial orientation from partner _____
   - Introductions _____
   - Review of face-to-face orientation and fielding of questions _____
   - Overview of each team member's background and role on the team _____
   - Overview of the customer's background _____
   - Overview of the team's norms and code of conduct, including remote team norms (phone etiquette and the like) _____
   - Review of software or other groupware and technology requirements, with tutoring, if appropriate _____
   - Review of how the new team member will be introduced during the next team session _____
   - Coaching through a first session with technology such as groupware, if necessary _____
   - Indication of where team notes from meetings are kept and fielding of any questions about them _____
3. Second orientation following the first team meeting _____
   - Review of the session and fielding of questions _____
   - Feedback on the use of team norms and code of conduct _____
   - Responses to questions about the roles of other team members, customers, and stakeholders _____
   - Discussion of best practices and lessons learned from the team _____
   - Indication of team repository for best practices _____
4. Ongoing activities _____
   - Review of best practices _____
   - Feedback on style, use of technology, and deliverables _____

Time Frame for the Orientation Process

The time needed to identify stakeholders, develop a charter, select team members, and hold an orientation session varies from team to team. In general, however, the more complex the team's task—measured in the number of people and the time and distance between them—the longer it takes. Team leaders should allow at least one month to identify stakeholders and develop charter and two to four weeks to select and orient team members. Less time may be needed for experienced virtual teams.

Ample time must be allocated for the orientation session. For a team that has a moderately complex charter, the orientation can take up to three days, especially if detailed work planning is an activity. For teams that have simple charters, only one day may be required. Because team leaders usually know more about the task and deliverables, they need to allow enough time for the team members to catch up. If the session is conducted remotely, the team leader may want to schedule two separate sessions.

Checklists 5.6 and 5.7 show the outcomes the team should strive for in the first two meetings.

Near Virtual Disaster

Sara had just been put in charge of a new group aimed at ensuring smooth execution of projects globally. The function of the team was to identify impediments to success for high-visibility projects, communicate those to the appropriate party, and then assist in removing the impediments. Her team's composition was diverse, with members from many different backgrounds and with varied types of experience. They were all fairly senior and had worked extensively in a virtual environment. As a result, Sara decided not to hold a face-to-face kickoff meeting. The team established norms and protocols over the phone and felt ready and empowered to move out. Some team members began to share their results with more senior leaders in regular staff meetings, mostly during normal reviews of team activities.

A few high-level project managers, mostly in locations outside the headquarters office, began a revolt: "How dare they come and examine my project without my permission!" In fact, the intent was the opposite—to help the project managers with problems they might be having.

The team had neglected to identify stakeholders in remote locations. Sara and a few other team members had done a good job of engaging stakeholders on a local level, but those out in the field did not have a clue what the team was about. Sara and the team suffered a huge setback due to these misperceptions. This could have been avoided by more careful attention to team startup and stakeholder engagement. This becomes even more important on a virtual team when there is no day-to-day or consistent contact with champions, sponsors, or stakeholders.

CHECKLIST 5.6. OUTCOMES FOR FIRST TEAM MEETING.

Outcomes

1. Team members understand the charter, mission, and scope of the team. _____
2. The team develops norms for team behavior and team processes. _____
   - How to schedule meetings; who has authority to schedule others; use of electronic scheduling or calendaring systems _____
   - How often voice mail and e-mail are to be answered _____
   - Etiquette for face-to-face meetings, audioconferences, and videoconferences _____
   - How agendas for team meetings will be developed and distributed _____
   - How minutes will be taken and distributed (timing and method) _____
   - Who will facilitate meetings _____
3. Team members understand their accountabilities and those of other team members. _____
   - Accountabilities of all team members are reviewed and agreed on. _____
4. The team develops a plan for the use of technology, including _____
   - Agreement on major type of work (parallel, sequential, or pooled sequential) _____
   - Technology needed given the type of work _____
   - How to exchange information and documents _____
   - Hardware and software needs of team members (e-mail, fax, telephone, video, and so on) _____
   - How information and documents will be stored (team Web site, shared files, or other) _____
   - When to mark e-mail messages and other documents "urgent," "important," or the like _____
   - Acquisition of new technology (for example, groupware, electronic meeting systems) _____
   - Training and orientation for team members in technology _____
   - Review of compatibility issues (MAC or PC, word-processing applications, Internet providers) _____
5. The team develops an external communication plan: _____
   - Which stakeholders, partners, champions, and others will get what information and when? _____
   - Which team members will coordinate with those individuals and answer questions? _____
6. The team determines how it will review progress: _____
   - Frequency of team meetings _____
   - Preliminary agenda for review sessions _____
   - Who will be required to attend _____
   - How meetings will be held (audioconference, videoconference, face to face, and so on) _____
7. Team-building activities are conducted, and team norms are reviewed. _____

CHECKLIST 5.7. OUTCOMES FOR SECOND TEAM MEETING.

Outcomes

1. The team reviews norms for team behavior and team processes and validates and updates them. _____
   - Review of etiquette for audioconferences, videoconferences, face-to-face meetings, and so on. _____
2. The progress of the team's work to date is reviewed. _____
3. Accountabilities are clarified, if necessary. _____
4. The team reviews technological issues and problems:
   - Exchange of information and documents, hardware and software needs of team members, information and document storage and access, e-mail and voice mail problems _____
   - Additional technology needs _____
   - Training and orientation _____
5. The team reviews progress regarding the external communication plan: _____
   - Is information getting to other team members, stakeholders, and champions? _____
6. The team assesses its work to date:
   - Progress of technical work, overlap or redundancy of roles and accountabilities _____
   - Availability of team members _____
   - Availability of information and documents _____
   - Access to technology _____
   - Access to stakeholders and other important team members _____
7. Additional team-building or trust-building activities are conducted, as appropriate. _____
8. The team reviews its current meeting effectiveness and plans for the next meeting. _____

Points to Remember

1. The team orientation process has six steps that teams can enter at any time.
2. An effective team orientation is essential to high performance.
3. It is best to conduct the team orientation meeting face to face.
4. The leader should ensure that all team members can attend the team orientation session.
5. The leader should ensure that team norms, technological plans, and communication plans are developed during the team orientation.
6. The leader should determine the types of team-building activities that are appropriate for the cultures and types of experience represented on the team.

TEAM MEMBER ROLES
AND COMPETENCIES

The need to balance coordination and collaboration with autonomy exists in any team situation. On a virtual team, this challenge is more complex because time, distance, and organizational boundaries separate team members. Frequently, when people work on a virtual team, they believe that it will be pretty much like working in a traditional environment or that they can multitask their way through, especially since they do not have to physically attend meetings or see other team members. Although they may correctly calculate the difficulty of the technical task of the team, they may underestimate the extra time and effort that they need to spend in coordination and collaboration activities. Consequently, they may overcommit themselves and end up trying to manage too many tasks.

Balancing Coordination and Collaboration

Successful virtual team members understand the importance of balancing coordination and collaboration with autonomy. Maintaining this balance may not be easy. Team members may be tempted to work independently because coordination and collaboration are more difficult in a virtual situation and because common interests seem less compelling than local needs and preferences. Virtual team members often need to behave autonomously to perform activities traditionally performed by the team leader, such as networking, resolving conflicting loyalties, and clarifying ambiguous situations.

However, the virtual situation also requires that team members take the initiative in coordinating and collaborating with other team members, with other people in the organization, and with external partners. Traditional organizational structures, reporting hierarchies, processes, and systems do not ensure coordination and collaboration in virtual teams.

Coordination and Collaboration Roles

Coordination and collaboration roles for virtual team members include the following:

1. Acting as ambassadors for the team by keeping local managers and stakeholders informed of the team's work
2. Acting as conveyers of information in order to keep the team members informed of the concerns, interests, and reactions of their functional areas, local stakeholders, and management
3. Coordinating and communicating with other team members to ensure that all are aware of who is performing what activities and that all have access to important documents and other information
4. Building and maintaining trust with other team members by demonstrating reliable performance, integrity, concern for others, and inclusion
5. Sharing lessons from their experiences with other team members and with their local organizations
6. Taking accountability for their inclusion in the virtual team, especially when they feel that they have been ignored or overlooked

Autonomy Roles

Autonomy roles for virtual team members include the following:

1. Acting as self-managing team members by assuming accountability and leadership in their areas of expertise and by delivering quality products on time
2. Taking responsibility for identifying and reconciling team needs and priorities with the priorities of other teams that they serve on and with local needs
3. Clarifying ambiguous tasks with the team leader and with other team members
4. Addressing conflicting loyalties between the team and other groups
5. Taking care of themselves in terms of their needs for meaningful assignments, inclusion, feedback, and career development

Many virtual teams find the balancing of coordination and collaboration with autonomy roles to be so important that their members regularly assess and discuss their performance. Too much coordination and collaboration might be overkill and take away from the technical task itself, while too much autonomy might lead to an effort that is not integrated between team members and cannot leverage learning optimally.

A sample team assessment is shown in Table 6.1, and an agenda for reviewing the data from the assessment is shown in Table 6.2. Prior to the assessment session, the team leader can send the questionnaire to the team members, summarize the team members' responses to the questionnaire, and post them on the team's shared Web site or via e-mail. If a team has access to an electronic meeting system (EMS), administration of the questionnaire and the subsequent discussion of ways to improve the team's performance can be conducted interactively. Allow ample time—at least thirty to forty-five minutes—during the meeting to discuss the results of the questionnaire and possible follow-up actions. The minutes of the meeting and a list of items to be followed up on in the next session should promptly be sent out to all team members.

The determination of whether or not the results of the assessment warrant attention will depend on the team's mission and its members' reactions to the survey results. For example, teams that require extensive external boundary spanning will consider this item more seriously than teams that focus on local issues.

TABLE 6.1. TEAM MEMBER ROLE ASSESSMENT.

Instructions: Under each statement, please circle the answer that best characterizes your activities on the team.

Coordination and Collaboration

1. How often do you interface with top management at your location about the team and its progress?

Never	Once in a while	Sometimes	Quite a bit	Continually

2. How often do you *systematically* report to the team about local concerns, interests, and reactions to the team's work?

Never	Once in a while	Sometimes	Quite a bit	Continually

3. How often do you report to other team members about progress on your work or on the success of deliverables?

Never	Once in a while	Sometimes	Quite a bit	Continually

4. How often do you gauge your actions against their impact on other team members?

Never	Once in a while	Sometimes	Quite a bit	Continually

(continued)

TABLE 6.1. (CONTINUED).

5. How often do you and other team members discuss the level of coordination and collaboration that is appropriate for the team?

Never	Once in a while	Sometimes	Quite a bit	Continually

6. How often do you and your team members take the time to share learnings?

Never	Once in a while	Sometimes	Quite a bit	Continually

Autonomy

1. How often do you participate in activities with the team where you use specialized expertise?

Never	Once in a while	Sometimes	Quite a bit	Continually

2. How often do you reconcile competing priorities between this team's needs, other teams' needs, and local needs?

Never	Once in a while	Sometimes	Quite a bit	Continually

3. How often do you clarify ambiguous tasks with the team leader and/or with other team members?

Never	Once in a while	Sometimes	Quite a bit	Continually

4. How often do you take the initiative to conduct networking and boundary-spanning activities on the team's behalf?

Never	Once in a while	Sometimes	Quite a bit	Continually

5. How often do you assess your progress on the team in relation to your personal goals?

Never	Once in a while	Sometimes	Quite a bit	Continually

Roles and the Impact of Culture

National culture can influence team members' perceptions of their team roles, such as dealing with ambiguous situations, defining accountability, acting on behalf of the team leader, and interfacing with people at higher organizational levels. The following is an example of this in Sara's team.

The members of Sara's team knew that for the team to succeed, all members had to perform ambassadorial behaviors and had to coordinate horizontally with other teams and functions. The team members even distributed a detailed timeline for

TABLE 6.2. AGENDA FOR TEAM MEMBER ROLE ASSESSMENT.

Agenda Item	Time
1. Review the purpose of the assessment: To reinforce our roles as team members and to take action in areas that need improvement.	5 minutes
2. Review the responses to each item, one at a time.	10 minutes
3. Ask team members whether they generally agree with the responses. Ask if there are any questions.	5 minutes
4. Go over the items, one at a time, and explore the team members' responses and reactions. Focus on the top two or three priorities. Be certain that there is agreement about what the *appropriate* response to each item should be, given the team's mission and the type of team.	20 minutes
5. For each item, brainstorm actions the team could take to improve the item scores.	15 minutes
6. Document actions and make plans to follow up. Adjust items on the questionnaire if appropriate.	5 minutes

communication and sent one another e-mail and instant messages about what to say to whom and when. What they did not consider was how differently they would interpret and carry out their roles in different cultural settings.

When Sara attended a progress meeting with upper management, one of the division vice presidents from Latin America acted surprised about the extent of the team's activities. He asked Sara if she had appropriate sponsorship for her team's work and complained that Sara had not informed him of the team's activities.

After the meeting, Sara checked her communication log and saw that indeed, this division vice president was listed as someone targeted for ambassadorial behavior. She called the team member accountable for this activity and asked what had happened. He replied that the division vice president was a high-level individual and that he did not feel comfortable communicating with the man directly. Consequently, rather than holding short face-to-face briefings with senior staff, as required by the team's communication plan, he had been sending the VP e-mail updates. This VP did not check his e-mail regularly and had missed the messages.

In hindsight, Sara felt frustrated with herself for not following up to ensure that proper communication was occurring.

Power distance is one cultural variable that can affect how well team members perform their collaboration and coordination roles. Sara's team member, although not at the bottom of the organization, was at a level where he would not feel comfortable setting up a face-to-face meeting with a senior manager. Sara and the team learned that some team members feel uncomfortable performing boundary-spanning tasks that require collaboration and coordination between team members and people at higher status levels. Although these team members may have the skills to perform such tasks, they consider doing so culturally inappropriate.

Another cultural variable, uncertainty avoidance, may also affect the ways in which team members carry out autonomy roles. Team members from cultures with high uncertainty avoidance are less likely to be comfortable in roles that are ambiguous. Members from low-uncertainty-avoidance cultures may view their teammates from high-uncertainty-avoidance cultures as needing too much definition and structure. Striking a balance that is appropriate for the cultural composition of the team and the team's task is tricky and may require candid discussions among all team members.

The definition of accountability also varies from culture to culture. It has a very clear meaning in the United States, where it implies individual responsibility for final outcomes. In other cultures, the meaning is less clear. For example, there is no word in Spanish that translates directly as "accountability." Members of Spanish-speaking cultures, as a result, may understand accountability differently from English speakers. In collective societies, sharing of accountability and goals by the entire team may be the preferred way to work. In more individualistic cultures, individual accountability for interdependent tasks may be preferred. Teams that have cross-cultural membership may want to discuss the meaning of terms such as *accountability, autonomy, coordination,* and *collaboration* to ensure that all team members share common understandings.

Functional culture might also affect people's perceptions of the meaning of collaboration, coordination, and autonomy. Team members from subcultures used to working in a more autonomous environment (such as people who work alone) might unintentionally shift the balance more toward autonomy than individuals from functional environments that are more collective.

Virtual Team Members' Areas of Competence

Virtual team members must acquire skills in six key areas of competence in addition to traditional team competencies that ensure success in collaboration and coordination and in autonomy roles.[1] The areas of competence are as follows:

1. Project management
2. Networking
3. Use of technology
4. Self-management
5. Spanning boundaries
6. Interpersonal awareness

Project Management

Project management skills include the following:

- Planning and organizing individual work to correspond to team schedules
- Developing and using methods to report progress and problems
- Monitoring and controlling costs
- Taking actions to get back on track
- Documenting and sharing individual lessons learned.

Competence in project management facilitates balancing collaboration and coordination with autonomy. Good project management techniques can enhance performance even on teams that are not project-oriented. Coordination and collaboration include carefully planning and scheduling work, keeping commitments, and reporting progress in relation to the plans in order to provide early warning of problems and delays to the team leader, affected team members, and outside stakeholders. Good planning discipline can help team members be autonomous and recognize when their work is off track or off schedule and can facilitate immediate action to get back on track or back on schedule.

Controlling the costs of labor, travel, and other expenses is another project management skill. If team members are spending beyond their budgets, they need to let someone know. If they underspend, they should offer the money for other team requirements.

Virtual team members also need to document new knowledge and key lessons and share them with their teammates. This is typically done at the end of most project management cycles but can also be accomplished through an ongoing knowledge management system. Successful teams distribute lessons within the team and beyond to the wider organization.

Networking

Networking skills include the following:

- Knowing the organizational landscape and who is in it
- Knowing what questions to ask to get others' perspectives
- Maintaining guidelines about when to see people face to face, when to send them messages, and when to avoid them altogether
- An ability to see other points of view or empathize with different groups

Virtual team members need to take the initiative to learn about their organizations and the people in them. They should be able to map who is powerful, who can provide information, who is usually skeptical, who might have a helpful but dissenting view, and who usually is supportive. They must be able to navigate inside and outside the organization and talk with all levels of management and with people from varied backgrounds about complex topics. They should also be knowledgeable about external sources of information, expertise, and support. Like farmers, they need to know their landscape, what grows well, and which areas may need further cultivation.

Virtual team members need to develop skills in networking and in communicating with and without face-to-face contact. Knowing when and how to use different types of technology to network and communicate effectively is a related skill. Savvy networkers seldom rely only on e-mail or voice mail to communicate complicated, highly political, or emotional material. Using change management techniques can be helpful in thinking about the approach and potential landmines. For example, before communicating with anyone, a team member must ask the following five questions:

1. What does this person have to lose by this decision or piece of information?
2. Does this communication change the power structure in the function or organization?
3. How would I react if this were presented to me?
4. Is this material or concept relatively easy to understand?
5. What is positive and attractive about this decision or information?

If any of questions 1 through 4 has a negative answer, the virtual team member must use a synchronous and information-rich communication medium. A face-to-face meeting is preferable; a telephone call is the minimum option.

Use of Technology

Technological skills include the following:

- Using the appropriate technology to communicate, coordinate, and collaborate, given the task and the backgrounds of other team members
- Knowing how to access training or help with new technology
- Knowing the etiquette of using technology
- Knowing how to plan and conduct remote team meetings
- Creating technology backup systems in the event that the planned technology fails.

Virtual team members need to develop skill in selecting and using technology to communicate, coordinate, and collaborate. Although competence is likely to vary with individuals' backgrounds and functional disciplines, all team members should be able to make informed decisions about when it is best to call, use e-mail, rely on instant messaging, or meet face to face. In addition, all must be able to access and use basic technology, which includes cell phones, videoconferencing, teleconferencing, voice mail, e-mail, basic word processing packages, document exchange applications, simple graphics, and Internet searches. Team members who have subteam leadership account-abilities also need to understand how to plan and facilitate remote meetings.

In addition, all team members should be aware of the etiquette and practice of working remotely. Sending e-mail messages or voice mail messages of appropri-ate length, leaving one's telephone number at the beginning of a voice mail mes-sage, and inquiring about format preferences before sending electronic files or e-mail messages are all good practices.

Team members who have technical backgrounds should remember that not all team members may be as experienced with technology as they are. The basic skills of all team members will increase over time, but team members should set their own minimum standards for their team, based on the team's needs. Finally, team members need to be open to experimenting with new technology and pursu-ing training to increase their proficiency.

Self-Management

Self-management has a number of different aspects and may vary, depending on what the team is working on and the specific situation of each team member. Four types of competence are extremely relevant in this category:

- Skill in establishing personal and professional priorities and goals
- Skill in prioritizing work and setting limits
- Skill in creating and executing opportunities for individual learning, growth, and career satisfaction
- Skill in taking the initiative to change working methods and processes to meet the demands of the work

A virtual team member's world consists of many potentially conflicting priori-ties. Dealing with ambiguity, prioritizing tasks, setting personal and professional limits, and saying no are critical self-management strategies. For example, virtual team members who work on project teams and report to a number of team leaders may have trouble saying no to requests for work. In the end, these team members may find themselves working all the time and not enjoying any job. The ability to say no when the quality of performance or the team member's work-life balance is sacrificed is a necessary skill.

Other important self-management skills include career management, promoting oneself, and learning. Maintaining state-of-the-art expertise is critical for virtual team members, who are selected primarily for their technical and teamwork expertise.

Staying current technically through extension courses or college courses is essential to skill maintenance. A further step is to participate in the creation of knowledge in team members' professional field by publishing or by presenting at professional conferences. Finally, virtual team members must be able to promote their own career development, often with managers whom they never see face to face. Being assertive about discussing career goals, asking for new assignments, and obtaining tasks with visibility are crucial skills for virtual team members. For virtual team members who wish to work on their own in the future, these activities are indispensable if they are to stay connected to their field and their career.

Finally, an accomplished virtual team member is able to conform or stretch to the requirements of the job. Adaptable team members understand the dynamics of the task and take the initiative to make changes in their accountability to meet shifting task goals. They take responsibility for ensuring that they are included in meetings and decisions. They make sure that there is a dial-in for them when they are the only remote team members in an audioconference, they make sure people remember to call them, and they speak up during meetings even when they might be the only team members on the phone or in a videoconference. They realize the importance of communicating these changes proactively with other team members, stakeholders, and managers.

Spanning Boundaries

Virtual team members need to be competent in spanning cultural, functional, and organizational boundaries. They need to be skilled in the following areas:

- Understanding how cultural perspectives influence work and collaboration
- Understanding how differences in national, functional, and organizational cultures affect working styles, team interactions, team members' expectations, and team dynamics
- Sensitivity to differences in business practices in different parts of the world
- Understanding how the organization works and how it is structured
- Taking a "big picture" view of the work and the enterprise

Cross-functional awareness includes some comprehension of how areas of expertise or diversity influence working styles. People who have engineering and science backgrounds, for example, often tend to work in a more linear style than individuals from marketing and sales functions. People who have backgrounds in human resource development, strategy, and quality improvement tend to view work from a systems perspective, whereas other team members may favor a task-specific approach. Although understanding differences in working styles attributable to functional backgrounds or individual diversity may seem burdensome, a competent virtual team member can leverage this diversity to benefit the team. A useful strategy is to solicit input from the members with diverse points of view or approaches and to enjoy the experience of learning how to work with diversity.

In cases where a department or function is virtual and embedded in a nonvirtual group, such as global technology in regional business units, boundary spanning becomes multilayered. This multilayering is particularly noticeable in matrixed, geographically dispersed organizations. Typical functions that are multilayered are human resource, finance, or headquarters functions. Team members need to pay attention to the local practices, regional practices, or practices associated with the entire enterprise.

If the geographical dispersion is global, national culture affects team members' working styles, expectations, and communication preferences. Experienced virtual team members who work on teams that span boundaries of national culture expect national differences between team members, can discuss them openly, and are open to new ways of working. A team member who is uncomfortable with uncertainty, for example, may volunteer to work on a task with less structure than he or she prefers and use his or her reactions as learning experiences. Taking a deep breath and letting another way of working take over is a sign of an experienced virtual team member who is comfortable in his or her skin.

Virtual team members must cultivate awareness of their personal cultural biases and the effect they may have on the team. All of us hold stereotypes and preconceptions of others. Awareness is the precondition for changing or at least managing these biases. The key to mitigating bias is to develop openness to other ways of thinking and acting and to suspend judgment about what is "good" and "bad." Openness is facilitated by gaining awareness through activities such as traveling, working with other functions, and talking with members of other cultures about reverse perceptions. Awareness of personal bias is also a component of overall interpersonal awareness.

Interpersonal Awareness

Interpersonal awareness skills include the following:

- Being aware of interpersonal styles and their impact on others
- Collecting feedback on one's interpersonal style from other team members
- Discussing one's interpersonal strengths and weaknesses with other team members and providing them appropriate feedback on theirs
- Being able to plan experiences that lead to improvement

The best-performing virtual team members are acutely aware of how others perceive them and how their behavior affects their team's productivity. They are skilled in anticipating the consequences of their own behaviors in many different situations.

They understand how they present themselves on the telephone and in writing and how people from different functions and cultures are likely to perceive them, especially across distances without face-to-face interpersonal cues. They gauge when to be friendly, when to get down to business, when to be talkative, and when to be quiet. They are also sensitive to issues that affect trust. Most important, they frequently seek and give feedback to one another. They understand that they have an impact on others and that how they choose to use technology, pay attention to team norms, and interact with other team members during meetings leaves an impression, even if people cannot literally see them. They also understand that this impression can be long-lasting and have an impact on team performance.

Some experienced virtual team members ask five simple questions after any meeting or major interaction to elicit feedback that will improve their self-awareness:

1. Was my behavior consistent with expectations?
2. What was productive about it for the team?
3. What was unproductive about it?
4. If the team were to give me advice about how to behave differently next time, what would it be?
5. Did cultural or functional differences affect perceptions of me?

Table 6.3 summarizes the knowledge, skills, and experiences that define competence in each of the six areas just discussed. Team members can use this list to solicit feedback on their behaviors.

Assessing and Developing Team Member Competence

The following checklists can assist team members in assessing their general levels of competence in all six areas. Checklist 6.1 can be used as a self-report form or as a 360-degree feedback instrument. Team members can use the results to create personal development goals. To improve the accuracy of the feedback, several people should assess each team member.

Checklists 6.2 and 6.3 can be used by team members to plan development activities in each area of competence. They can also help guide development prior to and after team assignments. Development should concentrate on the areas of importance to the team and the organization as well as those that are personally important to the team member. Developmental actions may include training, special assignments, reading, sharing lessons learned and best practices, mentoring, and on-the-job experiences.

TABLE 6.3. TEAM MEMBER KNOWLEDGE, SKILLS, AND EXPERIENCE.

Area of Competence	Knowledge	Skills	Experience
Project Management	Knows specific project management techniques for planning, organizing, and controlling work Knows different methods for documenting and sharing learnings	Can develop personal, project, and task plans, schedules, and cost estimates Can develop different strategies to get work back on schedule Can derive and document learnings from a number of different situations	Has developed project or task plans, schedules, and cost estimates Has shared learnings in formal and informal forums
Networking	Understands the formal and informal organization and where resources reside Understands how to interact and communicate with people from different functions and levels in the organization	Can identify important local stake-holders for the team Can plan and implement networking activities	Has worked in a number of different locations and functions within the organization Has worked with external partners, such as vendors and suppliers
Use of Technology	Is aware of major technological tools and when the use of each is appropriate Understands etiquette and practices associated with using technology	Can plan for the use of technology, given the backgrounds of team members and stakeholders and the demands of the team's task Can access training and skill-building activities in this area Can plan and facilitate remote meetings	Has experience using a number of different communication and collaboration technologies

(continued)

TABLE 6.3. (CONTINUED).

Area of Competence	Knowledge	Skills	Experience
Self-Management	Understands personal and professional priorities Understands personal limits Understands the need for development and learning	Can plan and prioritize personal work Can set limits and say no Has personal strategies for handling ambiguity Can identify learning opportunities	Has worked in a number of different teams simultaneously Has developed and executed personal-growth plans through formal education, on-the-job learning, and other strategies Has performed tasks that required learning new skills or changes in work habits
Spanning Boundaries	Understands the importance of cultural, functional, and organizational differences and how they can affect the team Is aware of own cultural biases	Can constructively discuss dimensions of cultural differences Is able to create ways of working that not only accommodate but also optimize differences Is able to plan team activities, taking into account how these processes interact with functions and cultures	Has worked in cross-functional teams Has worked in teams with cross-organizational and/or cross-cultural representation
Interpersonal Awareness	Is aware of how own behaviors affect others and the productivity of the team Is aware of areas in which further development is needed	Is able to collect and act on feedback from others about own interpersonal style Is able to give appropriate feedback, when solicited, to others regarding their styles Is able to foster interpersonal interaction about styles and their impact on others	Has worked in different virtual team situations and has modified own behavior to meet the demands of the situations Has participated in feedback sessions on personal behaviors

CHECKLIST 6.1. ASSESSING TEAM MEMBER COMPETENCE.

Instructions: Select the level in each area of competence that best characterizes the current skills and experience of the individual being assessed (your own skills and experience if this is a self-assessment).

Area of Competence	Skills	Skill Level (1 = low, 2 = medium, 3 = high)	Experience	Experience Level (1 = low, 2 = medium, 3 = high)
Project Management	Can develop personal, project, and task plans, schedules, and cost estimates Can develop different strategies to get work back on schedule Can derive and document learnings from a number of different situations	Score:	Has developed project or task plans, schedules, and cost estimates Has shared learnings in formal and informal forums	Score:
Networking	Can identify important local stakeholders for the team Can plan and implement networking activities	Score:	Has worked in a number of different locations and functions within the organization Has worked with external partners, such as vendors and suppliers	Score:
Use of Technology	Can plan for the use of technology, given the backgrounds of team members and stakeholders and the demands of the team's task Can access training and skill-building activities in this area Can plan and facilitate remote meetings	Score:	Has experience in the use of a number of different communication and collaboration technologies	Score:
Self-Management	Can plan and prioritize personal work Can set limits and say no Has personal strategies for handling ambiguity Can identify learning opportunities	Score:	Has worked in a number of different teams simultaneously Has developed and executed personal-growth plans through formal education, on-the-job learning, and other strategies Has performed tasks that required learning new skills or changes in work habits	Score:

(continued)

CHECKLIST 6.1. (CONTINUED).

Area of Competence	Skills	Skill Level (1 = low, 2 = medium, 3 = high)	Experience	Experience Level (1 = low, 2 = medium, 3 = high)
Spanning Boundaries	Can constructively discuss dimensions of cultural differences Is able to create ways of working that not only accommodate but optimize differences Is able to plan team activities, taking into account how these processes interact with functions and cultures of team members	Score:	Has worked in cross-functional teams Has worked in teams with cross-organizational and/or cross-cultural representation	Score:
Interpersonal Awareness	Is able to collect and act on feedback from others about own interpersonal style Is able to give appropriate feedback, when solicited, to others regarding their styles Is able to foster interpersonal interaction about styles and their impact on others	Score:	Has worked in different situations and has modified own behavior to meet the demands of the situations Has participated in feedback sessions on personal behaviors	Score:

Total number of 3s: _____   Total number of 3s: _____

Total number of 2s: _____   Total number of 2s: _____

Total number of 1s: _____   Total number of 1s: _____

Total: _____   Total: _____

Scoring

Instructions: Total the numbers in the "skills" and "experience" boxes for each competence. (For example, selecting 3 in all skill areas would give you a total score of 18 for skills.) Interpret the numbers as follows:

Skills

6 or less: You are probably just getting started in a virtual team setting. Your challenge is to gain skill in competence areas in which you scored 2 or below. This can be accomplished through training, reading, working with a mentor, and working in multiple virtual teams.

6 to 12: You have a solid understanding of the requirements of virtual team membership. Your primary challenge is to refine your skills for application in a number of different situations. This can be accomplished best by working in multiple virtual teams under the mentorship of experienced managers.

(continued)

CHECKLIST 6.1. (CONTINUED).

12 or more: You have excellent virtual-team-member skills. You may want to work on skill areas in which you scored 2 or less. You also may want to plan to help others acquire knowledge in the areas in which you are most skilled. This can be accomplished by working as a mentor/coach in multiple virtual teams.

Experience

6 or less: You probably have not had the chance to practice team membership in a virtual setting. Your challenge is to gain experience. This can be accomplished by working with a mentor or beginning to work in virtual teams under the guidance of experienced managers.

6 to 12: You have solid experience in a virtual-team setting. Your primary challenge is to broaden your experience in a number of different situations. This can be accomplished by working with a mentor or in multiple virtual teams.

12 or more: You have exceptional experience in virtual teamwork. You may want to expand your experience in any areas in which you scored 2 or less. You also may want to help others to acquire skills and experience. This can be accomplished by working as a mentor or coach in multiple virtual teams.

Near Virtual Disaster

The one role that team members often overlook is the role of ensuring that there are technology backup systems in the event that the preferred technology for a virtual meeting fails. This is particularly noticeable when the meeting is globally dispersed and the members of the virtual team are the top eight executive team of a global Fortune 100 company.

Sara learned her lesson the hard way. After moving up the ranks by hard work and outstanding accomplishments, the last thing Sara thought would derail her was the technology for a virtual team meeting. In fact, it was so far from her mind that she did not even consider the possibility until she had a near virtual disaster.

Sara was the lead on an annual five-hour strategic review with the senior executive team of her company. It was her first meeting with this team. The members of the executive team are geographically located in Delhi, Shanghai, Dubai, Paris, New York, Sydney, and Buenos Aires. This executive team meets regularly in the boardroom at headquarters, usually by teleconference. For this meeting, Sara had to present in person to the CEO and some of the executive team located in New York, with audio hookup around the world. Participants had a hard copy of the presentation at each location. The technology for the meeting was nothing fancy; it was to be a low-tech meeting. At the last minute, Sara had to change the meeting room in New York to a secondary venue because her team was too large to fit in the boardroom. She was under pressure to get ready: it was her first time in this venue, and she had a great deal to do—get the materials prepared, get the materials into the hands of the remote executive team, get the presenters ready, and settle her own nerves.

CHECKLIST 6.2. INDIVIDUAL COMPETENCE INVENTORY.

Instructions: In the next-to-last row, rate each area of competence as a high, medium, or low priority for your type of virtual team, using the information provided in the table. In the last row, rate each area of competence as a high, medium, or low priority for your self-development. The table lists the priority of each area of competence for each of the seven primary types of virtual teams. Developmental priorities are areas in which a medium-to-high team priority exists and your competence rating is medium or low.

Area of Competence

Type of Team	Project Management	Networking	Use of Technology	Self-Management	Spanning Boundaries	Interpersonal Awareness
Network	Medium	High	High	High	High	High
Parallel	High	Medium	High	High	Medium	High
Project or Product	High	Medium	High	High	Medium	High
Work or Production	Medium to high	Medium to high	Medium to high	Medium to high	Medium to high	High
Action	Medium to high	Medium to high	Medium to high	High	Medium to high	High
Service	Low to medium	Low to medium	Medium to high	Medium to high	Low to medium	High
Management	Medium	High	Medium	High	High	High
Priority for my team? (Yes/No)						
Priority for my development? (Yes/No)						

CHECKLIST 6.3. PLANNING DEVELOPMENTAL ACTIONS.

Instructions: For areas you listed as priorities for development for your team, use the following worksheet to plan training, on-the-job assignments, and/or other activities that can develop your skills and experience.

Area of Competence	Developmental Plans	Estimated Time to Complete
Project Management		
Networking		
Use of Technology		
Self-Management		
Spanning Boundaries		
Interpersonal Awareness		

The meeting began at 6:00 A.M. at the headquarters in New York. Unfortunately, within the first few minutes, all the remote locations said they could not hear well. Sara stopped the meeting to discuss what to do. Her team decided that the audio problem was likely the microphones in the room—or, jokingly, that the audio remote control panel was so complicated that no one knew how to use it. Because the meeting was occurring several hours before most people came to work in its time zone, there was no one to call locally to get technical help.

Visibly frustrated, the CEO decided to continue the meeting, given the number of topics the team had to cover, with the knowledge that the team members on the call could hear "somewhat." Sara was presenting, so she could not get up and try to alleviate or minimize the problem. The meeting continued with poor audio quality. She made it through the five-hour meeting; then she made a note to self.

Given the level of the audience, next time she would not assume that someone else had thought about what could go wrong or that there was an infrastructure of technology support for this level of meeting. She made herself an emergency list: conduct a dry run; check on the meeting room and the technology the day before; personally learn how to work the technology in the room; have a technology backup; ensure that each location has an alternative that can be switched to without disrupting the meeting, such as instant messaging; and schedule a technology professional and her secretary to be at work early to help her in the event that problems should arise.

Points to Remember

1. Virtual team members must balance coordination and collaboration with autonomy.
2. Culture can influence how members fulfill their obligations to the team.
3. Team members need to have basic skills in project management, networking, use of technology, self-management, spanning boundaries, and interpersonal awareness.
4. Virtual team members who are accountable to host a virtual meeting need to have a technology backup plan, especially when the stakes are high.

CHAPTER SEVEN

BUILDING TRUST IN VIRTUAL TEAMS

The ways in which virtual team members identify with one another, share power, communicate, and build trust are important in achieving team results and in the subjective experience of being a member of the team.[1] Effective virtual team members not only fulfill the team's task objectives but also, in the process, contribute to a trusting relationship among themselves. Trust is a critical structural and cultural characteristic that influences the team's success, performance, and collaboration.[2] Without trust, building a true team and maximizing output are almost impossible.

Because virtual teams, especially parallel, project, action, and network teams, often form and disband quickly, trust has to be built almost immediately. The qualities of the first interactions among team members set the tone. Indeed, first actions might impact long-term relationships not only on these types of teams but on longer-term functional teams.

Three Factors in Building "Instant" Trust in a Virtual Environment

The actions of the team leader and team members that affect trust fall into three categories.[3] Although trust is, to some extent, based on individual tolerances and experiences, people tend to trust others who perform competently, act with integrity, and display concern for the well-being of others. All three categories must exist consistently in order for a virtual team to sustain a high level of trust.

Performance Competence

Virtual teams exist to create results. The competent performance of team members is paramount for success. All of us want to know that we are working on a team with others who can produce results.

Reputation for Performance and Results. Sara has a reputation for "delivering" as a team leader. Her team members and many others throughout the organization know that her past projects have come in on time and within budget. She has received accolades from organizational leaders and customers. Sara is action-oriented and fulfills her commitments and obligations. Sara's competence contributes to the trust her team members place in her. Her team members know that she has the knowledge, experience, and skills to perform the work and achieve results.

If a team leader or team member appears to have little or inappropriate experience or a reputation for nonperformance, it may erode the trust that team members have in the importance of the team and their belief that it can perform effectively. On a virtual team, all that team members have with which to judge the probability of success are the team leader's and team members' credentials and the reputation of the team's sponsor. Other positive factors cannot compensate for poor performance.

Follow-Through. Timely follow-through on commitments is an important element in establishing a perception of performance competence. Promising something—whether it be information, a telephone call, or an e-mail message—and then not delivering, or not delivering on time, erodes trust. Follow-through may be more important to virtual team members than to members of traditional teams because virtual team members have fewer clues by which to decide whether other team members are committed to the team's performance. Developing a set of team practices for follow-through is one way for virtual teams to easily demonstrate a performance orientation.

Each of the members of Sara's team keeps a log of his or her commitments and checks them off in a timely manner. When a team member cannot meet a commitment, even a small one such as attending a meeting, he or she takes the time to explain this to the team. This norm was established in the initial team orientation session. If the commitment is critical, real-time communication with high social presence, such as a personal telephone call, is used, rather than e-mail or voice mail or rescheduling over the electronic calendaring system.

Obtaining Resources. The ability to obtain resources also contributes to the perception of performance, especially for the virtual team leader. Teams, virtual or not, are often derailed by believing that to meet their objectives, the organization must provide them with resources. Although this is true to some extent, especially at the onset of the team's work, high-performing teams track down or even create their own resources by taking creative approaches to problems. Team members regard virtual team leaders who are able to produce needed resources as performance-oriented and trustworthy.

Integrity

Integrity, the alignment of actions and stated values, creates a foundation for trust. Virtual team members watch and listen to determine whether others act in a manner that is consistent with what they say they will do. For example, team members who promise agreement during a review with top management and then do not act accordingly when the pressure is on do not engender trust. In a virtual environment, such actions have an even worse effect than they do in a traditional environment because inconsistencies in behavior are often not explained by environmental or contextual clues.

The perception of integrity complements the perception of performance. It is possible to believe that another person is competent and will perform well but to not believe that the person has integrity. Although there may be trust between two people in terms of getting the work done, there may be less in areas having to do with interpersonal relationships. Some team members find themselves working with people that they can count on to perform the task but whom they do not trust in areas such as acting in alignment with their stated values, taking individual credit for the team's work, and portraying the team in a positive manner.

The two primary behaviors that indicate integrity in a team are standing behind the team and all its members and maintaining consistent and balanced communication.

Standing Behind the Team and All Its Members. Integrity has to do, in part, with managing perceptions of team performance. Speaking poorly in public forums about the team's performance, about other team members, or about the quality of the team's product can not only destroy the team's reputation but also signal a lack of judgment and integrity. In a virtual environment, with the lack of other clues about performance, it does not take much negative information to ruin a team's reputation. Team members who do this, inadvertently or not, endanger the trust that other team members feel in them.

Sara does a good job of standing behind her team and its members with management, stakeholders, and other important members of the organization. She finds ways to act as an advocate for the project and for individual team members in good and bad times. She never speaks badly of the team or accepts information that indicates poor member performance or poor team performance without first investigating it thoroughly.

The team has also developed a norm to never send public electronic messages that could be construed negatively by others about the team and its performance. The team has heard of an incident in which one slightly negative e-mail destroyed a team's reputation. If Sara's team members have concerns or issues about their team's performance, they discuss them privately and in a nonbinding format.

Communication. Perceptions of integrity are built into the communication process. Ensuring that all team members receive critical information at the same time can foster integrity. In a virtual environment, it is difficult for team members to ascertain whether they have been systematically excluded by the team leader or other team members or just forgotten. In either case, trust can be eroded quickly when team members wonder if others have integrity.

It also is important that communications convey a balanced picture of the situation. Information that makes one party look better than another or that slants results inappropriately can destroy trust. It is better to examine both sides of an issue and take time to meet in an interactive session than to have team members wonder whether information is being hidden.

Sara's team members are conscientious about ensuring that important communications reach all team members at the same time, regardless of their locations. They know that people in remote areas or in partner organizations can feel left out and may believe that they are not communicated with as frequently as members who are closer to the center of the organization. So Sara's team members make special efforts to include everyone from remote locations and from partner organizations in audioconferences and videoconferences and to take all their comments and concerns very seriously. In addition, team members often check with one another when communicating controversial information, in order to make certain that they are presenting a balanced perception of the situation.

Concern for the Well-Being of Others

We trust people who are consistently responsive to our needs and to the needs of others in the organization. Four aspects of caring that appear to be critical to establishing and maintaining trust in a virtual team setting are (1) creating an environment of inclusion, (2) transitioning people on and off the team so that their careers are positively affected, (3) understanding the impact of the team's actions on people inside and outside the team, and (4) helping each team member commit to the task and the team's outcomes.

Creating an Environment of Inclusion. Trust can be eroded if members feel that they are systematically excluded from the team. The risk of this increases exponentially when a team is virtual. Leaders and other team members who practice inclusive behaviors can overcome these feelings and build trust in the virtual teams. Behaviors of inclusion for virtual teams include the following:

- Greeting each team member or asking each team member in the virtual meeting to introduce himself or herself.
- Making sure every voice is heard by asking everyone to participate and then reinforcing that with appropriate inclusive behaviors.
- Calling on people who have not spoken, so long as this is conducted in a culturally sensitive way without embarrassing anyone or putting someone on the spot.
- Creating an environment that seeks diverse points of view. This could include a structured approach of asking someone to play the devil's advocate or to take a contrarian view.
- Ensuring that each person's skills and potential are maximized by team assignments and new experiences.
- Practicing communication behaviors that lead to trust, such as respecting individuals, remembering and using the names that individuals prefer to be called, creating a dialogue instead of a monologue, and listening attentively.
- Practicing the spirit of forgiveness when someone makes a mistake.

Transitioning Team Members. An important aspect of trust is the belief that team leaders and members will display concern for team members who are new to the team or leaving the team for other assignments. Expressing concern for others includes explicit discussions about transitions, helping new members assimilate, and helping exiting members find next assignments. Virtual team members frequently remark that the manner in which they are transitioned on and off a team is representative of the trustworthiness of the team's leader and of the organization in terms of managing their careers. Helping new members assimilate and aligning team members' ambitions will augment trust in the team.

Impact on Others. Another factor in concern for the well-being of others is the team's awareness of its impact on other organizations, projects, functions, and remote customers and sites. Virtual teams that are "team-centric" and exhibit a disregard for nonmembers may have difficulty in convincing potential team members and others that they are trustworthy. A team decision that adversely affects another team, project, or function may easily undermine trust in the team. Furthermore, teams that project the exclusiveness of a clique or that put their needs before the needs of the organization have a hard time developing trust within the organization.

At the individual level, team members who assess how their behaviors affect other team members will most likely be perceived as having more concern for others. Team members who appear to be insensitive to others' personal situations and feelings will be perceived as less trustworthy.

On a virtual team, it is more difficult to form close relationships. For example, one virtual team member was both surprised and embarrassed to find out, upon asking another team member not to take a planned vacation during a crucial time in the team's work, that the other team member had scheduled the time off to get married! Because most of the interactions between these two individuals were task-focused and conducted by e-mail, little effort had gone into building an interpersonal relationship.

Commitment to the Task and Its Outcome. The last area of concern for the well-being of others involves ensuring that each member has an opportunity to perform tasks that will make a difference on the team. Many teams suffer when a subset of the team or a particular person is perceived to be given all the best assignments. This is intensified when the select group is closer to the team leader and the more remote members are not considered. When members feel involved in and excited about what they are working on and all other factors of the virtual team are working well, the group will feel a greater commitment to the task and its outcome and perform at its best. A committed team does not watch the clock or worry about extrinsic rewards. The work itself is motivating and rewarding.

Using the Three Trust-Building Factors

The checklists presented here are tools that virtual team members can use to create and maintain trust. Teams can use Checklist 7.1 as a trust-building exercise during their initiation activities and on a regular basis thereafter. It highlights the development of team action in the three trust-building factors. Checklist 7.2 is a trust log that aids in individual understanding and analysis of how one's promises and actions can affect other team members. Checklist 7.3 exemplifies how elements from the three trust factors can be used to create a trust audit. Team members can use it to provide real-time feedback about how they are feeling about trust issues.

Trust Radius

Robert Shaw created the concept of a trust radius that is analogous to the human eye taking in light.[4] When the human eye takes in light, the pupil expands. The more light that enters the eye, the larger the pupil becomes in relation to the iris. A person's trust radius also increases as the person takes in team members, partners, and sponsors from across traditional boundaries (see Figure 7.1).

A large radius of trust means that people are willing to trust others who are not from their own locations, cultures, functions, and organizations. The virtual team, at least initially, reflects the trust radius that each member brings to the team. Take as an example working on a virtual team with members from an external consulting firm. At the end of each day, team members would send their work to members of the consulting firm, who would integrate it with previous work and send it back the next day. The integrated work almost never looked the same as the original information sent in by the team members. This made the team leader feel as if her efforts and those of the other team members were not being fairly represented. This affected her trust in the members of the team from the consulting firm. Such an experience could decrease a person's radius of trust with other external partners.

CHECKLIST 7.1. TRUST BEHAVIORS.

Trust Exercise

Instructions: The following steps constitute a one-and-one-half- to two-hour session with a virtual team and its leader to introduce the topic of trust. The exercise is intended to be used in a face-to-face session, if possible.

1. Introduce the topic of trust as an important element of leadership in the team and in the organization.
2. Ask the team members how trust promotes an effective work environment. (Responses may include facilitation of risk taking, learning, creativity, and innovation.) Also discuss the consequences of a low-trust environment.
3. Introduce the three factors of trust: performance and competence, integrity, and concern for the well-being of others. Provide some examples of each.
4. Divide the team into three subgroups. (If the session is being conducted by videoconference or audioconference, assign individuals to work on specific trust factors.) Ask each subgroup (or individual) to create a list of behaviors or actions in the team that contribute to trust.
5. Reconvene the total group and discuss the lists.
6. Distribute the trust checklists and review the examples in each trust category. Link these items to the items presented in step 3. Add items if appropriate.
7. Split the team into three subgroups. Assign each group (or several individuals if the session is remote) one of the trust categories: performance and competence, integrity, or concern for the well-being of others. Have the subgroup members discuss the items generated in step 4 and the items in the trust checklist in relation to each of the elements in their category and decide how they could be implemented in the team.
8. Reconvene the total group and have subgroups present their results from step 7. Discuss which items might be implemented quickly and which will be more long term. Assign time frames to actions and accountabilities.
9. Ask each person to work individually to select one item/action from each trust category that he or she will commit to. Ask for volunteers to discuss their actions.
10. Close the session.
11. Follow up on action items.

(continued)

CHECKLIST 7.1. (CONTINUED).

Trust Checklist

	Trust Factors	Examples	My Actions
Performance Competence	Develop and display competence.	Focus on individual and team results. Keep current in your technical area of expertise. Continue reading and learning about new skills, processes, approaches, and so on. Be open to new ideas and methods. Be able to say, "I don't know." Allow others to be experts. Foster expertise and sharing on the team—for example, set an agenda item for sharing learnings and establish a project Web page to share learnings.	
	Follow through on commitments and show results.	Keep a log of commitments and make them visible to the team through e-mail or another means. Have a method to ensure follow-through. Keep promises even if circumstances have changed. Keep your commitments in cost, schedule, and technical areas. Inform team members well in advance if you will be late in any area.	
Integrity	Ensure that your actions are consistent with your words.	Align your behaviors at meetings, during reviews, and at other critical times to the values and expectations you want to promote within the team. Have team members you trust watch you and give you feedback on the consistency of your words and actions. Conduct regular trust audits. If your actions are not consistent, explain why to your team members.	
	Stand up for your convictions; display integrity.	Do the right thing in the best interest of the team or its members. Be able to say, "I don't agree" to those above you. Speak up for what you believe in with the team and with management. Continue to do the right thing, even in a crisis or firefighting mode. When appropriate, openly discuss your work-related convictions and values with team members and with management. Have an agenda item about this in team meetings.	
	Stand behind the team and its people.	Keep up to date so that you can catch problems before you have to defend the team or any of its members. Always investigate problems with the team before commenting to others about possible reasons for them. Never speak negatively about the team to others.	

(continued)

CHECKLIST 7.1. (CONTINUED).

	Trust Factors	Examples	My Actions
Integrity (continued)	Communicate and keep everyone informed about progress.	Hold a regular audioconference, videoconference, or other meeting once a week and have an agenda that covers bad as well as good news. Don't forget people in remote locations and extended team members. Post information and decisions so that everyone has access to them. Ensure that everyone receives information in a timely manner. Use multiple, synchronous, asynchronous, and redundant communication methods.	
	Show both sides of an issue.	Formally present both the pros and cons of issues. Post them on a Web site for the team members to read. Create an environment for and schedule time for discussion and debate in team sessions. Start a chat room or other means for asynchronous discussions.	
Concern for the Well-Being of Others	Help team members with transitions.	Have standard processes for selection, rewards, assignments, and sharing of information that do not favor certain people, functions, cultures, organizations, or locations. Rotate the "good" and "bad" team jobs. Help team members to transition off the team and to new assignments. Assign partners to new team members for orientation and reassignment.	
	Be aware of your impact on others.	Be aware that people are watching what you do, especially when you are a team leader. Take your role seriously. Take time to develop interpersonal relationships with team members, especially if team membership is permanent or long-term. Ask someone you trust to describe how you affect others on the team in different situations (for example, in crises or with demanding customers).	
	Integrate team needs with other team, department, and organizational needs.	Map how decisions on the team will impact other functional areas. Ask others for their opinions about how the team's behaviors impact functional areas before implementing changes. Have team members explore this as a team assignment. Keep track of how decisions evolve and how they affect others on the team. Have team members report on how their decisions may affect other team members.	

CHECKLIST 7.2. TRUST LOG.

Instructions: All virtual team leaders and members should keep trust logs of items that are important to them and/or to the team. The idea is to select one or more of the trust elements from the checklist and to begin to explicitly track actions, words, and decisions and their consequences in terms of creating a foundation for trust, building trust, and maintaining trust. This written record can help each individual to weigh the consequences of actions, words, and decisions. It also facilitates sharing information with others.

Sample items from a team leader's trust log are provided below. You can construct one for your own use or for the entire team.

Sample Trust Log

Trust Area	Situation	Actions, Words, Decisions, and Consequences
Keep commitments and show results.	I told all members of the core team that they would be able to attend major customer reviews and that everyone would have a role in presenting the product. The original schedule was for early March, when there was plenty of travel money. The client is located in Santa Clara, California. Team members are from around the world. The presentations are now scheduled for late November, and travel money has been cut. There is only enough money for the team leader and the lead technical person to present in person. Not everyone in the team likes the lead person. Team members have really sacrificed for this project. They were looking forward to attending.	I should never have promised this, but it was the right thing to do at the time with the information I had. I need to ensure that everyone understands the situation and has his/her contributions recognized with the client and with his/her management. Actions: 1. Have everyone sign the final product. 2. Write letters of commendation to all team members' managers, the team members, and the client. Copy other important people. 3. Consider a videoconference report with the client, with team members online. 4. Explain to the team in a face-to-face or electronic meeting the situation and my feelings about it. 5. Plan a success party and honor team members.

CHECKLIST 7.3. TRUST AUDIT.

A trust audit is a useful way to obtain real-time and ongoing feedback about actions that are important to the virtual team. After the team has determined items that are meaningful to it from the trust checklist, questionnaire items can be constructed that provide the team and its leader with feedback on how the team is doing. The questionnaire can be put into an e-mail format and administered on a regular basis. The results serve as a point of departure for the team members to debrief how they are performing in each trust area.

New items can be added as the team matures and as new issues arise. Rotating the responsibility for summarizing results and leading the team's debriefing and action-planning session can give everyone a sense of participation in building trust. When debriefing, use an agenda that everyone has agreed to and be certain that all responses remain anonymous and that all items are thoroughly discussed and resolved. No item or response is too minute or unimportant to be addressed.

If debriefing sessions are conducted by audioconference or videoconference, schedule at least two hours. If necessary, obtain the help of a meeting facilitator. Always find a way to follow up on actions in a timely manner.

An example of items from a trust audit is shown below. It is not necessary to have a large number of items. Instead, pay attention to creating a questionnaire that is meaningful, easy to respond to, anonymous, and focused on the team's unique concerns and issues.

Example of Areas for a Trust Audit

Trust Element: Keep Commitments and Show Results

1. Team members meet all deliverable cost and schedule requirements.

Never	Once in a while	Some of the time	Most of the time	All the time

2. On this team, we notify one another if we can't meet our commitments.

Never	Once in a while	Some of the time	Most of the time	All the time

3. This team does a good job of posting commitments on the network when they affect the team.

Never	Once in a while	Some of the time	Most of the time	All the time

4. When circumstances change, all team members hear about it in a timely manner.

Never	Once in a while	Some of the time	Most of the time	All the time

FIGURE 7.1. TRADITIONAL TRUST RADIUS.

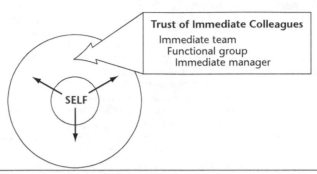

Source: Adapted from R. Shaw, *Trust in the Balance.* San Francisco: Jossey-Bass, 1997. Used with permission of John Wiley & Sons, Inc.

CHECKLIST 7.4. DEFINING YOUR TEAM'S TRUST RADIUS.

This exercise provides virtual team leaders and team members a way to begin to discuss how each team member's experience and background affects his or her trust radius. The idea is not to develop a definitive statement about each team member's radius but to use what each person reveals as a starting point for a team discussion about trust.

This exercise can be used by a virtual team leader at the team's orientation session or at one of the follow-up sessions. It can be conducted online if the team uses an electronic whiteboard or collaborative groupware with graphics capability. It can be conducted in an audio conference if each team member has faxed his or her trust radius to the others prior to the session. It also can be conducted in a face-to-face setting and is probably preferable in that mode if team members are just getting to know one another.

Instructions: Have each team member draw three circles on the following template that best characterize the radius of team membership in their last three project or work teams (the circles farther out indicate a larger trust radius than those closer to the middle). Have team members use solid lines to represent their most recent teams, dotted lines to represent their next most recent teams, and lines with arrows to represent the teams before that.

Next, lead a team discussion about what the current team's trust radius needs to look like. Does this team need a large trust radius or a smaller one? Who should be included in that radius (other teams, partners, other individuals or groups)? After the team has reached agreement, draw that radius on each team member's worksheet, using two double lines.

(continued)

CHECKLIST 7.4. (CONTINUED).

Have each team member compare his or her previous trust radii with the trust radius required for the current team. Lead a team discussion with the following questions:

1. Is the current team's trust radius requirement larger or smaller than your previous teams' requirements? _____

2. If it is larger, who is included now who was not included by the previous teams? _____

3. What are the implications for building trust in this team? _____

   _____

4. With whom do we need to network and build bridges? _____

   _____

5. What are the implications for getting to know more about one another?

   _____

Following this discussion, review what team members can do to build trust with one another. Use the trust checklist in this chapter as a guide.

Trust Radius Worksheet

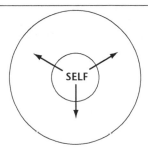

Source: Adapted from R. Shaw, *Trust in the Balance.* San Francisco: Jossey-Bass, 1997. Used with permission of John Wiley & Sons, Inc.

FIGURE 7.2. EXPANDING THE RADIUS: TRUST FOR VIRTUAL TEAMS.

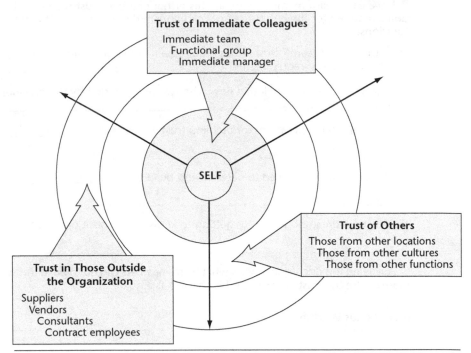

Source: Adapted from R. Shaw, *Trust in the Balance.* San Francisco: Jossey-Bass, 1997. Used with permission of John Wiley & Sons, Inc.

It is up to the team to help expand the trust radius of each individual team member and hence of the whole team (see Figure 7.2). The activity in Checklist 7.4 allows a team to examine its trust radius and to make plans to expand it.

Trust in a Multicultural Context

The three factors in trust—performance competence, integrity, and concern for the well-being of others—appear to be acceptable to individuals in most cultures. Our proj-ects with multicultural organizations often address issues related to trust. In all cases, it appears that all cultural groups accept the three factors as meaningful and important. The ways in which they are enacted and perceived, however, are affected by cultural influences. For example, there is the possibility that individuals from more collective cultures may believe that concern for others and certain aspects of integrity, such as standing up for the team, are more important than performance competence. Because collective societies have a stronger focus on the importance of relationships, trust may be influenced more by factors related to building and sustaining relationships.

Power Distance

People from high-power-distance cultures may have more of a tendency to accept that decisions will be made by higher-status individuals on the team without consultation with other team members. This can erode trust with members from low-power-distance cultures, who expect to work and make decisions more participatively and to be consulted about decisions. When they are not, they may perceive a lack of concern for or trust in them or their perceived competence.

Uncertainty Avoidance

The cultural dimension of uncertainty avoidance has to do with how comfortable people are in ambiguous situations. People from cultures with high uncertainty avoidance may tend to feel and act anxious in uncertain or unknown situations. People from cultures with low uncertainty avoidance may easily misinterpret this anxiety as low trust in their or other team members' abilities or competence. In fact, the anxiety may have more to do with a need for structure. Helping individuals from high-uncertainty-avoidance cultures feel comfortable may involve paying closer attention to predictability—developing written rules, procedures, and structures, especially in the beginning stages of the team's life.

Individualism–Collectivism

Individualistic cultures tend to value autonomy; collective cultures place the needs of the group before those of the individual. People from cultures that are strongly individualistic are more likely to expect to look after themselves than individuals from cultures that are strongly collective. As a result, their expectations of the team leader in terms of assistance with career development, coaching, and communicating with management may differ, depending on their cultural backgrounds.

In general, team members from more collective cultures expect more interaction and relationship-focused behavior than team members from individualistic cultures. Keeping in touch with other team members and finding out about their lives may be perceived as appropriate in more collective cultures and as inappropriate in more individualistic cultures. When team members from individualistic cultures do not do this, they may be perceived as having less concern for others.

Behaviors such as taking individual credit for the team's output and speaking inappropriately of other team members probably have a negative impact on trust in any culture. In a collective culture, however, they may be more damaging. It is possible that trust in collective cultures is based more on showing concern for others and acting with integrity than it is in individualistic cultures. Individualistic cultures, whose members see themselves working as individuals within the team, not as tightly linked with the team's or another team member's identity and history, may focus less on, and place less value on, the relationship aspects of trust.

Long-Term Versus Short-Term Perspective

A long-term perspective is evidenced in the tendency to display perseverance and thrift. A short-term perspective may be evidenced in the tendency to make decisions that are immediately profitable. The tension that arises between these two ways of looking at things can cause distrust on a team if certain members are seen as compromising the future to look good in the short term, while others are seen as having no sense of urgency or risk taking. One way to solve this is for the team to agree to make all short-term actions and decisions based on the longer-term perspective—in other words, keeping both perspectives in mind all the time.

High Context Versus Low Context

Context has to do with people's preferences for the amount and type of information in the communication process. People from high-context cultures prefer more information and detail than people from low-context cultures do. It is possible that requests for information that originate from a high-context team member about a low-context team member's idea or plan may be misinterpreted. The low-context team member may see the need for more information as irrelevant. Worse yet, it may be perceived as an insult to his or her competence and as a signal that the high-context team member does not trust him or her. A preference for more information-rich communication may be interpreted as distrust.

The Impact of Technology

Although research on the topic has not been extensive, it is clear that technology interacts with the three trust factors. First, technology can be used to send subtle messages about who is considered a high performer and who is not. High performers on teams tend to send more one-on-one electronic messages than low or moderate performers do. They also tend to send more one-on-one messages to other high performers than to low-performing team members.[5] This formation of electronic "in groups" can communicate who is perceived as competent and who is not. Being left out of one-on-one communication patterns could indicate that a team member is perceived as less competent than others.

Second, technology can be used to facilitate the integrity of team processes and decision making. The integrity of team members' opinions and ideas can be preserved using groupware with anonymity features, especially when the team members are discussing topics on which there may be disagreement or when one or two team members may be in the minority. This technology allows all opinions to be voiced without fear of recrimination. Scheduling software and similar features also facilitate timely follow-up and the feeling that other team members are meeting their commitments. Electronic distribution lists or postings make it easy to get the same information to everyone in a timely manner.

Third, because virtual teams operate in isolated environments rather than in social ones, there is less need for social posturing than in traditional settings. This may, however, create a tendency to display less concern for others. It is not uncommon for team members to ignore social mores and make blunt remarks that would never be uttered face-to-face or even over the telephone. One study showed that computer-mediated groups communicate more negative messages than face-to-face groups do.[6] Teams should guard against this and reserve criticisms and challenges for face-to-face meetings (or at least audioconferences) so that they are not misconstrued. As mentioned earlier, just one negative e-mail message from a team member early in the team's life can destroy the trust that the team has in this individual for a long time.[7]

Finally, virtual teams that are also functional groups have the potential for a higher trust factor due to goals that tend to be more closely aligned and the existence of a single accountable manager at the head of the function who has direct authority over the virtual team members.

Virtual Near Disaster

Sara was the victim of one of the most common and unfortunate forms of near virtual disasters; virtual blindness. She was on a videoconference with three locations. Each location had a large group of people sitting around the table who were part of the virtual team. It was rare that so many members of the team gathered in one meeting. There had been some infighting and undercutting of the team members on a sensitive and highly political project that the team was assigned. The team leader thought it was best for the team to come together and go through the project plan in the spirit of transparency; everyone could see what everyone was working on. Sara had been at odds with Jim on a assignment that she was leading.

When the meeting began, the leader asked for a role call. Everyone said his or her name. Sara and Jim were in different locations. Sara was late and came in after the role call. She took the last seat in the corner of the room. The video camera was only wide enough to get a partial view of the group, and unfortunately, the view did not include Sara. When the controversial assignment that the team leader gave Sara came up, the leader started the conversation. Jim interrupted the leader immediately, not knowing Sara had joined the virtual meeting. "Sara has been leading this project without asking for everyone's opinion," he said. "She needs to step back and realize that some of us have been here a long time and have valuable input. I know that I am not the only one who feels this way. Maybe the assignment should be given to someone who will ask us what we think." Sara couldn't contain herself, and at the end of his sentence, she jumped in, much to Jim's surprise. "I have asked for input from everyone including you, Jim, but you did not respond." The meeting went on, but the damage was done. Sara was furious that Jim would try to speak ill of her. She became even more angry after she had pieced together what had just happened. She realized that Jim did not know Sara was there and took that opportunity to talk about her—a bit cowardly, she thought. Sara never trusted Jim again.

Virtual blindness happens all the time. You respond to an e-mail by clicking "Send to All" when you really just wanted to respond to the sender. You are on a call and you don't know who is listening in at every location. You trust the person you send a voice mail to, and the recipient broadcasts it to the entire team, perhaps inadvertently. Unlike a face-to-face meeting, you don't always know who is in the room or who will hear or read your words. The lesson is to always assume that virtual meetings or forums are public, realizing that you have no certainty about who is on the call. As in the Sara and Jim debacle, once you breach trust with virtual blindness, it is hard to regain it.

Points to Remember

1. Developing trust is a crucial activity early in the life of virtual teams.
2. Trust depends on three factors: performance competence, integrity, and concern for the well-being of others. These factors apply across cultures but may be interpreted differently in different cultures.
3. A virtual team's trust radius needs to be larger than a traditional team's.
4. The use of technology has implications for trust building in virtual teams.

PART THREE

MASTERING VIRTUAL TEAMS

CHAPTER EIGHT

VIRTUAL TEAM MEETINGS

Knowing how to facilitate and lead meetings is an essential skill for anyone in business. All groups need to share information, coordinate, collaborate, discuss, make decisions, and produce products. Facilitating these processes to be effective and efficient is central to the success of high-performing virtual teams.

The right technical tools enhance our ability to share concepts, merge ideas, and use synergy to accomplish our goals. They also give us the option of interacting synchronously or asynchronously. Meetings can occur over a number of hours or days, and team members can attend the same meeting at different times. "Store and forward" technology allows us to hold a videoconference in China one day and ship the entire meeting, video and data, to Brazil in time for the next business day.

However, meetings will always be composed more of people than of technology. Virtual team leaders and members need to learn and use facilitation techniques that work for virtual teams. Technology cannot make up for poor planning or ill-conceived meetings. In fact, it can make the situation worse.[1] Without proper facilitation, virtual teams that meet on an ad hoc or short-term basis, such as virtual network and parallel teams, exchange information much less effectively than face-to-face teams do.[2] Functional virtual teams or long-standing project virtual teams have a better opportunity to create efficient and effective facilitated meetings over time than ad hoc virtual meetings. They can create a cadence and a familiarity that ad hoc teams cannot. Even so, certain types of meetings still benefit from good facilitation skills.

Effective facilitation can help ensure that relationships between team members and productive patterns of interaction develop and are nurtured so that they continue. Over time, with the proper selection of technology and effective facilitation, the exchange of information and the decision-making processes in virtual teams can be at least as effective as those of face-to-face teams.[3]

Who Does What in a Virtual Meeting: Four Roles

Julia Szerdy and Michael McCall present four roles that are relevant for all virtual meetings: owner, facilitator, participant, and technology.[4] Depending on the purpose of the meeting, some roles may overlap. The owner of the meeting may also be a participant. Often the owner takes the role of facilitator. However, it is useful for clarity to discretely outline each role.

Owner

The owner or client defines the objectives and outcomes of the meeting. He or she determines who should participate and the types of background information the participants will need. In addition, the owner should work with the facilitator to develop the agenda, select the technology to be used, and conduct the meeting. During the meeting, the owner should interact with the facilitator (if one is present) to ensure that the objectives for the meeting are met and that necessary decisions are made. Finally, he or she must decide the best way to follow up with next steps and action items.

Participant

Participants need to take responsibility for preparing for the meeting, including reading the background material and becoming familiar with the technology to be used. During the meeting, participants should be willing to speak out (or respond using electronic methods) as well as to listen and consider the ideas of others. In remote meetings, it is easier to "hide" than it is in face-to-face meetings. The participants must take active responsibility for making suggestions and decisions as well as for following up on meeting actions.

Facilitator

The facilitator is the person who conducts the process of the meeting. In a virtual meeting with members at remote locations, this role involves more technology than in a face-to-face meeting. The facilitator matches the technology to the goals of the meeting and to the items on the agenda, tests the technology before the meeting, and checks the technology throughout the meeting.

In addition to selecting the technology, the facilitator is responsible for the meeting process. Process considerations for virtual team meetings are similar to those for face-to-face meetings and include the following:

- Understanding the desired meeting outcomes and matching the agenda to them
- Communicating the agenda and meeting process
- Keeping the group focused and moving through the agenda during the meeting
- Modifying the agenda, if necessary, and removing barriers to success, such as nonparticipation by some people
- Addressing issues of team dynamics during the meeting
- Summarizing decisions and actions to be taken and reviewing the effectiveness of the meeting at its end

One of the biggest mistakes that owners can make is blurring the line between owner and facilitator. The owner has the accountability for the outcome of the meeting. The facilitator has the accountability to assist the leader—the team member who is accountable for the team's output—by employing methods to enable the meeting to be more effective and efficient. Keeping these roles clear is as important for the participants as it is for the owner and the facilitator.

Technology

It cannot be overemphasized that technology should serve the meeting, not dominate it. Technology enables virtual team members to meet and to accomplish what would be difficult or impossible without it. It should increase productivity. Technology should not be in the way when it is not needed or is inappropriate. During meetings that use real-time data-conferencing systems with text and graphic support, for example, there are times when the facilitator may ask the participants to stop typing and to just talk with one another. (In some cases, where the technology is complex, a separate facilitator, or "technographer," is sometimes used to focus solely on the technology. This frees the facilitator to focus on the meeting process.)

What Is Done in a Virtual Meeting: Three Activities

All virtual meetings require three types of activities:[5]

1. Selecting the appropriate technology and type of interaction (real-time or asynchronous), given the purpose of the meeting

2. Planning for "people issues" (such as who will participate), scheduling the meeting around the availability of the participants, and dealing with meeting logistics
3. Developing an effective agenda and facilitating the effective use of technology

Selecting the Technology and Type of Interaction

One of the primary determinants in selecting technology is the level of interaction a meeting demands. The purpose of getting people together in a meeting can vary from just catching up to producing deliverables. There are four major types of meetings:

1. *Information-sharing meetings,* in which information is shared and discussed among team members. Such meetings can range from one-way presentations to multiple-path exchanges of information. Examples are regular progress reviews and updates.
2. *Discussion meetings* that include the exchange of information but also promote dialogue, the generation of ideas or options, and discussion of issues or problems. Such meetings include discussions about technical approaches to problems and discussions about system issues, plans, and policies.
3. *Decision-making meetings,* in which issues are discussed and decisions are made collaboratively. An example is a meeting in which a final decision is made about a project schedule, technical approach, or policy.
4. *Product-producing meetings,* in which "hands-on work" is done and tangible products are produced, such as the analysis of data or work on a document or an engineering design. These meetings require the most collaboration.

Categorizing meetings on a continuum of low to high interaction can be useful in deciding what technology would be most effective for a particular type of meeting (see Table 8.1).[6]

An example from Sara's experience illustrates the waste of time that can result from selecting inappropriate technology.

Sara just got out of a meeting that was supposed to be a regular progress review with her team. One team member had talked her into testing a new type of Web-based electronic meeting system that her organization had just started to use. The system looked great during the demonstration and had more functionality than the systems Sara was used to. It allowed team members to brainstorm anonymously, to categorize and prioritize their ideas, and to vote on the best ones. It also allowed team members to turn on and off anonymity as they desired, so that if people's opinions were important, team members could know who said what. It allowed team members to move documents from shared databases in and out of the system.

A person from the information systems group who had just been trained on the system helped Sara with the technical part of the session. He did a good job before

TABLE 8.1. MEETING INTERACTION CONTINUUM.

Information Sharing	*Brainstorming and Decision Making*	*Collaborative Work*
Low Interaction	**Moderate Interaction**	**High Interaction**
Voice mail	Electronic bulletin board	Real-time data conference with audio/video and text and graphics
E-mail	Chat rooms	Whiteboards with audio/video link
	Videoconference	Electronic meeting system (EMS) with audio/video and text and graphics
	Audioconference	Collaborative writing tools with audio/video links
	Real-time data conference	

the meeting in working with Sara to develop an agenda and with the team members to prepare them to use the software. He handled the technology during the session. Sara thought that if her team members worked with him long enough, they would be able to plan and facilitate their own sessions.

Unfortunately, the agenda and the technology turned out to be too complex for the meeting. In trying to use all the capabilities of the EMS, her team wasted valuable time. Although the team members had fun using the system, they complained that the process was not really adding value. Brainstorming, prioritizing, and voting on each section of the report was too complicated, given the purpose of the meeting. In addition, the topics were not controversial enough to warrant anonymity. A simple audioconference would have done the job. The team members could have received materials via e-mail prior to the meeting, reviewed them, sent their comments back to Sara, and then discussed issues and next steps during a one-hour telephone conference. Although Sara wants to draw out some of the quieter members of the team, this was not the way to do it. Sara wants to use the EMS again, but this time she will select a more appropriate meeting.

Sara's experience can teach us the following lessons:

- Be clear about the purpose of the meeting. Is it to share information with two-way dialogue and discussion, to generate ideas and discuss them, to make a decision, or to produce a product?
- Don't overcomplicate the situation. Select the simplest technical solution, given the purpose of the meeting. The technology and the agenda should support the purpose of the meeting, not the other way around.
- Don't try out new technology during an important and time-critical session. Test new technology yourself before you subject the team to it.

From these lessons, we can construct a decision matrix that allows a team to match the technology to be used to the goal of the meeting (see Table 8.2). It allows the team to rate the effectiveness of each meeting technology on a continuum from not effective to highly effective, given the goal of the meeting.

The general rule is that for meetings that require rich discussion to gather or generate unique and new information, use synchronous methods with a number of information-rich communication channels, such as a videoconference with text and graphic capabilities. Synchronous methods work best when the issue is ambiguous and cannot be solved using data alone. The potential for conflict and the need to debate and discuss different approaches or methods are indicators that real-time conferencing is the best option. In extreme cases, where issues are highly emotional or ambiguous and when the team is newly formed or short-lived, none of the technological approaches listed might be appropriate. In such a case, if possible, schedule a face-to-face meeting.

Asynchronous meetings are appropriate if team members need time to ponder or consider an issue or if they need time to collect additional information in order to make recommendations or finish a product. Asynchronous meetings also work best if the issue is rather clear-cut and can be solved using data. Simple idea generation can be accomplished using asynchronous methods such as bulletin boards.

Planning for "People Issues"

Virtual meetings need participants. The team leader (perhaps with the assistance or guidance of the facilitator) selects the attendees, schedules the meeting, and attends to meeting logistics.

Selecting the Participants. Because communication and collaboration technology can allow us to interact with more people than face-to-face methods can, and also because people do not have to travel to participate, the temptation is often to invite all team members, stakeholders, and partners to every meeting. This is a mistake.

First, although collaboration is important, sometimes everyone does not have to know everything at the same time. The team leader should decide who should have access to what information and when.

One team was working out a technical problem using a real-time data-conferencing system when its customer joined the meeting and reviewed some of the work. She was furious when she detected what she believed to be a potential slip in the schedule about which she had not been informed. She described the project and team as "out of control." In reality, the conference communication did not tell the whole story, and the problem was immediately solvable. It took the team a long time to recover from this, and the customer remained somewhat suspicious throughout the rest of the project.

TABLE 8.2. MEETING SELECTION MATRIX.

Type of Technology	Information Sharing	Discussion and Brainstorming	Collaborative Decision Making	Collaborative Product Production
			Purpose of Meeting	
Voice mail	Somewhat effective	Not effective	Not effective	Not effective
Audioconference	Effective	Somewhat effective	Somewhat effective	Not effective
E-mail	Effective	Somewhat effective	Not effective	Not effective
Bulletin board	Somewhat effective	Somewhat effective	Not effective	Not effective
Real-time data conference (no audio/video)	Effective	Somewhat effective	Not effective	Somewhat effective
Videoconference without shared documents	Effective	Somewhat effective	Effective	Not effective
Real-time data conference with audio/video and text and graphics	Effective	Effective	Effective	Effective
Electronic meeting system with audio/video and text and graphics	Effective	Highly effective	Highly effective	Effective
Collaborative writing with audio/video	Effective	Effective	Somewhat effective	Highly effective

Explain to those who are not invited to attend why it is not a good idea for them to attend and when (or if) they will receive information from the meeting. If the client or owner is not invited, make sure that this person knows when he or she will receive the results of the meeting.

Second, because people do not have to travel, it is easy to assume that team members always have the time to attend all meetings. During the planning phase of the team, decide, as a team, who will attend which meetings and for which meetings attendance will be optional. That way, there will be no surprises. Some teams create a folder on a team Web site in which important documents and other information are kept so that people who do not attend meetings can keep up-to-date on decisions that affect the team.

Scheduling the Meeting. An electronic group calendaring and scheduling system should be part of any virtual team's technology package. The use of such a system can save the team's leader or facilitator days of effort in trying to coordinate people's schedules. The following are the steps taken to schedule a meeting using a scheduling system:

1. After you have decided who should attend the session, create a preliminary agenda or at least a list of desired outcomes. Determine how long it will take to work through the agenda. Also determine whether the meeting will be synchronous or asynchronous. If it will be asynchronous, notify the attendees about the periods of time in which you want them to "attend" the session or to conduct an activity, such as review and comment on a document.

2. If the meeting will be synchronous, select a time for the meeting. This should include starting and ending times. Be aware that scheduling systems are sometimes tricky to use across time zones. The person who is scheduling the meeting should be cognizant of differences in time zones and should not schedule any team members to attend in the middle of the night! Most scheduling systems offer a composite of schedules for all possible attendees. After a time is selected, an icon will appear next to each person's name. Most systems also contain an automatic time selection feature that determines the first available time slot for everyone on the team.

3. Send a notice about the meeting to each person who is selected to attend. Ask the potential attendees to respond to you by a specific date about whether or not they can attend.

Dealing with Meeting Logistics. Although we tend to ignore logistics because they are boring, they can make or break a meeting. If the agenda is not distributed before the meeting, the participants are likely to be ill-prepared to discuss agenda items. In addition, not anticipating issues regarding system compatibility or the unreliability of hardware and software can quickly ruin a meeting.

The agenda sent out prior to the meeting should inform the participants about what they will be expected to contribute during the session. Tell them whether you expect a high degree of participation or their input on one or two issues. If possible, let each participant know what his or her specific role will be. Regularly scheduled meetings should have standard agendas so that everyone knows what to expect.

If materials are distributed for preparation or prework, tell the participants how the materials will be used and whether any items are to be reviewed and returned to you and by when. Let people know where to find information they need on Web sites. If documents will be discussed during the meeting, especially during an audioconference or videoconference and not Webcast, make sure that pages and important sections are well labeled so that people will not be flipping through documents trying to find the appropriate pages. It is a good idea to indicate page or section numbers on the agenda. If materials will be printed from e-mail files, use hard page breaks so that people who have different printers will be looking at the same pages. Nothing is more frustrating than to be disagreeing about a point only to find out that you are referring to different pages!

If the meeting deals with a detailed review of a document or product, gather as much information about people's reactions as possible prior to the session. Collect answers to questions you can anticipate before the meeting so that you can summarize reactions and direct the conversation. This way, if there are strong commonalties and themes, they can be reviewed but not become the focus of the meeting. The focus can be on areas or ideas that need more discussion. Virtual meetings, like face-to-face meetings, if not properly planned, run the risk of just rehashing old information.[7]

Ensure that all team members have access to and are comfortable with the technology that is needed for the meeting. Make sure that attendees have the right hardware and software configurations; make a list ahead of time and send it to them. Schedule training and provide technical support, especially for people who are not experienced in using the technology. After several meetings, the team members may be able to handle the technology on their own.

Ask for a demonstration prior to selecting new technology, and test it again one or two hours before the actual meeting so that you have time to work out any problems. Also, have a backup plan for each site in case of technical problems.

When introducing new technology, it is a good idea to consult with someone who is an expert in using the system prior to the meeting to plan the best way to use the system. Never assume that everything will work well. Check to see that any technological systems you plan to use are compatible with one another. Some approaches, such as EMS, whiteboards, and collaborative writing, are used less frequently by virtual teams than other forms of collaboration, such as e-mail. Today, although compatibility is improving, there is no single system that will interface with and support all the components desired (such as different data, graphics, and video) in all types of meetings.[8] Be aware of any differences in the participants' computer monitors. Some people may have slightly different displays than others and may become confused if they are not viewing the same information as everyone else.

According to research by David Pauleen and Pak Yoong, successful virtual team members selected technology "channels" based on the team task.[9] For example, team members used e-mail for coordinating and transacting information but relied on more complex technology, such as desktop video, when interaction and group collaboration were required. The study also found that team members used the telephone for building relationships and getting interpersonal cues from other team members. Many times, team members find that simpler technology is better suited and more cost-effective than more advanced and complicated technology.

Lisa Kimball and Amy Eunice suggest ways to improve the effectiveness of virtual teams that are easy and low in cost.[10] Their suggestions include making sure the whole team is visible to every member. This can be accomplished by ensuring that a picture of the team or team members is posted or by posting a map that shows the location of each team member. They also suggest that the team create a "line of sight" for each member. Ways to do this include using a journalism style to capture meeting notes rather than a minutes format; creating a "virtual water cooler" for sharing stories and small talk, and ensuring that conversations are rich and diverse rather than predictable and stale.

Developing an Agenda and Facilitating the Use of Technology

Although academic research and practical experience regarding virtual teams is still maturing, it is possible to discuss what is known about virtual team meetings, with a focus on maximizing the exchange of information and discussion of ideas.

What Is Known Virtual teams have a variety of technology channels available to create the appropriate team environment. According to Charlene Solomon, the key is to choose the right technology for the type of work and to know when to use it.[11] Again, the research shows that the more team members can interact with voice and audio, the more likely they are to overcome barriers to time and distance. Solomon acknowledges that virtual teams need to have access to other forms of technology.

Many factors affect the transaction of information in virtual meetings. These include the member's familiarity with the information, the opportunity for inclusion and engagement in the meeting, and the hierarchy of the team members.

Social status also affects the exchange of information.[12] Often people who have higher status, such as managers, dominate conversations in meetings. Social status may also relate to cultural dimensions. For example, individuals from high-power-distance cultures may feel more inhibited about participating when people of higher status, such as managers, are participating in a meeting.[13]

People must have the motivation to participate. Most people find it difficult to be motivated to offer input or new information that is counter to the primary sentiment of the group.[14] It takes energy to contribute if you know that your opinion is going to be in the minority. Also, an opinion that is offered first often dominates the entire meeting, which makes it difficult for others to offer conflicting ideas. People can lose motivation very early in a meeting when they realize that their views will likely not be heard, let alone discussed. People who are not committed to the team or who have conflicting priorities may also not be motivated to contribute to the meeting.[15]

Finally, if a person contributes and then is ridiculed or punished in some way for voicing a dissenting opinion, that person will not be motivated to participate in the future. Anonymous procedures, such as balloting, can be used when discussion topics are very controversial in order to ensure that each team member provides input.

The total amount of information exchanged in virtual teams (especially in newly formed ones) is often less than that exchanged in face-to-face groups.[16] Communication channels often limit the opportunity to offer input. The absence of nonverbal clues during audioconferences and other electronically mediated meetings limits communication and inhibits the normal give-and-take of face-to-face conversation. If team members are typing their comments during a virtual meeting, the opportunity to provide information is limited by their typing speed. In teams with members who speak different native languages, issues arise around accents and jargon, the ability of some individuals to type quickly in their nonnative language, and a general apprehension about jumping into a conversation when the majority of participants may not understand you.

Virtual teams can also find it more difficult to coordinate their activities and to exchange information than face-to-face teams do.[17] It takes more effort and motivation by a virtual team to reach understanding and complete tasks than it does for a traditional team. Virtual teams run the risk of spending more time talking about the procedural aspects of a meeting, such as where the team is on the agenda, than traditional teams do.[18] This may lead to less opportunity to contribute and less motivation to do so as participants become tired of focusing on procedural topics.

The good news is that especially for virtual team members who work on a long-term basis, select the right technology and agenda, and become familiar with one another, some of these problems can disappear or be overcome.[19] With the right task, agenda, and facilitation, virtual teams can actually surpass in-person teams in many areas.

Obtaining facts and reminding people of decisions made in earlier sessions can increase recall and move a meeting along. Real-time access to databases, search engines, articles, and other information prior to and during meetings can help team members remember previous decisions and resolve disagreements. These features are often present in Web-based conferencing tools and other groupware products.

One team, working at the headquarters level on a policy issue, had developed a strategy that it thought would address a competitive threat. Some team members seemed to remember a similar strategy that was developed earlier by a field operation but was not accepted by upper management. The team was able, online, to search and access the previous group's recommendations in the company's resource library. It reviewed the results and realized that it was reinventing a strategy that had proved ineffective.

Virtual team members can have the opportunity to participate more openly and fully than face-to-face team members.[20] Under the correct conditions, such as using EMS groupware with anonymity features, virtual team members express more extreme views and more unusual ideas and can contradict one another more than team members who are meeting face to face, perhaps because they feel less social pressure.[21]

Another team, tasked with developing market projections, used groupware to raise concerns during a meeting about market projections in Asia that were much more discouraging than those revealed during a face-to-face sales planning session with top management. When they were face to face, the team members were uncomfortable delivering "bad news." Team members from collective cultures and those from high-power-distance cultures are generally more able to present divergent ideas in remote meetings than in face-to-face meetings.[22] This is important, because divergent thinking is desirable for generating new and unique ideas and for identifying problems with existing ideas.

Electronic polling systems, which are often features of EMS, are useful in the middle of a meeting to redirect discussions. They can assist at any time in making immediate decisions. Having team members anonymously criticize ideas or rate a topic improves decision quality as social pressure is diminished.[23] Electronic polling systems can also motivate members to make decisions that may be too painful to make face to face.[24] A decision about closing a facility or dropping an unprofitable product line can be made anonymously. Polling can also demonstrate agreement on the team and can help a group get past unnecessary debate and discussion.

Using technology to more effectively structure collaborative tasks is another gain that virtual teams may realize. Group editing of a document, for example, can be structured in three different ways: (1) sequentially (the document is passed from person to person), (2) in parallel (a part of the document is worked on by different authors and reassembled electronically), and (3) reciprocally (collaborators work to create a common document, edit it together, and adjust it in real time).[25] The use of electronic document-writing tools to perform the latter two options, along with a tightly structured agenda, makes these editing options possible. The technology can produce significant gains in productivity over the usual process of passing a document from person to person. These gains exist, in part, because the technology facilitates a process in which team members have a structured opportunity to contribute. Motivation is increased because participation increases ownership of the final product.[26]

These findings, along with lessons from experience, have implications for the ways in which team leaders and facilitators plan and carry out virtual team meetings.

Planning the Agenda and Linking Technology to Specific Agenda Items

The meeting owner and facilitator must know what the meeting is to accomplish—a decision, a plan, a document, a product, and so on. On your agenda, map out how you will use the technology to achieve each result. Teams that use collaborative writing tools, for example, gain from using a structured process that links the use of specific electronic tools to activities on the agenda.[27] Generating the document outline, for example, is linked to the use of a group outlining tool. Feedback and discussion about the outline then connects with a collaborative annotation or a parallel discussion tool. The participants must perceive how the use of technology is related to specific outcomes and activities; otherwise, they may think it a waste of time.

Table 8.3 provides a format that can be used to link agenda items to technology to be used during a meeting. It also shows how agenda items and technology relate to the four factors that facilitate the exchange of information in a virtual setting. The table uses agenda items as the anchor and then links the meeting process to the agenda item. Meeting process refers to factors such as who will participate in what activity. The third column lists the technology that might be used to accomplish the agenda item using the selected process. The fourth column provides a final check by listing how the agenda, process, and technology work together to facilitate the four factors associated with successful virtual team meetings: recall, input opportunity, reduced social pressure, and motivation. Technology and processes that consistently do not contribute to any of these factors should be reconsidered carefully.

Using Technology to Maximize the Contribution of Every Team Member

Technology should increase a participant's ability and motivation to recall and contribute relevant information and opinions. It should also reduce social pressure and increase motivation. Structure the agenda and the technology to maximize these factors. If there is a large amount of information to cover, have databases or other supporting information available online to enhance recall. Use anonymity features when trying to encourage the generation of new ideas and risky thinking or when

TABLE 8.3. EXAMPLE OF A PLANNING FORMAT FOR ALIGNING AGENDA, GROUP PROCESS, TECHNOLOGY, AND FACILITATION GOALS.

Purpose of meeting: Identify trends that affect strategic plan.

Agenda Item	Process	Technology Selected	Facilitation Goals
Introductions	Round-robin introductions	Audioconference and EMS	Increase opportunity to input Reduce social pressure Increase motivation
Identify trends that will affect business in the future	Ask participants to brainstorm trends anonymously for five minutes: any trends that will affect the business	Use anonymous parallel-input feature that allows people to see everyone else's input on the screen	Increase opportunity to input Increase recall of information Reduce social pressure
Begin prioritization of items listed	Ask participants to review the list, comment, and prioritize the top five items	Use commenting tool and ranking	Increase opportunity to input Reduce social pressure
Discuss new list	Ask participants if they have any comments about the list so far	Topic commentator in EMS Audio/video link	Increase opportunity to input Increase motivation
Use new prioritized list as a beginning, adding any items	Ask members to review the highest-ranked items Ask them to add any additional items that relate to the top ten	Use EMS anonymous brainstorming Use bold to highlight new items	Increase opportunity to input
Sort top ten items into categories	Ask members to create categories related to themes of items and put items into "buckets" that represent categories	Use EMS organizer feature	Increase recall of information Reduce social pressure

(continued)

TABLE 8.3. (CONTINUED).

Agenda Item	Process	Technology Selected	Facilitation Goals
Rate each of the categories regarding importance vis-à-vis future trends	Use multicriteria evaluation process	Use multicriteria evaluation process	Reduce social pressure Increase opportunity to input
Decide how confident the team is that these are the themes or categories	Ask team members for vote of confidence if these are the correct themes or categories	Use EMS voting	Increase recall of information Increase opportunity to input Reduce social pressure
Discussion	Discuss results of voting	Use audio/video link	Increase opportunity to input Increase motivation
Close and plan next steps	Ask participants to volunteer for follow-up, such as distributing minutes and reviewing results with local management Set follow-up date	Use audio/visual link Use e-mail for follow-up	Increase motivation and "buy in" to results

social pressure might be an issue. Use anonymous voting to obtain views about a topic or idea, to discover how comfortable people are with a plan, and to redirect the agenda. Increase people's motivation by using tools, such as group document editors, that allow everyone to participate in a timely manner and according to their own schedule.

Table 8.4 offers suggestions for leveraging technology to facilitate recall, contribution, and motivation and to reduce social pressure.

Using Agenda Topics and Subtopics to Manage Interaction Listing topics and subtopics on the agenda not only fosters meeting organization but also promotes the opportunity to contribute.[28] It allows participants to choose the topic or subtopic they are working on as their focus. They can also choose to arrive at the meeting space at the time that their topic is being considered.[29] In this way, they can see the work completed so far and then add their own contributions.

For each meeting topic, determine the outcomes and decide how long the topic will be under consideration and the process that will be used to manage the agenda item. For example, if you are using an EMS, this may include open discussion, side discussion, voting, idea generation, and research into an existing database.

Achieving a Balance Between Formality and Informality Formal, preset agendas have been found to inhibit the free flow of information and collaboration, especially in regularly scheduled meetings.[30] Other analysts recommend that agendas be structured tightly.[31] This presents the facilitator with a dilemma: how to foster informality and at the same time ensure productivity and a sense of accomplishment.

Especially with a new team or one that is working on a short-term project, prior to the meeting, encourage informal interaction by asking that participants collaborate on a task. Assign people to work with one another to develop a portion of the agenda or a product to present during the meeting. Taking their cultural biases into account, have them exchange photographs, biographies, or work histories that can become the basis for small talk during the meeting.

Build some informality or fun into the agenda. Discuss the weather. Play a word game at the beginning of the meeting. Develop ways to nurture the feeling of social presence and inclusion or a sense of "being there." Invent new methods and channels for sharing communication clues, and use them. This is especially necessary when using chat rooms and other electronic approaches that provide no verbal or visual clues. With the team's input, develop ways to signal emotions. For example, many virtual team members use signals such as all caps to indicate strong feelings or acronyms such as IMHO for "in my humble opinion" and BTW for "by the way" to speed communication. These create a sense of familiarity and belonging.[32] Encourage the members

TABLE 8.4. FACILITATION TIPS TO INCREASE RECALL OF INFORMATION, OPPORTUNITY TO INPUT, AND MOTIVATION AND TO REDUCE SOCIAL PRESSURE.

Focal Area	Facilitation Tips
Help people to find and remember information	• Provide an agenda well in advance. • Ask participants, prior to the meeting, to think about specific questions or issues. • Provide a format with which to respond to questions or collect thoughts that relate to meeting objectives. • Provide information about where to find information, e.g., databases, documents, search engines. • Use online documents during the meeting. • Have results of past decisions available. • Provide "think breaks," especially if there are nonnative speakers present.
Provide the opportunity for people to contribute	• Use anonymity features for brainstorming. • Use anonymity features for voting and reaching consensus. • Structure the agenda so that people can work in subteams. • Have people send in opinions prior to the meeting to avoid spending unnecessary time during the meeting and to increase the probability of divergent input. • Allow ample time; schedule two sessions if necessary. • Use communication technologies that provide enough interaction. If there is a need for extensive give-and-take, do not use technologies that allow only typing as input.
Increase motivation to participate	• Structure the agenda so that everyone has the opportunity to contribute. Go "around the room" virtually. In an audioconference or videoconference, ask each person for his or her opinion; vote using EMS. • Use technology, such as group editing and collaborative writing, to obtain "buy in" on final product from everyone. • Structure the agenda so that people can come in and out of meetings according to their needs for information and input.
Reduce social pressure that limits participation	• Use anonymity features for voting, brainstorming, and reaching consensus. • Use data-only technology to gather input from team members from high-power-distance cultures. • Collect divergent views prior to the meeting.

to make up signals that are unique to the team. Also encourage the team members to write more informally. Formal writing takes a long time and limits the number of ideas.

Varying Interaction Styles Repeating the same type of activity can have a dampening effect on even the most creative thinkers.[33] Mix electronic and verbal interaction modes during the meeting if you are working with a system in which both are possible. Use various ways to generate ideas. For example, use the nominal group technique in one activity and the Delphi technique in another.[34] Have members anonymously vote to demonstrate their confidence in an idea rather than asking people to say that they agree or disagree with it. Many groupware products and electronic meeting systems are very capable and allow great flexibility in skilled hands.

Another option is to occasionally mix the mode of interaction from meeting to meeting. If you have held audioconferences for a while, switch to a video format or use a whiteboard or editor for group writing. Also mix ways for team members to work with one another. For large tasks, divide the work among subgroups and vary, within their expertise, who works together.

Actively Facilitating Meetings There are a few general facilitation techniques that are useful in any meeting. Some of them are as follows:

- Check frequently that the team is staying with the agenda and actually making progress. It may be necessary to say that time is running out for discussion of a specific topic. Guide the discussion toward resolution or postponement. Let the team members decide if they want to keep discussing an item after its allocated time, but be certain that it is a group decision.
- Notice if some team members have not spoken, and ask if they have anything to contribute before the discussion of each item is closed. Think of new ways to use technology to draw them out.
- If the meeting is conducted in a language that is not the native language of several team members, provide them with "think breaks" to get their thoughts together. Often it is more difficult to keep up with a discussion if it is not in your first language.
- Pay attention to the team's process—how the members interact during the meeting—and raise relevant issues at an appropriate time. Are some members dominating the discussion? Are cliques forming? Is the group avoiding a controversial topic? Are members nitpicking or getting bogged down in details? As a process observer, you can help the group improve its meeting effectiveness by calling attention to such process issues.

- At the end of the meeting, summarize the discussion and make sure that any decisions, recommendations, and actions are recorded. Obtain commitment on who will do what by when.

- Try to have the minutes of the meeting available within a day or two. Be sure that you know how to get the minutes to each participant. Take particular care to ensure that the minutes are correct. In a virtual setting, it is easier to take liberties with interpretation of other people's input.

Adopting Best Practices for Meetings Using Different Technological Techniques There are best practices that can make audioconferences, videoconferences, chat rooms, and other meeting techniques more effective. Checklist 8.1 presents meeting management and facilitation tips for using different types of technology. Some of the tips may appear to be common sense, but they often are forgotten or overlooked in actual meetings.

CHECKLIST 8.1. FACILITATION TIPS FOR VARIOUS TYPES OF TECHNOLOGY.

Voice Mail

1. State your name and telephone number at the beginning and end of the message. _____
2. Keep the message short and to the point; make your request clearly and limit it to one or two items. _____
3. Be clear about what you need, when you need it, and how you want to receive it. _____
4. State whether the person should respond to you. _____
5. If you are sending a broadcast message, think carefully about who may receive it accidentally. _____

Audioconference

1. Define a specific purpose and time. _____
2. Limit participation to no more than seven or eight active participants. More can listen in. _____
3. Distribute the agenda and any prework prior to the session (allowing enough time for participants to complete any prework) and draw attention to important pages. _____
4. Gather opinions about more mundane items before the meeting so that people will not need to take time to discuss unimportant topics. _____

(continued)

CHECKLIST 8.1. (CONTINUED).

5. During the meeting, tell people who (the team leader or the facilitator) will be in charge of the process. _____

6. Ask who is online at the beginning of the session and ask everyone to introduce himself or herself. _____

7. Request that mute buttons be used when people are not speaking. _____

8. If someone has to leave, ask him or her to tell the group beforehand. _____

9. At the end, summarize the conversation and distribute the minutes within two days. _____

Videoconference

Use the guidelines for audioconferences. In addition,

1. Make certain that everyone has access to the equipment and test it beforehand. _____

2. Ensure that everyone has access to a database or hard copy of the meeting materials. _____

3. If you are using the Internet or desktop conferencing, consider whether bandwidth problems are going to be too annoying. Sometimes an audioconference works just as well. _____

4. Note that people's display monitors might be different. Try to reconcile this prior to the meeting. _____

Chat Room

1. Be clear about the purpose of the chat room. Limit it to a few topics or questions. _____

2. Let participants know the level of output and detail that you want. Conversations can become lengthy and stray from the point. _____

3. Let people know who will have access to the information. _____

4. Decide whether you want anonymous input. _____

5. Summarize the meeting (sort topics into themes) and send copies to the participants. Scrolling through discussion items is difficult and time-consuming. _____

E-Mail

1. Be specific about what you want from people, a return e-mail, a phone call, review of a document, and so on. _____

2. Send messages only to people who need to be included. Don't overload the system. _____

3. Use urgent and important tags only for those items that really are. _____

4. Ask for confirmation of receipt of messages and documents. _____

5. If possible, ask for confirmation of receipt of the file on important items (some e-mail systems have this). _____

6. Ask for confirmation that the person has actually read the information. _____

7. Note how you would like each participant to annotate a document (using underline, color, and other techniques). _____

(continued)

CHECKLIST 8.1. (CONTINUED).

8. Note who has what privileges to review or change a document. _____

9. Tell participants how to get the document back to you (by e-mail, fax, or other means). _____

10. Ask the IS department to set up a system that provides returned mail for "bad addresses," preferably with the correct addresses. _____

11. If you are using the system for workflow, get training and support for team members. _____

Electronic Meeting System

1. Ensure that the system works appropriately and is compatible with everyone's equipment. _____

2. If necessary, move applications as well as files to users prior to the meeting. _____

3. Make certain prior to the meeting that everyone can access the software as well as the shared files that may be needed. _____

4. Develop the agenda with a skilled facilitator, especially for the first few meetings. _____

5. Subdivide the agenda into parts and link each section to how you will use the technology (for example, for voting). _____

6. Decide when input will be anonymous and when it will not be. _____

7. Rotate activities, such as sorting information and voting, to avoid boredom. _____

Collaborative Composition

1. Decide what type of composition is best: sequential (output is passed from one person to another), parallel (the work is divided so that collaborators work on different parts of the document at the same time), or reciprocal (people work on the same document at the same time, adjusting their activities to take into account one another's input). _____

2. For sequential composition, e-mail or other forms of document exchange can be used. For parallel or reciprocal composition, use collaborative writing tools. These, at this point in time, will most likely require other modes of interaction in addition to the collaborative writing tools. _____

3. When the writing task gets in the way of progress, assign people to a subteam to work on the document and let the rest of the group move forward. _____

4. Tell the participants not to spend time formatting the document; have them use the time to focus on content. _____

5. Much of collaborative writing to date has been done using sequential methods or face-to-face collaborative methods. Little is really known about collaborative writing in a synchronous, distributed environment. _____

Near Virtual Disaster

Sara was the frustrated leader of a virtual team who could not seem to get its act together. Meetings rarely started on time. Many members, despite having agreed to the time and date of the meeting in advance, did not show up at all. Unfortunately, their participation was critical to the team's work and joint decision making. Sara scratched her head. Perhaps she was not setting the proper agenda. For the next meeting, she did everything right on the agenda and still had the same problems. Next, she decided that maybe the technology was inappropriate or not enabling the meeting as much as it could. For the next several meetings, she "experimented" with new and exciting technological approaches. Although they worked better than the ones she had been using, this seemed to make matters worse by frustrating the participants. Next, she tried to be sure to work on the "people" issues, including ensuring that language was not a barrier, encouraging dissenting views, and so forth. Still the attendance and quality of the dialogue did not improve. She finally decided to enlist the help of a facilitator. They spent several hours redesigning the next meeting. The result was as poor as the other attempts: two members of the five did not show up at all, one could stay for only ten minutes of the one-hour meeting, and the dialogue splintered into so many directions that neither she nor the facilitator could get the meeting back on track. That night, Sara and the facilitator went to dinner and talked at length about what was wrong.

Sara realized that her problem was not the meeting agenda, the technology, the facilitation, or maximizing the contribution of every member. The dysfunction came from the fact that the wrong level of people were on the team, given the nature of the task at hand. After months of anguish and near virtual disasters, Sara realized that virtual meetings can suffer from the same issues as nonvirtual meetings. Unfortunately, sometimes when we are working virtually, we go to the technology or the nature of the virtual space to solve the problem. There are times when the problem comes back to old-fashioned "Meetings 101." Had Sara realized that the problem was in the team makeup itself, she could have saved herself and everyone involved a great deal of anguish and wasted time.

Points to Remember

1. Facilitating a virtual meeting includes managing the agenda, the participants, and the technology.
2. Select technology that is appropriate for the outcome of the meeting. Match the use of technology to specific agenda items.
3. Leverage the agenda and the use of technology to maximize recall, the opportunity to contribute, and motivation and to reduce social pressure.
4. Make use of social protocols and best practices for using the selected technology.
5. Make certain that logistics cover issues such as compatibility of technology, training in using new systems, and backup plans.

CHAPTER NINE

VIRTUAL TEAM DYNAMICS

Dynamics of a virtual team are likely to manifest over the team's life cycle. It is important to understand the factors that influence and are affected by team dynamics in a virtual setting. Helpful strategies and tools facilitate virtual team dynamics. These tools help leaders and team members assess the health of their virtual team.

Technical and Adaptive Environments

Virtual teams can exist in technical or adaptive environments. In a technical context, work is usually planned and executed according to a timetable, with schedules and project plans. The knowledge necessary to solve a problem usually exists and may even be codified in policies, processes, or procedures. In this situation, the team acquires the knowledge and applies it to the team's task.

In an adaptive environment, situations are unique and do not have defined or routine solutions. The challenge is to devise a solution to a problem or a strategy that does not yet exist. Along the way, team members and organizational stakeholders may need to make painful adjustments in their attitudes and expectations. The specific character of a team's dynamics depends in part on whether the team's task environment is more technical or more adaptive. Clearly, this is a continuum; most tasks include problems for which partial solutions already exist. However, most virtual teams face situations that require behaviors toward the adaptive end of the continuum.

Traditional Models of Team Development

Bruce Tuckman's model of team development, the most widely quoted one, incorporates the stages of forming, storming, norming, performing, and adjourning.[1] The model explains that most teams go through a series of stages and that there may be conflict and interpersonal issues along the way. The assumption is that the team progresses over time toward better communication, maturity in relationships, and better performance. This model has proved quite useful to many practitioners and team leaders in traditional settings, in which team members are all in the same place and engaged in predefined work tasks. However, this model and others like it are not as useful when applied to teams that are virtual, exist in adaptive environments, or involve multicultural complexities.

For long-standing teams or functional intact virtual teams, the stages still apply. However, the team may go more slowly through the different stages or even backtrack to earlier stages when the context of the work is changed, new projects are assigned, or something interrupts the routine workflow. Moreover, Tuckman's model works at the microcosmic level of teams, at the introduction of a new task or relationship even if the people involved have worked together for some time.

Virtual teams require a new model that accounts for the complexities of their work environments. Virtual team leaders and members who are skilled in using such a model will be better equipped to influence the performance of their teams and make informed choices about when, how, and how often they should intervene.

A New Model of Team Development

As with Tuckman's model, a sequence of stages can be used to encapsulate the dynamics associated with a team's task, especially a team that uses technology to communicate and collaborate.[2] A parallel series of stages is related to the team's social dynamics—how team members interact, resolve differences, and make decisions.[3] Team leaders and members must navigate the task dynamics and social dynamics to ensure good performance and feelings of being part of the team.

Productivity is important in all teams that are formed to produce a result. The goal of well-managed task dynamics is productivity.

The goal of well-managed social dynamics is a feeling of team unity. This feeling, although not always a prerequisite for high performance, helps team members maintain motivation, perceptions of trust, and interaction quality. It also contributes to positive attitudes toward future participation. Because face-to-face contact is not part of everyday life for virtual teams, unity may be more difficult to attain and manage.

It is possible to be productive without having the feeling of being a team, and it is possible to feel a sense of unity without being productive. In the end, many of our most satisfying experiences are on teams that balance task performance and social dynamics. The dynamics work together to create the team experience. Both are necessary for effectiveness.

The virtual environment does not contain many of the traditional means of managing the task and social aspects of team dynamics. Virtual team members and leaders consequently need to be more cognizant of how they develop and implement strategies to manage those dynamics. They need to understand the stages of each type of dynamics. Table 9.1 lists the task and social stages and the dynamics associated with each.

TABLE 9.1. TASK AND SOCIAL STAGES OF VIRTUAL TEAMS.

Stage	*Task Dynamics* Description	Task Activities	*Social Dynamics* Description	Social Activities
1	Inception	Select goals Generate preliminary plans Generate ideas	Interaction/ inclusion	Ensure team member inclusion Ensure opportunity for participation Define initial roles
2	Problem solving	Select technical problems to be resolved Solve problems with correct, known answers Solve ambiguous problems	Position status/role definition	Address status of team members Clarify and refine roles and expertise
3	Conflict resolution	Resolve conflicts about different points of view Resolve conflicts stemming from different interests	Power/ resource allocation	Address power differences between team members Address interpersonal relationships Address how different solutions affect power allocation to different functions, regions, and countries
4	Execution	Perform tasks Address organizational barriers to performance	Interaction Participation	Ensure equal participation Ensure effective interaction and communication

Task Dynamics

The four stages associated with task dynamics are as follows:

Stage 1: Inception. This stage involves the generation of ideas related to defining the goals of the team, how the goals might be accomplished, and the overall plans to achieve them.

Stage 2: Problem Solving. This stage involves choosing the correct means by which to address issues and solve technical problems. Issues and problems can have knowable and "correct" answers or can be unique, with no existing answers.

Stage 3: Conflict Resolution. This stage involves the resolution of conflicts that emerge from different points of view. Team members may have different approaches to technical problems. Conflicts can also be the results of different cultural, functional, and organizational perspectives.

Stage 4: Execution. This stage involves performing the team's work and overcoming organizational barriers that inhibit performance. Barriers include power struggles between functions, issues of ownership over the final product, and conflict over allocation of resources.

Virtual teams that are addressing simple, repeatable, prescriptive tasks may be able to move from stage 1, inception, to stage 4, execution, after a minimal planning period, as shown in Figure 9.1.

Stages 2 and 3 may or may not be required, depending on the circumstances. For example, teams working on technical tasks that have been successfully completed before may move directly to the execution stage. Service, work, and production teams that are involved in routine activities probably can skip stage 2, selecting the means to solve problems, because solutions already exist. Stage 3 may also not be required, because conflicts stemming from different points of view and different interests have been settled in the past. On the other hand, teams that are addressing problems that are new or unique or that involve the potential redistribution of power or resources between functions or organizations might have to devote much more time to stages 2 and 3, as shown in Figures 9.2 and 9.3.

Complicated patterns are more likely to occur in teams working on complex tasks in adaptive environments or in teams that have a number of team members or stakeholders with polarized functional, organizational, or cultural interests.

FIGURE 9.1. TECHNICAL PATHWAY A: INCEPTION TO EXECUTION.

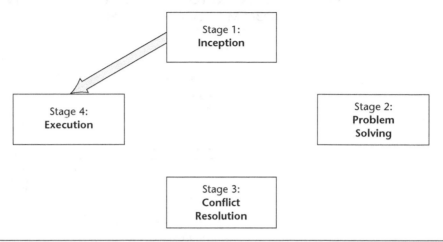

Source: Adapted from J. McGrath, "Time Matters in Teams." In J. Galegher, R. E. Kraut, and C. Egido (Eds.), *Intellectual Teamwork: Social and Technical Foundations of Cooperative Work.* Hillsdale, N.J.: Erlbaum, 1990. Used with permission.

FIGURE 9.2. TECHNICAL PATHWAY B: INCEPTION TO PROBLEM SOLVING TO EXECUTION.

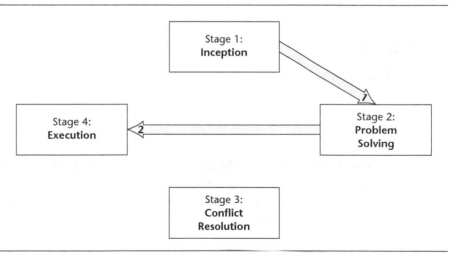

Source: Adapted from J. McGrath, "Time Matters in Teams." In J. Galegher, R. E. Kraut, and C. Egido (Eds.), *Intellectual Teamwork: Social and Technical Foundations of Cooperative Work.* Hillsdale, N.J.: Erlbaum, 1990. Used with permission.

FIGURE 9.3. TECHNICAL PATHWAY C: INCEPTION TO PROBLEM SOLVING TO CONFLICT RESOLUTION TO PROBLEM SOLVING TO EXECUTION.

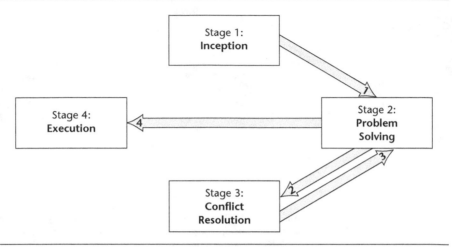

Source: Adapted from J. McGrath, "Time Matters in Teams." In J. Galegher, R. E. Kraut, and C. Egido (Eds.), *Intellectual Teamwork: Social and Technical Foundations of Cooperative Work.* Hillsdale, N.J.: Erlbaum, 1990. Used with permission.

Social Dynamics

The social dynamics of virtual teams parallel the task dynamics and include four stages.

Stage 1: Interaction and Inclusion. Team members define their individual contributions to the team and begin to interact as a group to develop the team's charter and work plans.

Stage 2: Position Status and Role Definition. Team members interact to define or redefine their roles and status in relation to one another. The focus may be on their roles as experts or as organizational representatives. It may be on their personal or expert status in relation to other members, particularly in determining the solutions to problems.

Stage 3: Allocation of Resources and Power. The team addresses issues regarding the allocation of resources and power that result from the team's activities or from particular approaches to problems. This stage can be contentious if the team contains members from many different stakeholder groups.

Stage 4: Interaction and Participation. This stage involves participation and interaction among team members in performing work and in overcoming barriers that inhibit team productivity.

The team may move through these stages in the same manner as it moves through the task stages. Some virtual teams move directly from stage 1, inclusion and interaction, to stage 4, interaction and participation, as shown in Figure 9.4.

A second path may include involvement in stage 2, status and role definition, prior to moving into stage 4, as team members determine who has expert status, as shown in Figure 9.5.

A third path involves more complicated movement back and forth through the stages as team members address the issues of power, role definition, status, and allocation of resources, as shown in Figure 9.6.

Teams that are addressing solvable problems or repeating production work or are functional virtual teams are likely to have fewer issues regarding team member role definitions and status because of templates provided from previous work cycles. Workflow processes often define roles and accountabilities for these types of tasks. Teams that are working on more unique and adaptive tasks for which the outcomes may

FIGURE 9.4. SOCIAL PATHWAY A: INTERACTION AND INCLUSION TO INTERACTION AND PARTICIPATION.

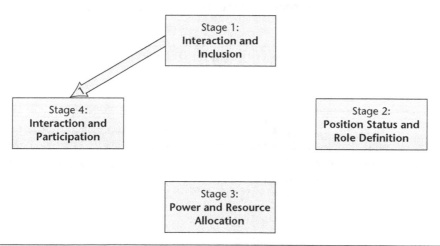

Source: Adapted from J. McGrath, "Time Matters in Teams." In J. Galegher, R. E. Kraut, and C. Egido (Eds.), *Intellectual Teamwork: Social and Technical Foundations of Cooperative Work.* Hillsdale, N.J.: Erlbaum, 1990. Used with permission.

FIGURE 9.5. SOCIAL PATHWAY B: INTERACTION AND INCLUSION TO POSITION STATUS AND ROLE DEFINITION TO INTERACTION AND PARTICIPATION.

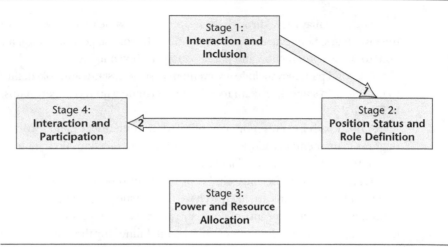

Source: Adapted from J. McGrath, "Time Matters in Teams." In J. Galegher, R. E. Kraut, and C. Egido (Eds.), *Intellectual Teamwork: Social and Technical Foundations of Cooperative Work.* Hillsdale, N.J.: Erlbaum, 1990. Used with permission.

change the power distribution among functions, organizations, or partners often have to deal with more complex social dynamics related to power and status.

Three Factors That Affect Virtual Team Dynamics

In a virtual environment, team leaders may have less access to the traditional clues that indicate how the team is progressing through the stages. Team dynamics are determined by complicated variables that relate to three factors: time, team environment, and team composition (see Figure 9.7). The leader of a virtual team must exercise diligence to determine whether or not the team's dynamics are healthy and whether intervention is necessary.

Time

Team dynamics are affected by the passage of time, especially in parallel, project, and action teams.[4] Connie Gersick, in her work with task and project teams, found that most teams undergo major transitions about halfway through their life cycles, no

FIGURE 9.6. SOCIAL PATHWAY C: INTERACTION AND INCLUSION TO POSITION STATUS AND ROLE DEFINITION TO POWER AND RESOURCE ALLOCATION TO POSITION STATUS AND ROLE DEFINITION TO INTERACTION AND PARTICIPATION.

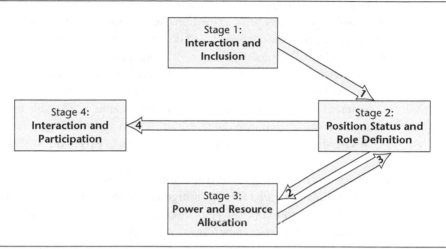

Source: Adapted from J. McGrath, "Time Matters in Teams." In J. Galegher, R. E. Kraut, and C. Egido (Eds.), *Intellectual Teamwork: Social and Technical Foundations of Cooperative Work.* Hillsdale, N.J.: Erlbaum, 1990. Used with permission.

FIGURE 9.7. THREE FACTORS THAT AFFECT TEAM DYNAMICS.

matter how much time the teams have allotted for their tasks or how many times they have met.[5] The transitions take many forms, such as adopting new perspectives regarding technical problems; reengaging with top management, outside stakeholders, and other organizational functions; redirecting plans; and dropping old patterns of behavior. Many teams come up with new approaches to their tasks and execute new plans at this transition point. Just prior to the transition, teams typically experience conflict, changing alliances, role confusion, and debate about technical approaches or solutions to problems. During the transition, old approaches and viewpoints are cast aside as new ones take their places. It is almost as if teams "punctuate their equilibrium" and, after a period of stability, progress through a more revolutionary period of change.

All teams need to understand the midpoint dynamic and be able to identify the characteristics associated with the transition. There are four events that the virtual team leader should look for that signal the transition to execution (see Figure 9.8):

1. Abandonment of much of the team's early work, including plans and agendas
2. Task completion and a feeling of urgency to finish on time. Virtual teams go through a first round of task completion and seek task closure. It is at this point that teams often develop new insights and approaches about the overall task and may reassess their earlier assumptions.
3. Renewed contact between the team and its organizational environment, most often the sponsor or a member of senior management
4. Specific new agreements on the ultimate direction the team should take

FIGURE 9.8. THE TRANSITION TO EXECUTION.

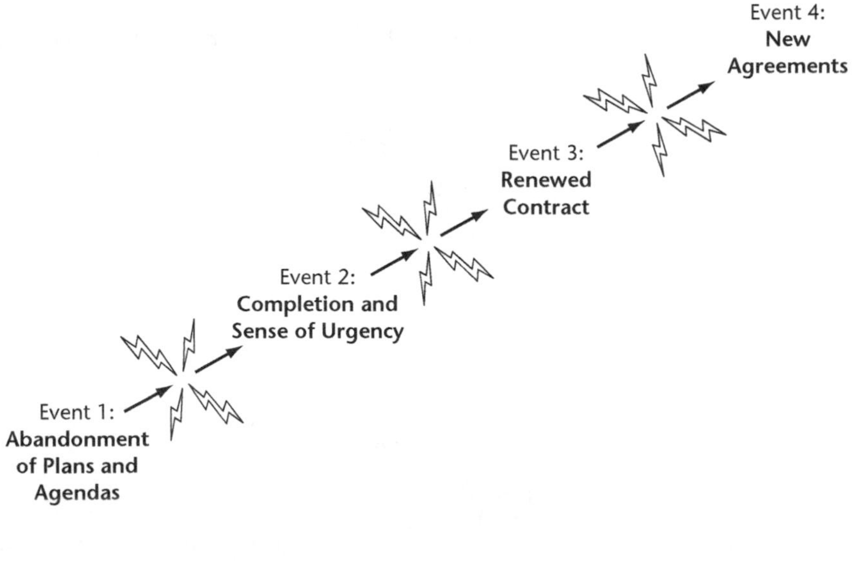

Teams that have experienced conflict prior to the midpoint often find that they transition to collaboration and participation. For teams that start fast and develop solid plans, the transition may be a time to pause, analyze current work, debate, and then make improvements. For teams that start more slowly and are addressing disagreements, power struggles, and other uncertainties, the transition may signal a period of pulling together and focusing on execution. Teams that do not make the transition to collaboration may find that the team leader or the sponsor unilaterally determines an answer and executes the work.

Virtual team members and leaders need to be aware of and anticipate these time dynamics. They should not be alarmed if the team exhibits sudden changes in direction or a preoccupation with time pressure midway through its life. A virtual team may want to facilitate this by scheduling a face-to-face session toward the middle of the team's life cycle. Checklist 9.1 can serve as a guide in diagnosing whether or not events signal a healthy transition.

Environmental Influences

The second factor that influences team dynamics is the environment. One variable that has been associated with performance is how "embedded" or rooted the team is in the organizational setting—the extent to which the team affects and is affected by

CHECKLIST 9.1. TRANSITION POINT HEALTH CHECK.

Instructions: Indicate the response that best represents the team's transition behavior.

Does the team drop the established agenda or plan?	Yes	No
Does the completion date drive the team to change approaches or plans?	Yes	No
Do team members feel that they need to review contracts with sponsors?	Yes	No
Are some team members becoming revitalized?	Yes	No
Is this period accompanied by renewed energy and creativity?	Yes	No
Are new contracts shared with important stakeholders and customers?	Yes	No
Is the team aware that it is experiencing a transition?	Yes	No
	Total yes: _____	Total no: _____

Two or more of your responses should be yes during your team's midpoint transition.

the organization's structure and processes and by other teams in the organization and in partner organizations. The second variable is the nature of the team's assignment or task. The third is the impact of technology.

Embeddedness. Teams can be described as being embedded in the organization when the organization's structure, processes, communication channels, management, and reward structure support and nurture the team's activities.[6] Teams can also be described as highly embedded if the work they are doing has a high impact in one area or many areas of the organization.

A team that is not highly embedded in its organization often has difficulty obtaining access to information, scheduling time with management, and obtaining support from other functions. A team that is highly embedded in its organization has appropriate top-management support and attention, access to resources, a well-defined task, and rewards for team members for their performance in their local organizations. In addition, the team's outcome often affects the ways in which people do their work in many different places in the organization and may even affect suppliers and vendors.

The degree of embeddedness of a virtual team affects the team's dynamics. Because virtual teams do not have physical boundaries, those that are not at least moderately embedded in their organizations in other ways (such as through linkage to strategy or the management structure) may experience confusion regarding their purpose, how their work fits with other efforts, and the overall value of their contributions. As a result, such teams may spend more time in the task and social dynamics stages 2 and 3, dealing with issues related to problem solving, roles, status, and conflict.

Of course, there is the danger of being too embedded. Too much attention can result in micromanagement. Overly embedded teams may also lose the independence and freedom necessary to innovate.

Nature of the Task. The more complex the team's task, the greater the chance of conflict and disagreement about roles, approaches to problems, and definition of outcomes. Teams that exist in adaptive environments are more likely to dwell on resolving power differences, status differences, and conflicts about technical approaches and allocation of resources. Repeatable and simple tasks, for most virtual teams, equate to less time spent in activities such as conflict resolution, role definition, and authority relationships in the group.

Impact of Technology. Because virtual teams interact by means of electronic communication and collaboration technology, it is important to anticipate its effect on team dynamics. (Information about the effect of technology on team meetings is covered in Chapter Eight.)

The use of some technology (for example, group decision support systems) can increase the team's depth of analysis and clarify vague and ambiguous problems.[7] If used effectively, technology can decrease the time it takes a team to move to stage 4, execution. Using EMS technology that includes idea generation capabilities, for example, can increase a team's ability to generate plans quickly. EMS can also be used to avoid unproductive personal conflict about different approaches to problems by employing anonymity features for voting and polling. The use of shared databases, whiteboards, and other presentation software can facilitate the exchange of documents and ideas between team members. The effective storage of information and the use of distributed databases can help teams resolve conflicts and select technical approaches using best practices and lessons learned from other teams. This enhances task-oriented communication and the quality of information available for analysis and as a result may facilitate movement to stage 4.

There may be some negative aspects of technology for task-related team dynamics. The combination of the lack of normal conversational give-and-take and the drama of using technology to generate a large quantity of ideas or to quickly exchange documents may sometimes suboptimize the quality of solutions. Some adaptive tasks require deep thought and debate that require time, face-to-face contact, and productive conflict. More than one team has been happy with the quantity of ideas and plans it has generated using technology, only to discover later that there should have been deeper thought about the quality of the ideas. Having more information, or too much information, can also slow a team's decision-making process.[8]

Technology can also affect social dynamics. The impact of social pressure on participation is often reduced by using technology such as chat rooms, EMS, and distributed databases. The implication is that using technology may foster equal participation and inclusion. It may also reduce conflict over roles and status, because everyone has a chance to contribute anonymously. Using e-mail and other methods to distribute information to everyone at the same time may also facilitate inclusion.

The effect of technology on social dynamics can also be negative. Most technology, because it does not provide the metaverbal cues of face-to-face communication, may get in the way of building trust and resolving interpersonal conflicts. The lack of such cues may lead to bad feelings that fester until they are not resolvable, even face to face. For example, one member of a parallel virtual team voiced a negative opinion of the team's work during every audioconference. He also sent sharply worded e-mail messages to team members and to managers. This slowed the team down and made the people who were doing most of the work feel as if they were doing their jobs badly. Soon most team members simply ignored whatever he said. The team leader started to schedule meetings when this member could not attend. The lack of attention given to the conflict was fostered, in part, by the lack of give-and-take in audioconferences and the difficulty of confronting him over the telephone.

Virtual teams need to pay attention to these environmental factors so as to be able to predict the probability of negative team dynamics, such as conflict, role confusion, and lack of team unity, that keep teams in stages 2 and 3.

Team Composition

The third factor that affects team dynamics is the composition of the team.[9] People from very different backgrounds and experiences bring different behaviors, routines, and assumptions about work and the world to the virtual team. People develop routines and assumptions that make it easier for them to predict what others will do. These routines and assumptions also make coordinated action possible, as people from similar backgrounds normally do not have to talk about them, thereby saving time and energy. This is also true of long-standing teams or functional virtual teams that have a history of shared experiences. However, this is not often the case for other virtual teams, with their varied membership.

Although routines can facilitate quick and coordinated action, once they become habitual, they are very difficult to change. In fact, under pressure, most of us unconsciously resort to our old habits. Assumptions, behaviors, and routines that served as shortcuts before joining the team may be disruptive to the team and lead to conflict between team members. Those that stem from the same cultural and functional backgrounds of team members can have negative effects on team dynamics. The same risk is true with long-standing teams or functional virtual teams. They can develop orthodoxies or individual team models that serve them well but can also impede innovation when approaching adaptive challenges.

Cultural Differences. The team members' cultural backgrounds include differences that can affect team dynamics. The cultural assumptions and perspectives embedded in team members' behaviors can be much harder to discuss and change than those associated with functional backgrounds and organizational cultures. This is especially true for individuals who do not have a great deal of cross-cultural experience or for those who do not have strong technical backgrounds that can help mitigate cultural behaviors. Cultural dimensions that appear to have the greatest potential to affect virtual team dynamics are individualism–collectivism, power distance, and uncertainty avoidance.

Individualism–Collectivism. Team members who are from individualistic cultures, such as the United States and Great Britain, may be much more assertive about performing independent work and desire less interaction and participation than team members who are from more collective cultures. It is important that virtual team members define the degree of interaction and participation that is appropriate for each task. This will help members from both individualistic and collective cultures know what is expected of them. The definition should include the amount and type of interactive behavior, such as the frequency of team interactions and the amount of participation that team members should expect from one another. Focusing on these factors early in the team's life contributes to healthy social dynamics of interaction, inclusion, and participation. It can help move the team members through the stage 1 dynamics, in which different expectations about the amount and type of interaction among team members may be influenced by culture.

Power Distance. Cultural differences regarding power distance can also affect a virtual team's dynamics. The risk of disruption is higher if team members come from different levels in the organizations. Team members who come from lower-power-distance cultures, such as Canada, the United States, and Great Britain, may be much more assertive about stating their opinions and disagreeing with other team members from higher organizational levels than team members from higher-power-distance cultures, such as China and Thailand. Differences in power distance can affect the team's social dynamics of interaction, participation, and inclusion. One result may be that team members from low-power-distance cultures assume that they are moving out of stage 2 or 3 because there is no conflict when in fact team members from high-power-distance cultures have different ideas about approaches to problems but have failed to mention them.

The use of technology can assist with differences in power distance. Although people from high-power-distance cultures may be less apt to speak up in a group when people of higher status are present, they will use e-mail and other "less aggressive" means to state their opinions. Technology has the potential to increase the focus on ideas and decrease the focus on culture, personalities, and titles. Many virtual team leaders use computer technology to poll team members about their opinions and perspectives, sometimes anonymously, before making decisions. The use of collaborative software that allows team members to contribute to or comment on a document is also a good way to obtain team members' opinions about other people's work, especially if the higher-status members of the team produced the work. Technology also helps avoid the perception of criticism as a personal attack by members of certain high-power-distance cultures, for which personal integrity and credibility are based on maintaining a positive public face.

Some virtual team leaders have used the power hierarchy in these cultures to help their members disagree with higher-status individuals. A person who is working with a team member who is having difficulty saying no directly or disagreeing with other team members can contact that individual's local manager to elicit the manager's help in encouraging the team member to speak up or say no. Because the encouragement is coming from a direct superior, it may override typical power distance behaviors.

Uncertainty Avoidance. Uncertainty avoidance frequently affects team dynamics. People who are from cultures with high uncertainty avoidance feel more comfortable operating with defined plans and roles than people who are from cultures with low uncertainty avoidance. These cultural preferences may cause conflict about planning activities in the team initiation stages, including how well the team members' roles need to be defined, the level of technical plans required, and the rigor of processes and documentation. The virtual team should balance the preference for more certainty with the demands of the task. This balancing process may require teams to occasionally allow more discussion of plans than the task deserves, in order to meet the needs of members from cultures with high uncertainty avoidance.

Handling Team Conflict. Handling team conflict is an area in which the impact of culture is evident.[10] Many people who are from high-power-distance and collective cultures see open conflict as a loss of face or an affront to their group. The North American strategy of getting the entire team together to work openly on a conflict may be perceived as very inappropriate and threatening by people from high-power-distance cultures. In addition, team members from some cultures send more information during times of conflict than members from other cultures. This leaves the team leader with less formal information to use in managing the conflict.

Differences in Functional Background. Functional background can greatly affect a person's behavior. For example, cross-functional product development teams that have members from engineering, marketing, finance, and manufacturing functions usually agree that using a standard product development process is a good business practice. They disagree, however, about the importance of each stage of the process.[11] The stages of the process that are marketing-oriented, such as conducting customer focus groups early in the project, are much more important to team members from the marketing function than they are to engineers. Although both recognize the importance of focus groups, they may disagree on their emphasis. This can result in conflict regarding allocation of resources and the relative importance of different team members' roles in stages 2 and 3.

In addition, team members from high-context functions, such as human resources and marketing, may need more background information than team members from low-context functions, such as engineering and finance. This may promote misunderstandings about problem definition, technical approaches, and the amount and type of information that team members need in order to move forward. In short, differences in functional backgrounds, assumptions, and routines may cause the team to have task and social dynamics that keep it in the stages of problem solving and conflict resolution.

Team Size. The number and composition of team members also affect a team's dynamics. Clearly, the team needs to be large enough to have the skills and expertise to get the job done. In addition, the heterogeneity of the team needs to be appropriate for the task. If the task requires a large amount of input from local regions, team members must have sufficient diversity to fulfill this requirement. Whenever there are more than two team members, coalitions and subgroups will begin to form. These may be based on location, function, or cultural background (or some combination of these). People who are from the same country or who work in similar functions often form subgroups. Although this is normal and facilitates a sense of belonging for some team members, if the subgroups are allowed to polarize too much along functional or cultural lines, they can disrupt healthy team interactions.

Team size also affects the use of technology, and vice versa. Technology such as EMS actually increases performance in idea generation and other tasks with groups of more than twelve people.[12] With smaller groups, technology does not help as much. With larger groups, it seems as if technology makes it easier for people to build on one others' ideas, to feel less inhibited about offering new thoughts and opinions, and to offer suggestions at any time. This has implications for using technology to maximize inclusion for large virtual teams and for generating ideas in order to solve problems and generate new approaches.

Checklist 9.2 provides a quick check of team composition in areas that may affect team dynamics.

CHECKLIST 9.2. TEAM COMPOSITION QUICK CHECK.

Instructions: Assess the characteristics of your virtual team by responding to the questions below.

1. Are more than two different national cultures represented in your team?	Yes	No
2. Do the majority of team members have little or no experience working cross-culturally?	Yes	No
3. Are more than two functions or organizations represented in your team?	Yes	No
4. Does your core team have more than twelve members?	Yes	No
5. Are all team members located in different places?	Yes	No
	Total yes: ____	Total no: ____

If you have more than two yes answers, your team's dynamics may be affected by the team's composition. Note the areas where you checked yes, and make plans to carefully observe your team in areas that may become problematic.

Measuring Team Performance

On traditional teams whose members see one another every day, it is easier to perceive problems with team dynamics that are affecting performance. Bickering over status or resources and conflict over roles or technical approaches can be observed in meetings and in hallways. Leaders of virtual teams, however, report that recognizing conflict and performance problems is one of their most difficult management tasks. Many times, inexperienced virtual teams do not know that they have problems until extremely dysfunctional team dynamics occur, task output is affected, or members leave the teams. By that time, it may be too late.

Although the checklists provided so far in this chapter can alert a virtual team to potential problems, the team leader and its members should regularly assess the team's interaction processes and level of effectiveness. J. Richard Hackman suggests paying particular attention to indicators of team performance such as signs of problems or unexploited opportunities and criteria for effectiveness at different stages in a team's maturation.[13]

Signs of Problems or Unexploited Opportunities

It is important to assess the degree to which the team experiences problems in collaborating or in developing strategies for task execution and the extent to which team members appear to be exploiting or not exploiting opportunities for synergy, collaboration, and the sharing of expertise.

General trends to look for include evidence of collaboration, such as team members reporting that they have checked with one another before finalizing a product or making a decision, and other evidence that technical expertise on the team is being utilized.

These are some of the symptoms of problems:

1. *Use of air time.* Do some team members dominate most of the conversation time during audioconferences, data conferences, videoconferences, or face-to-face sessions? Do some team members take a disproportionate amount of the team leader's time?
2. *Group pressure.* Do some team members appear to give in to the larger group or to aggressive or higher-status team members? This may be a sign that the team has not addressed issues involving roles or status or an indication of cultural differences in the team.
3. *Free riding.* Do some team members appear to be doing most of the work?
4. *Incomplete use of information.* Do some team members appear not to be using information that has been disseminated to them? Indications of this include not remembering that they received documents or e-mail messages and not reviewing them in sufficient detail prior to meetings.

Criteria of Effectiveness

There are two types of effectiveness criteria: intermediate and final. Intermediate criteria measure the degree to which team members apply sufficient time and effort to task completion and use strategies that appear to be appropriate for the task.

When some team members seem to be doing all the work, participating the most in audioconferences, or making most of the comments, the leader may question whether other team members are expending sufficient effort on the task.

Late deliverables or missed milestones further confirm that there may be problems. Experienced virtual teams keep a very close watch on deliverables and other milestone schedules. When a pattern begins to develop, they intervene immediately.

It is more difficult to assess whether the team is applying task-appropriate strategies. Although they do not want to micromanage their team members, effective leaders understand how the members are approaching their jobs. One team was shocked to discover that one member was using an external vendor with a vested interest in the outcome of the team's work to help gather information critical to the team's recommendation on a new training curriculum. The vendor had a lot to lose from any change and hence an incentive to slant the results. The team member should have been doing the analysis without outside assistance.

Final Criteria of Effectiveness

Final criteria assess both task and social dynamics. First, they help evaluate whether the team's output or service meets the requirements of those who review or receive it, such as the client or top management. Second, they determine whether the work satisfies the team members' personal growth objectives and the team members' and team leader's perceptions that working on the team was a positive experience.

Virtual Interventions

Using Hackman's performance indicators is more difficult for a virtual team. The use of online questionnaires for team members and of observation guides for audioconferences and videoconferences can be useful in assessing social dynamics. It also is useful to have a professional observer from outside the team use guides or protocols during audioconferences or videoconferences to examine the team's processes and dynamics. This provides an impartial perspective and allows the team members to concentrate on the demands of the task. The observer can feed observations back to the team leader and the team. The team can then plan interventions based on the results.

Checklist 9.3 presents process observation guides for audioconferences and videoconferences that allow a team member, team leader, or other observer to assess signs of unexploited opportunities, intermediate effectiveness, and potential problems with team dynamics. It includes observation, over the course of a meeting, of factors such as whether or not one person is dominating the discussion, whether or not there is healthy debate, and whether there is too much agreement. Teams should feel free to insert factors that are important to them. The virtual team leader or member needs to intervene if team dynamics are not healthy.

CHECKLIST 9.3. PROCESS OBSERVATION.

Instructions: Have a professional facilitator use this observation form during an audioconference or videoconference. Add behaviors that are appropriate for your team. Note how often the targeted behaviors occur during the session.

Then have the observer review the results with the team leader and then with the team during the next status review session. Examine the patterns and determine whether they are healthy, given the task, your expectations of the team members, and the point in the team's life cycle. Compare these observations with your own and with those of other team members to validate "hunches" and personal opinions. It is important to have more than one source of data when working in a virtual environment.

Behavior	Frequency			
	Less than two times	Two to four times	More than four times	Total
1. The team leader dominates the conversation.				
2. One or two team members dominate the conversation.				
3. One or two team members appear to negatively criticize the work of others.				
4. Debate appears to be excessively negative.				
5. Some team members appear to agree with everyone.				
6. Some team members appear to be left out of the conversation.				
7. Some team members appear to be lost or not in touch with the team and its agenda.				
8. Some team members appear to be confused about information they should have received.				

Negative results from a process observation, team assessment, or online questionnaire may indicate problems with team dynamics. These can be separated into four general categories:

1. Indications that the team is stuck in one of the first three stages and is not moving into task stage 4, execution, in a timely manner. For example, conflict about technical approaches or about which member has expert status that arises well past the team's scheduled midpoint transition is an indication of problems.
2. Signs of unexploited opportunities, such as underused expertise of team members, conflict between team members from different functions or cultures, free riding, team members taking up too much air time, and incomplete or inadequate use of information.
3. Intermediate effectiveness criteria not being met. Examples are missing interim deliverables and using inappropriate task strategies.
4. Final effectiveness criteria not being met. Examples are poor reviews of the team's deliverables by senior management and negative perceptions of the team experience gathered from team members by formal or informal means.

Checklist 9.4 gives some tips for managing conflict on a virtual team. Checklist 9.5 outlines interventions that a team leader can use in a virtual environment.

CHECKLIST 9.4. CONFLICT MANAGEMENT TIPS.

1. Conflict on virtual teams is hard to spot and may simmer for a long time before you notice it. Keep your eyes and ears open: if you suspect an issue, there probably is one. Make measuring and discussing team dynamics an integral part of the team from the beginning. Get people used to reporting and discussing when disagreement becomes nonproductive.
2. If you observe nonproductive conflict, check your perception with others (such as your team's facilitator) before you take action.
3. Discuss your observations either face to face or over the telephone with each person individually to gather opinions. Do not use fax, e-mail, or voice mail for this.
4. If an intervention is necessary, conduct it face to face or at a minimum over the telephone with the participants, not with the entire team. Set strict ground rules beforehand, and send each person an agenda. Use a facilitator if you can. Jointly solve problems and set specific expectations for each person. Follow up with each person by telephone after the session.
5. Be aware of the need to save face in some cultures. Do not address conflict in public with persons from such cultures.
6. Be aware that people from some cultures have different perceptions regarding the importance of deadlines. If any team members are from such cultures, clarify goals and objectives specifically.

CHECKLIST 9.5. TEAM INTERVENTIONS.

Symptom of Team Problem	Possible Interventions by the Team Leader
The team cannot get out of the inception and inclusion stage.	Teams that get stuck in the first stage have larger underlying issues. Review the team's composition and the team's charter. Ensure that the right people are on the team and that they understand the charter. The inception phase requires creativity and less control. Be sure that you are modeling creativity and not overcontrolling the members. If possible, bring in a member from the organization who is innovative to challenge and spark the team.
The team appears to be stuck and is not moving toward execution.	Assess the team in terms of task and social dynamics. Discuss the problem with the team. Look at environmental factors that may be causing the team to slow down. Also look at the team's work practices and determine if the members need help in establishing priorities or a reasonable work schedule. Hold a session to review expectations. Map the team's progress and problems to see if any patterns appear that need to be changed in order to allow the team to move forward.
A few team members seem to be doing all the work.	Talk to the working and nonworking members separately to determine the reasons for the differences. Are tasks allocated appropriately? Are the working members creating an exclusive environment, because of national or functional cultures, that is keeping the others out? Do the nonworkers feel that there is something wrong with the team or its leadership?
Team members do not appear to be applying sufficient effort to the team's task.	Address this problem quickly. First, talk to the team members who are not applying the required effort and determine whether the problem lies with them or with another factor, such as unrealistic expectations. If the problem is the individuals, find out why they are not putting forth the effort. If the problem stems from lack of skills or resources, get them the training or resources they need. If it stems from attitudes, talk to them about it. Do they feel the work is meaningful? Are they receiving timely feedback on their work? Are the results of their work recognized?
The team misses or almost misses a deadline for deliverables.	If the team is likely to miss a deadline, find out the reason. Put the mechanisms in place to fix the problem. Communicate to your sponsor that you have corrected the problem. During the next cycle, stay close to the team. It is better to be accused of micromanaging than to miss a deadline

(continued)

CHECKLIST 9.5. (CONTINUED).

Symptom of Team Problem	Possible Interventions by the Team Leader
	for a deliverable. Talk with and monitor the team members. When their progress becomes satisfactory, you can pull back.
Conflict arises that derails the team's progress.	Discover the reason for the conflict. If it is task-related, review the work plan and seek input on how to improve the problem. If it is social in nature, determine the cause and determine if differences in culture are indicated. If it is between two individuals, speak with both of them individually. If the conflict involves you, ask an outside facilitator to help to resolve the problem.
Team members who are not co-located seem to be fading into obscurity.	Virtual team members can fall into obscurity quickly. Keep a record of when you have contact with members. Set up a schedule and be sure to talk with or meet with each team member regularly through e-mail, telephone calls, visits, and so on. Go to where the members are sometimes; don't always ask them to come to you. If some members are not in the team on a full-time basis, their other priorities many be taking them away from the team. Talk to their supervisors and review the agreements that you made before they were assigned to your team. Sometimes it is necessary to ask team members who are located together to meet informally to keep up morale.

Adjournment Dynamics

Many teams have defined end points. The adjournment of a team requires its own ritual. William Bridges, in his work on transitions, discusses the need to allow people time to celebrate accomplishments, mourn loss, and move on.[14] Virtual team members, although they may never have met, also need this time. There is nothing as demotivating as teams that just fade away after months of hard work.

Teamwork can be all-encompassing and energy-draining. At the end, there may be a feeling of loss or disillusionment that affects team members' perceptions of the experience of working on the team and also affects the amount of energy they have to focus on new assignments. Virtual team leaders should adopt proactive strategies to address this effect. The team leader can set aside money in the team's budget for all team members to meet and celebrate. Some teams have remote parties over video links. Many team members take the time to call one another to offer their thanks and best wishes. Some team leaders contact local managers to express their gratitude for their team members' participation. Some write formal thank-you notes to all team members and copy individual managers and the team's sponsor. Most make sure that team members have the opportunity to discuss everyone's new assignment and to make plans to keep in touch.

Near Virtual Disaster

Sara's company just dramatically changed strategic direction. The new strategy required employees to practice many new skills and behaviors. The senior council of the company asked Sara to lead a virtual team to identify the new rewards and recognition program that would help reinforce these new skills and behaviors.

After Sara and the team had several virtual meetings, it became clear that this was going to be a difficult task and that there was no precedent for it. First, each department had its own rewards and recognition program, so understanding and removing these was going to be both difficult and unpopular. Second, setting up a company-wide program that all of the leaders would agree to was not going to be easy. Sara and her team realized that the quick project that they thought they were given was really a longer and more complex task. And the CEO wanted periodic updates on their progress.

After several meetings, they developed proposals that they felt very deeply about. They really wanted to have a finished product to show the CEO. Sara scheduled a first meeting with the CEO and the team. It could not have gone worse. The CEO could not agree to some of the team's premises and assumptions; consequently, the presenters did not even get to the team's proposals. Sara regrouped the team and held a meeting to discuss how to get back on track. For the first time, some of the members did not show up. The work continued, but some team members missed essential deadlines. Finally, the project recommendations were accepted, but with more resignation than celebration. The team disbanded and went on to work on new projects. Months of work had gone into the team, but the outcome was very unsatisfactory.

Sara reflected on what she could have done differently. First, she should have been clear on the outcome and beliefs of the CEO: the task of the team. Second, she needed to pay more attention to the social dynamics of the team, notably that members were linked and embedded in their own groups' ways of doing business, thus causing conflict about an optimal solution. Third, she should have set up intermittent and final criteria for effectiveness. Fourth, recognizing that the task was adaptive and not technical would have caused her to adopt more realistic expectations about the amount of time the team would need to work on the task. Finally, she should never have disbanded the virtual team without providing closure for the work the team had performed, including making sure that even if it was not accepted in its entirety, some of the work would move forward. Team members most likely left this team feeling that they had not accomplished the task.

Points to Remember

1. Virtual teams pass through sequential stages of task dynamics and social dynamics. They do not have to pass through all the stages all the time. Virtual team dynamics are affected by time, the team's environment, and the team's composition.
2. Teams should watch for midpoint transitions.
3. Teams should maximize the use of technology to help with inclusion, participation, and decision making.
4. Team performance can be measured by paying attention to problems and unexploited opportunities, criteria for intermediate effectiveness, and criteria for final effectiveness.

CHAPTER TEN

WORKING ADAPTIVELY

Consider a world in which cause and effect are erratic. Sometimes the first precedes the second, sometimes the second the first. Or perhaps cause lies forever in the past while effect in the future, but future and past are entwined.

—ALAN LIGHTMAN, *EINSTEIN'S DREAMS*[1]

Most virtual teams exist in adaptive environments. Their work is always changing, there are always new problems on the horizon, and the solutions to problems are often one-of-a-kind. When Einstein observed that we cannot solve the problems we have created with the same type of thinking that created them, he was referring to the adaptive world.

To understand adaptive environments, it is useful to contrast them with technical environments.[2] Technical environments have structures and known rules. Teams can address work in such environments with tested methods and expert knowledge. Variables are contained, surprises are minimized, and planning and control are paramount. It is a world of process mapping, predictability, and repetition.

Adaptive environments do not follow rational, structured rules. Adaptive work consists of situations in which teams have not yet developed satisfactory responses to the problems they face. In fact, the problems might be so complex that team members may not even know what questions to ask. There is no specific plan of action or tool of logic that can solve these types of problems.

Many people prefer technical environments; these feel more comfortable because they tend to provide answers. Adaptive environments are riskier, require more effort, and generate uncertainty and discomfort. It takes a measure of courage to work in an adaptive environment. Many virtual teams work in adaptive environments or face adaptive situations.

Eight Principles of Working in an Adaptive Environment

Helping virtual teams face adaptive situations is a process of mobilizing and enabling, rather than one of planning and control. Traditional styles of leadership do not work well in adaptive situations. According to Ronald Heifetz and Donald Laurie, adaptive environments require leading and working from a different perspective. Doing so involves the following eight principles:

1. Get on the balcony.
2. Identify the adaptive challenge.
3. Regulate distress.
4. Maintain disciplined attention.
5. Rely on distributed intelligence.
6. Encourage leadership by all members.
7. Encourage robust communication.
8. Create a learning obligation.

Table 10.1 summarizes the actions required by team leaders in adaptive environments in applying each of the eight principles. Let's look at each one in greater detail.

Get on the Balcony

Virtual team leaders and members must move back and forth between the content of their work and the overarching plan. This is like moving between the field of action and a balcony from which the whole field can be seen.[3] It is important to become skilled in discerning patterns from the balcony, seeing the overall context. Patterns that can be seen from the balcony can be translated into strategies of action and decisions. Leaders in adaptive environments may fail if they spend all their time in the trenches and don't view the action from high enough to see the overall pictures.

Leading-edge product developers base their new products on broad trends and patterns that they perceive as unfolding in the market. The adaptation of the telephone into a personal communication device combining features of computers, MP3 players, and cameras is a good example: developers discerned a pattern of consumer needs and merged them into a product to address those needs. Like smart product developers, virtual teams can transform what appears to be chaos and confusion into usable patterns.

TABLE 10.1. ADAPTIVE LEADER ACTIONS.

Principles	Virtual Team Leader Actions
Get on the balcony	• Don't stay in the trenches. • Move between the balcony and the field of action. • Look at what is happening from an overall point of view. • Look for larger patterns. • Give the team a background sense of history and values.
Identify the adaptive challenge	• Determine whether there is a precedent for the problem. • Talk to as many people as possible about the challenge, especially people outside normal networks and comfort zones. • Assess the roles of team members from high-uncertainty-avoidance cultures to minimize the adaptive content. • Assess the roles of team members from low-uncertainty-avoidance cultures to maximize the adaptive content. • Determine the degree of adaptive change required of each team member. • Discuss and negotiate appropriate boundaries for work and tasks.
Regulate distress	• Determine the distress capability of each team member and a method for handling it. • Let the team feel the external pressure within a range it can tolerate. • Maintain healthy levels of stress. • Develop behaviors that help to suspend decisions while looking for unprecedented solutions. • Define communication strategies to aid team members who are experiencing stress. Arrange face-to-face meetings with team members and stakeholders who are undergoing the greatest degree of adaptive change.
Maintain disciplined attention	• Develop communication strategies and technologies suitable for regular discussions to keep the work focused. • Frame the key issues and continually ask questions about them. • Focus and create a sense of urgency. • Ensure that communication technologies can communicate focus and sense of urgency. Develop strategies to deal quickly with distractive behaviors from outside and inside the team.
Rely on distributed intelligence	• Get team members into the habit of talking about their findings, even if they think they are not relevant. • Encourage team members to network outside of comfort zones and conventional areas. • When discussing a problem, ask every team member for information that is relevant. • Admit that the leader does not have all the answers. • Create an environment of developing solutions as a team.

(continued)

TABLE 10.1. (CONTINUED).

Encourage leadership by all members	• Identify leadership roles for team members to assume. • Allow leadership to emerge close to the action. • Clarify team accountabilities and vision with each team member. • Acknowledge and maintain overall accountability. • Practice redistributing leadership roles, given the problem at hand and the team member's area of expertise.
Encourage robust communication	• Communicate failures as well as successes. • Create richly connected networks of mutually involved people. • When in doubt, overcommunicate. • Rely on emerging technologies for virtual team communication.
Create a learning obligation	• Make learning a part of the team's process from the beginning. • Ask the team members what they have learned from various experiences. • Use novel approaches to gain information. • Encourage team members to discuss problems and thoughts with a wide variety of people inside and outside the organization. • Capture learnings and underscore the importance and benefits of learning in virtual teams. • Look for the larger learning patterns, not necessarily the discrete steps that lead to the learning.

Identify the Adaptive Challenge

Determining whether a problem is technical or adaptive is central to a virtual team's success. Teams can address many problems using technical solutions but may miss the potential to catapult the team to higher levels of success. Often the mere existence of the virtual team indicates that the task requires far-flung answers and expertise. If the problem were purely technical, the organization would probably solve it in one specific region, time zone, or location. The challenge is to resist the temptation to provide quick answers—only partly because there are none—while leading the team to look for opportunities and possibilities.

We recently worked with the incoming president of a major firm who was seeking a new business strategy. The company's business leaders, operating in a mature market for over a decade, had not been forced to make strategic choices during that time, and as a consequence, the business was not growing. The new president introduced the mandate for change and asked his leadership team to help generate the range of choices that they, as the business leaders, should consider. This confused the team members, who were used to strong leadership. They expected the president to present them with choices, but even he was not sure what the choices were. His acknowledgment of this made the team members even more uncomfortable. They worked through the problem by realizing that their business environment was complex and adaptive and that no one person could have all the answers. They needed to look for openings, not closure. They realized that they would have to learn the answers as they went along. Once they came to this realization, they became more comfortable with not being given the answers by the president.

Virtual teams can learn from this example by accepting that the continual search for answers is part of working adaptively. The challenge in working adaptively is just to realize that this is the situation the team finds itself in.

Regulate Distress

Adaptive situations generate for all team members a range of personal stresses that affect how rapidly they can discard old information and attitudes and assimilate new information, attitudes, and responsibilities. The natural tendency is to avoid distress, moving as quickly as possible into the safer realm of the known, but virtual team leaders and team members need to be able to operate for prolonged periods within a productive range of distress. This is the zone in which optimal learning and performance occur. A certain level of stress actually stimulates learning and the integration of new information and skills. Operating in this zone requires that the team keep uncertainty alive for longer than is typically comfortable. The task is to become comfortable with uncertainty and to use it to generate the motivation for learning and performance. Often virtual team leaders must address the balance between generating enough discomfort to change with moving people into a level of distress that inhibits action.

The executive committee of a large global organization created a new corporate vision. The process of creating a vision statement entailed a large amount of uncertainty and a lot of faith. But vision statements, by their very nature, are adaptive. If they are well conceived, no one, not even the CEO, knows how to accomplish them. The executive committee came up with a very ambitious goal. When the members finally said the goal out loud, they became distressed. It seemed safer to strive for a more easily achievable goal, but the CEO was sure that the more ambitious vision was exactly what the company needed. He helped the committee members become comfortable with what they had generated. He first asked them if it was too big. They discussed it. Then the CEO stated that he thought it had to be big enough to bring forth energy—a call to arms. After a great deal of conversation, the executive committee affirmed the vision. The boldness of the vision became a rallying cry for the organization to do the impossible. This team, like many others in adaptive environments, used uncertainty and personal discomfort as clues that it was on the right track to a transformation solution appropriate in an adaptive world.

Maintain Disciplined Attention

A virtual team needs to guard against distractions that can multiply with diverse members, priorities, and distance. It is important to develop strategies to minimize distractions. Staying focused on the work is aided by communication and technology strategies. For example, the process of framing key issues needs to be accomplished using technology that minimizes social presence distractions. At the same time, the technology needs to have enough social presence to allow for the give-and-take necessary for good conversation.

It is crucial that virtual team leaders maintain a sense of urgency. Team members find it difficult to stray into side considerations when an urgent solution is needed. This must be balanced with enabling the team members to wonder in order to generate creative solutions. Targeted agendas and good meeting management practices can help attain these goals.

A key principle of working in adaptive environments is to guide the flow of dialogue and interaction. Working and leading in an adaptive world requires acting much like a good host, tapping into commonalties between guests and starting the right conversations between them. Maintaining disciplined attention entails getting teams past hurdles and on to discussing the right things with the right people, often from unexpected places.

Distractions that a team can create for itself include denying problems, passing the buck, and changing the subject to technical details and solutions that keep the team suspended in an unceasing technical state. Other distractions may emerge from the organization. These distractions include the traditional technical organization trying to rein in virtual teams through hierarchy, overly structured processes, and other mechanisms that neutralize creativity and innovation.

Rely on Distributed Intelligence

A good metaphor for virtual teams is a puzzle. The pieces are scattered over time and space. Everyone in the team has a piece of information that, when joined with other pieces, creates a complete understanding. The complexities of tasks in virtual teams warrant using all members to understand the whole. This is not true of technical tasks, for which each person has a specialty and a body of knowledge that applies solely to his or her part of the work. Technical tasks are strung together like a chain, sequential and linear, with outputs passed down the chain to become inputs. In contrast, virtual teams in adaptive work environments search for puzzle pieces and try them out until they fit. Each team member has knowledge that affects the whole.

To optimize distributed intelligence, team members should get into the habit of talking about their findings, even the ones they feel are not relevant. When discussing problems, all team members should be encouraged to add information, even if it seems tangential. Team members need to work outside their routine networks. This opens up areas of discussion and problem solving that may be unavailable to the team unless members get outside their comfort zones. Team leaders need to become comfortable in admitting that they do not have all the answers, thereby creating environments in which solutions are generated by their teams.

Encourage Leadership by All Members

Because teams in adaptive environments rely on distributed intelligence, each member of the virtual team must adopt a leadership perspective when working on adaptive challenges. There are intervals in which the leadership shifts, given the specifics of the task, to a team member who has certain expertise or access to a unique body of knowledge or who is closest to the action. Leadership emerges and is redistributed as expertise becomes relevant and as problems arise and shift. The team's leader facilitates these shifts, like a choreographer, as the situation dictates. Of course, the team leader is always accountable for the work of the team. On virtual teams, the process of shifting leadership from one team member to another is challenging. Team leaders need to stay acutely aware of when the shifts should occur and facilitate this process.

Encourage Robust Communication

When every team member has a piece of the puzzle, robust communication pulls the pieces together and plays a key part in solving problems. Communication is paramount in an adaptive world and is essential to collaboration. Communication includes the exchange of information in both the task and interpersonal realms. In adaptive environments, team members use and rely on varied and robust communication using a variety of electronic transmission and collaboration technologies.

Communicating failures as well as successes is essential to survival in adaptive environments. Other team members can learn from mistakes that their colleagues have experienced. Often failures are not discussed or are hidden. When in doubt, it is better to overcommunicate. In adaptive environments, one member's failure may solve a problem that another member is facing.

Leaders can encourage robust communication by creating richly connected networks of mutually involved people. Team leaders can connect people who can help one another. Leaders can also encourage the use of technology with high social presence to help the team members communicate lessons learned and can encourage the use of technology with high information richness to store these data.

Create a Learning Obligation

Adaptive problems rarely repeat themselves. Creating an obligation to learn is essential to solving one-of-a-kind problems. Teams should make learning an obligation from the beginning. The learning from each problem rests in the higher-level patterns used to solve the problem, not in the discrete steps.

Teams should create mechanisms to capture their lessons learned. It should be routine that they use these lessons to apply new insights to problems they are facing.

One virtual team leader chartered a team with members throughout Europe to create a leadership course for entrepreneurs in eastern Europe. His manager, a short-sighted technical manager, told him that there were no funds available in the organization's training budget to create the course. The adaptive leader, undaunted, started turning over rocks and looking for unconventional places to find the funds. He talked to everyone he could about the problem, looking for pieces of information that he could string together for a solution. The solution came from an unconventional place. He went through the firm's philanthropic foundation to get the funds, altering the output to help both the organization and a nonprofit agency that the foundation was sponsoring. Going to the firm's philanthropic foundation was an unorthodox and creative solution.

What is important about this example is not the solution but how the leader solved the problem and the learning that occurred. This leader accepted an impossible challenge. He talked to everyone he could find about the problem, including people outside his normal network. He used novel approaches to gain information. He went to an unconventional source and found an ideal solution for his problem. He learned as he went along. Great, adaptive leaders and team members thrive on doing the impossible and the untried, using unconventional means.

The Tent Exercise

The experience of leading a team through an adaptive problem the first time is a character-building experience. In the right environment, the eight principles are applied to create a unique and rewarding event. The following describes a face-to-face exercise that simulates working in an adaptive environment. It can be used in face-to-face team orientation sessions to demonstrate the principles of adaptive work. With some cleverness and skill, it can also be turned into a distributed graphics package.

Sara attended a workshop on leading in adaptive environments. The instructor asked her and the other participants to look around the room and memorize its configuration and then divided them into teams and asked them to put on blindfolds. The instructor said that the team members had a task to perform while blindfolded: they had sixty minutes in which to properly assemble an unknown object that awaited them down the hallway in an adjacent room. In the adjacent room, each team had its own ten-by-ten-foot workstation, roped off to ensure that separate teams did not collide. During the sixty minutes, Sara's team members could talk to one another and move around but could not remove their blindfolds. The instructor assigned people to three roles: nine team members, two safety assistants, and one leader. Sara was asked to be the leader.

The instructor told them to start. After a few moments, the team members began to move toward a common spot. Sara was very unsure about what they were doing. She had the added pressure of being the team's leader, a ridiculous concept given that she could not see and did know what her team would be building.

After a comical journey to the next room, the team found its workstation. Individuals began to feel around to see what was there. Sara heard someone say that he had found something on the floor. The team members began to move closer to his voice. Sara moved there too, shuffling so that she would not stumble. She bent down and began feeling around the floor. She felt an object. It was a smooth, flexible, metal tube, about one inch in diameter. She could not tell how long it was. She described the tube to her team members. Others described the objects they found. As she listened, it occurred to Sara that they would have to describe, in minute detail, everything they found. Communication was critical to the team's success and had to be even more robust than usual because the members could not see and did not know what they were building.

Sara said, in her best leadership voice, "I have a suggestion. We are all finding different items. As we find them, we need to take turns saying out loud what we have found and what we think they are. If we do not communicate like this, we will never build this thing."

The members agreed and started announcing what they found as they felt around their space. It was unnerving not to know whether or not they had all the pieces and when they could stop looking and start building.

The team members all started going in different directions, some building with the pieces they had, others walking around to see how far their boundaries went. Some chatted on the sidelines.

They heard the members of another team cheering. Had they finished? Even though the instructor did not say so, Sara's team members felt as if they were competing and now were behind. Sara had to get them focused and pull them together.

She started by getting the team to determine if it had found all the pieces. She said, "Let's take five minutes and sweep our space. As you reach what you think is a boundary, call it out. Along the way, pick up anything you find and bring it here, to the center." In this way, the team gathered all the pieces.

After a few minutes, one member announced, "I think this is some sort of tent."

"Yes," another member said, "I have a large piece of fabric."

Sara thought about what was happening. "Has anyone here ever put this kind of tent together?" she asked.

One member said that it appeared to be an igloo-shaped tent and that she had put one up in the past. Sara asked her to explain how to put it together. No one paid attention. Everyone scattered and started doing different things. Finally, Sara asked the team members to stop what they were doing and to listen.

The experienced tent builder explained, "The trick is to take these long poles and find the sleeve that they fit in. The fabric sleeve is shorter than the pole, forcing it to arch over the tent. There are four poles that meet at the north pole of the tent. You have to feed them through these sleeves and insert the top end of the pole into the round sturdy plastic piece that stays on the tent's north pole, the epicenter of the tent. Then it is important to put the other end of the pole into the flap at the base. This flap secures it so that the pole bends up over the tent and does not slip out. The four poles cross over the top, causing it to develop the shape of the tent."

The team members all said that they understood. They experienced a burst of creativity.

Sara recommended that one person perform the role of builder. The builder would describe what he was doing as they put the pieces together, so the whole team could follow and help, where required. Sara selected the builder. He took his position and began assembling the tent, with the help of the other team members. They had little success and became distressed. The tent did not seem to be going together. Sara sensed the members' frustration. She suggested that each of the people that had one of the four poles try to insert it in the sleeve. When one was successful, he or she could tell the others how to do it. They all tried. Finally, one person was successful and explained it to the others. She was careful to communicate not only the steps that she took that succeeded but also the ones that failed.

Miraculously, the team members erected the tent. When they had finished, the instructor told them to return to the original room. Only then could they take their blindfolds off. They quickly made it back. The instructor then allowed the teams to go look at their tents. The teams felt very proud of what they had accomplished.

Sara started to think about what she had learned from the experience that she could apply in real life.

The tent exercise is an adaptive learning exercise developed in part by Robert E. Quinn at the University of Michigan. We have conducted the exercise with hundreds of team members from many nationalities and all kinds of teams.

When conducting the exercise, it is essential to designate two members of each team as safety assistants. Their role is to ensure that no one is hurt. However, when the safety assistants see how pathetic their blindfolded colleagues look trying to erect the tent, they become sympathetic and want to help. The safety assistants must be told explicitly that they cannot help their team members complete the task.

A valuable part of the exercise is asking the teams to get to their workstations while blindfolded. As the teams plan their treks, a lot of adaptive learning occurs. Some teams never make it to their workspace. One team designated two team members to be human breadcrumbs. They positioned them at intervals along the path so that when the team was ready to return, the two members could call out to the others. Another team got to a large architectural column in the room and proceeded to circle it several times before the members realized what they were doing. They quickly appointed a new leader.

In completing this exercise, functions follow stereotypes. Manufacturing groups approach erecting the tent very technically. A marketing group from emerging economies finished in record time; working adaptively had become second nature to the members. Sales groups have the most rework. They change direction continually, to the detriment of creating any synergy that could lead to a breakthrough.

Part of the value of the exercise is that people can have fun while learning how to work in adaptive environments. Amazingly, most teams learn to erect their tents. You can videotape the teams and play the tape for them as a learning technique or just to have some fun.

The story of Sara and the tent exercise is a good illustration of working with the eight adaptive principles. Sara had to first get up on the balcony to understand the adaptive problem. Sara's blindfold made it easier for her to adopt a new point of view. She could not see the details unfolding and had to visualize the whole picture in her head.

Sara identified the adaptive challenge early in the process. She used a technical approach by asking whether anyone had ever erected a tent before. Once she did that, she realized that the rest of the exercise was adaptive and directed it in that way. She did not force a linear model of reasoning on the team. She allowed it to generate the answers and to experiment with ideas.

Sara had to regulate distress. First, she had to regulate her own distress. She believed that leaders should know where they are going and have all the answers. She learned that in adaptive environments, this is not the case. Once she managed her own distress, she turned to the team's. She knew that she had to let the members explore their boundaries and experiment before they could be productive. She listened, and when things became too stressful, she intervened.

When another team started cheering, Sara had to maintain disciplined attention with her team. Even though the facilitator did not set it up as a competition, to the members it felt competitive. She had to bring them back together and refocus them.

This exercise clearly shows how distributed intelligence comes together to solve adaptive problems. At the beginning, each member felt around on the floor and found one or two pieces of the tent. They had to bring the pieces together to build the tent.

The role of leadership changed in this exercise. Sara had to encourage others to take leadership roles at different times: the person experienced in building a tent and the person designated as the builder. However, Sara remained the overall leader. She enabled the team to succeed. She defined and redefined boundaries. She helped the team understand why it was important for every member to describe exactly what he or she had found. Virtual teams go through the same realization. They have to adopt new communication techniques and understand how to use them in the most efficient and productive manner.

Finally, Sara helped her team create a learning obligation. The team accepted that no one person had the answer. When some of the team members had successes, they shared them. They were also careful to share failures. In the tent exercise, as in adaptive virtual environments, communicating failures is as important as communicating successes.

Virtual Tent Experiences

The experience that Sara had was not virtual, but it was an adaptive challenge. Virtual teams who work on adaptive challenges and succeed are plentiful. Consequently, team members and leaders are becoming more familiar with working on adaptive, virtual teams. The lessons from adaptive problem solving are excellent foundations for anyone to learn, but they cannot replace repetition and experience.

Much of the work that we engage in on a daily or weekly basis is virtual, adaptive work. When the first edition of the book was published in 1999, we were on a global, virtual team that had a significant adaptive problem to solve. We were chartered to take a complex strategy and deduce it down to the simplest essence that could be taught to and adopted by twenty thousand employees. The adaptive nature of the problem centered on customizing the content for every job grouping in a fast and cost-effective manner.

Our virtual team spent nearly nine months working through how to do this. We created a discovery map, a game with a metaphor-based message that teams could complete in one hour. It was a very successful solution but a long and hard process to get there. We spent the first month trying to understand our charter—what we were supposed to be doing—and had many frustrating moments along the way. For a while, it seemed like we were in a negative learning loop, rehashing the same issues over and over and never progressing to the next stage

Five years later, we had a similar adaptive assignment, to take innovation tools and processes and instill to the individual level, again variable to the job and level. The virtual team that succeeded in developing the overall approach took much less time to get to a defined space and realized at every step that the vagueness and frustration we were feeling was normal.

This second team came up with a different but equally successful answer. This team's time to completion was less than half of the first team's, with less angst and rework involved. We are convinced that a lot of institutional learning on approaching adaptive problems with virtual teams had occurred in the intervening five years. As in the tent exercise, members on the second team acquired the skill to apply all eight principles of working in an adaptive environment.

Many virtual teams address adaptive problems, even if they do not call them that. There are increasing numbers of team members who have served on different types of virtual teams and have gathered or developed institutionalized knowledge about how to address adaptive problems. Mastering virtual teams requires a working knowledge of both virtual teams and adaptive challenges.

The Acausal World

In a world without causes, scientists are helpless. Their predictions become postdictions. Their equations become justifications; their logic, illogic. Scientists turn reckless and mutter like gamblers who cannot stop betting. Scientists are buffoons, not because they are rational but because the cosmos is irrational. Or perhaps it is not because the cosmos is irrational but because they are rational. Who can say which, in an acausal world? In this world, artists are joyous. Unpredictability is the life of their paintings, their music, their novels. They delight in events not forecasted, happenings without explanation, retrospective.[4]

Understanding adaptive environments is counterintuitive for most people. A causal, linear world changes to an acausal, chaotic one. As the time available to complete projects decreases, as complexity increases, and as environmental factors force teams into virtual space, both the art and science of adaptive work become important. People who succeed will be able to excel in virtual, adaptive worlds.

Points to Remember

1. Get on the balcony.
2. Identify the adaptive challenge.
3. Regulate distress.
4. Maintain disciplined attention.
5. Rely on distributed intelligence.
6. Encourage leadership by all members.
7. Encourage robust communication.
8. Create a learning obligation.

NOTES

Chapter One

1. J. B. Quinn, *Intelligent Enterprise: A Knowledge and Service Based Paradigm for Industry*. New York: Free Press, 1992.
2. D. J. Grimshaw and F.T.S. Kwok, "The Business Benefits of the Virtual Organization." In M. Igbaria and M. Tan (eds.), *The Virtual Workplace*. Hershey, Pa.: Idea Group, 1998.
3. Ibid.
4. Quoted in R. Pastore, "A Virtual Visionary," *CIO,* July 1993, p. 46.
5. M. Apgar IV, "The Alternative Workplace: Changing Where and How People Work." *Harvard Business Review,* May-June 1998, pp. 121–139.
6. Ibid.
7. G. O'Dwyer, A. Giser, and E. Lovett, "GroupWare and Reengineering: The Human Side of Change." In D. Coleman (ed.), *GroupWare: Collaborative Strategies for Corporate LANs and Intranets*. Upper Saddle River, N.J.: Prentice Hall, 1997.
8. C. Perey, "Desktop Videoconferencing." In Coleman, *GroupWare.*
9. Ibid.
10. Apgar, "Alternative Workplace."
11. Grimshaw and Kwok, "Business Benefits of the Virtual Organization."
12. Ibid.

Chapter Two

1. J. E. McGrath and A. B. Hollingshead, "Putting the 'Group' Back in Group Support Systems: Some Theoretical Issues About Dynamic Process in Groups with Technological Enhancements." In L. M. Jessup and J. S. Valacich (eds.), *Group Support Systems: New Perspectives.* Old Tappan, N.J.: Macmillan, 1993.

2. Ibid.

3. J. Short, E. Williams, and B. Christie, *The Social Psychology of Telecommunications.* London: Wiley, 1976.

4. F. Jabman and L. Sussman, "An Exploration of Communication and Productivity in Real Brainstorming Groups." *Human Communication Research,* 1978, *4,* 337; McGrath and Hollingshead, "Putting the 'Group' Back."

5. C. Egido, "Teleconferencing as a Technology to Support Collaborative Work: Its Possibilities and Limitations." In J. Galegher, R. E. Kraut, and C. Egido (eds.), *Intellectual Teamwork: Social and Technological Foundations of Cooperative Work.* Hillsdale, N.J.: Erlbaum, 1990.

6. R. L. Daft and R. H. Lengel, "Information Richness: A New Approach to Managerial and Organizational Design." *Research in Organizational Behavior,* 1986, *6,* 191–233.

7. McGrath and Hollingshead, "Putting the 'Group' Back."

8. Ibid.

9. M. S. Poole and M. H. Jackson, "Communication Theory and Group Support Systems." In Jessup and Valacich, *Group Support Systems;* R. E. Rice, "Computer Conferencing." In B. Dervin and M. J. Voight (eds.), *Progress in Communication Sciences.* Norwood, N.J.: Ablex, 1980.

10. Poole and Jackson, "Communication Theory"; H. A. Innis, *The Bias of Communication.* Toronto: University of Toronto Press, 1991.

11. S. Khoshafian and M. Buckwitz, *Introduction to GroupWare, Workflow, and Workgroup Computing.* New York: Wiley, 1995.

12. D. Coleman, "GroupWare: The Changing Environment." In Coleman, *GroupWare.*

13. Categories from ibid., augmented by us.

14. R. Quick, "Hi Is Yr Office Turning into a Chat Rm? Fone Me!!" *Wall Street Journal,* May 29, 1998, p. B1.

15. D. G. Vogel and J. F. Nunamaker Jr., "Design and Assessment of a Group Decision Support System." In Galegher, Kraut, and Egido, *Intellectual Teamwork;* D. Coleman, "The Evolution of Web-Based Conferencing and Workflow." In Coleman, *GroupWare.*

16. J. F. Nunamaker Jr., B. O. Briggs, D. D. Mittleman, D. G. Vogel, and P. A. Balthazard, "Lessons from a Dozen Years of Group Support Systems Research: A Discussion of Lab and Field Findings." *Journal of Management Information Systems,* Winter 1996–1997, pp. 163–207; J. F. Nunamaker Jr., B. O. Briggs, N. Romano Jr., and D. D. Mittleman, "The Virtual Office Work Space: GroupSystems Web and Case Studies." In Coleman, *GroupWare.*

17. Coleman, "Evolution of Web-Based Conferencing."

18. D. Blundell, "Collaborative Presentation Technologies: Meetings, Presentations, and Collaboration." In Coleman, *GroupWare.*

19. C. Perey, "Deploying Videoconferencing." In Coleman, *GroupWare.*

20. M. J. Abel, "Experiences in a Distributed Organization." In Galegher, Kraut, and Egido, *Intellectual Teamwork.*

21. Ibid.

22. Khoshafian and Buckwitz, *Introduction to GroupWare.*

23. C. Knudsen and D. Wellington, "Calendaring and Scheduling: Managing the Enterprise's Most Valuable Resource—Time." In Coleman, *GroupWare.*

24. P. Turner, S. Turner, S. Green, and P. Mayne, "Collaborative Notebooks for the Virtual Workplace." In Igbaria and Tan, *The Virtual Workplace.*

Chapter Three

1. G. Hofstede, *Culture's Consequences: International Differences in Work-Related Values.* Thousand Oaks, Calif.: Sage, 1980.

2. Ibid.; G. Hofstede, *Culture and Organizations: Software of the Mind.* New York: McGraw-Hill, 1991.

3. G. Hofstede and M. H. Bond, "The Confucius Connection: From Cultural Roots to Economic Growth." *Organization Dynamics,* 1988, *16*(3), 4–21.

4. E. T. Hall, *Beyond Culture.* New York: Doubleday/Anchor, 1976.

5. Ibid.

6. E. H. Schein, *Organizational Culture and Leadership.* (2nd ed.) San Francisco: Jossey-Bass, 1992, p. 12.

7. R. E. Quinn, *Beyond Rational Management: Mastering the Paradoxes and Competing Demands of High Performance.* San Francisco: Jossey-Bass, 1991; K. S. Cameron and R. E. Quinn, *Diagnosing and Changing Organizational Culture.* Boston: Addison-Wesley, 1999.

8. L. Copeland and L. Griggs, *Going International: How to Make Friends and Deal Effectively in the Global Marketplace.* New York: Random House, 1985.

9. Hofstede, *Culture's Consequences,* p. 273.

10. H. C. Triandis and R. W. Brislin, "Cross-Cultural Psychology." Paper presented at the annual convention of the American Psychological Association, Anaheim, Calif., 1993.

Chapter Four

1. Apgar, "Alternative Workplace."

2. A. Clark, C. Downing, and D. Coleman, "GroupWare at the Big Six Firms: How Successful Was It?" In Coleman, *GroupWare.*

3. R. T. Hightower, L. Sayeed, M. E. Warkentin, and R. McHaney, "Information Exchange in Virtual Work Groups." In Igbaria and Tan, *The Virtual Workplace.*

4. Nunamaker and others, "Lessons."

5. M. O'Hara-Devereaux and R. Johansen, *Globalwork: Bridging Distance, Culture, and Time.* San Francisco: Jossey-Bass, 1994.

6. Ibid.

7. C. Handy, "Trust and the Virtual Organization." *Harvard Business Review,* May-June 1995, pp. 40–50.

Chapter Five

1. M. Hayward, *Using the Web to Build Project Teams*. Santa Clara, Calif.: Project World Proceedings, 1997.
2. G. P. Landrow, "Hypertext and Collaborative Work." In Galegher, Kraut, and Egido, *Intellectual Teamwork;* A. H. Van de Ven and A. L. Delbecq, "Determinants of Coordinative Modes Within Organizations." *American Sociological Review,* April 1976, pp. 322–338; J. F. Nunamaker Jr., presentation to the NASA Shared Experience Conference, Hagerstown, Md., 1998.
3. Turner and others, "Collaborative Notebooks."
4. Ibid.
5. S. Reder and R. G. Schwab, "The Temporal Structure of Collaborative Activity." Paper presented at the Conference in Computer Supported Cooperative Work, October 7–10, 1990.
6. D. Ancona and D. Caldwell, "Bridging the Boundary: External Activity and Performance in Organizational Teams." *Administrative Science Quarterly,* 1992, *37,* 634–665.
7. Ibid.
8. Ibid.

Chapter Six

1. W. O. Anderson, "Human Resource Development Challenges in a Virtual Organization," and C. Henri-Amherd, Z. Su, and D. Pulin, "Towards a Better Human Resources Management Within the Virtual Corporation." In *IEMC Proceedings: Managing the Virtual Enterprise*. Vancouver, British Columbia: IEMC, 1996.

Chapter Seven

1. R. B. Shaw, *Trust in the Balance: Building Successful Organizations on Results, Integrity, and Concern*. San Francisco: Jossey-Bass, 1997.
2. Ibid.
3. Shaw, *Trust in the Balance*.
4. Ibid.
5. T. Finholt, L. Sproull, and S. Kiesler, "Communication and Performance in Ad Hoc Task Groups." In Galegher, Kraut, and Edigo, *Intellectual Teamwork*.
6. S. Kiesler and L. Sproull, "Group Decision Making and Communication Technology." *Group Decision Making,* 1992, *52*(special issue), 96–123.
7. Jarvenpaa and Leidner, "Organization."

Chapter Eight

1. Nunamaker and others, "Lessons."
2. Hightower and others, "Information Exchange."
3. Ibid.; Nunamaker and others, "Lessons."
4. J. Szerdy and M. McCall, "How to Facilitate Distributed Meetings Using EMS Tools." In Coleman, *GroupWare*.

5. Ibid.

6. Blundell, "Collaborative Presentation Technologies."

7. Hightower and others, "Information Exchange"; H. Lamm and G. Trommsdorff, "Groups Versus Individual Performance on Task Requiring Ideational Proficiency (Brainstorming): A Review." *European Journal of Social Psychology,* 1973, *3,* 267–387.

8. Blundell, "Collaborative Presentation Technologies."

9. D. J. Pauleen and P. Yoong, "Relationship Building and the Use of ICT in Boundary-Crossing Virtual Teams: A Facilitator's Perspective." *Journal of Information Technology,* 2001, *16,* 205–220.

10. L. Kimball and A. Eunice, "The Virtual Team: Strategies to Optimize Performance." *Health Forum Journal,* May-June 1999, p 58.

11. C. M. Solomon, "Managing Virtual Teams." *Workforce,* June 2001, p. 60.

12. S. P. Weisband, S. K. Schneider, and T. Connolly, "Computer-Mediated Communication and Social Information: Status Salience and Status Differences." *Academy of Management Journal,* 1995, *38,* 1124–1151; Nunamaker and others, "Lessons."

13. B.C.Y. Tan, R. T. Watson, and K. K. Wei, "National Culture and Group Support Systems: Filtering Communication to Dampen Power Differentials." *European Journal of Information Systems,* 1995, *4*(2), 82–92.

14. D. Gigone and R. Hastie, "The Common Knowledge Effect: Information Sharing and Group Judgment." *Journal of Personality and Social Psychology,* 1993, *65,* 959–974; D. C. Myers and H. Lamm, "The Group Polarization Phenomenon." *Psychological Bulletin,* 1985, *83,* 602–627.

15. Hightower and others, "Information Exchange."

16. R. T. Hightower and C. Hagmann, "Social Influences on Remote Group Interactions." *Journal of International Information Management,* 1995, *4,* 17–32.

17. R. T. Hightower and L. Sayeed, "The Impact of Computer-Mediated Communication Systems on Biased Group Discussion." *Computers in Human Behavior,* 1995, *11,* 33–44; J. E. McGrath and A. B. Hollingshead, *Groups Interacting with Technology: Ideas, Evidence, Issues, and an Agenda.* Thousand Oaks, Calif.: Sage, 1994.

18. Hightower and Sayeed, "Impact of Computer-Mediated Communication."

19. Hightower and others, "Information Exchange"; McGrath and Hollingshead, *Groups Interacting with Technology.*

20. Nunamaker and others, "Lessons."

21. S. B. Weisband, "Group Discussion and First Advocacy Effects in Computer-Mediated and Face-to-Face Decision-Making Groups." *Organizational Behavior and Human Decision-Making Processes,* 1992. *53,* 352–380.

22. Tan, Watson, and Wei, "National Culture and Group Support Systems."

23. Nunamaker and others, "Lessons."

24. Ibid.

25. M. Sharples, "Adding a Little Structure to Collaborative Writing." In D. Diaper and C. Sanger (eds.), *CSCW in Practice: An Introduction and Case Studies.* New York: Springer-Verlag, 1992.

26. Nunamaker and others, "Lessons."

27. Ibid.

28. Ibid.

29. Szerdy and McCall, "How to Facilitate Distributed Meetings."

30. R. E. Kraut, R. Fish, R. Root, and B. Chalfonte, "Information Communications in Organizations: Form, Function, and Technology." In R. M. Baecker (ed.), *Readings in Group-Ware and Computer-Supported Cooperative Work.* San Mateo, Calif.: Morgan Kaufman, 1993.

31. Nunamaker and others, "Lessons."

32. Hightower and others, "Information Exchange."

33. Nunamaker and others, "Lessons."
34. D. L. Ford Jr., A. Delbecq, and A. Van de Ven, "An Applied Group Problem-Solving Activity," and D. L. Ford Jr. and P. M. Nemiroff, "Applied Group Problem Solving: The Nominal Group Technique." In J. E. Jones and J. W. Pfeiffer (eds.), *The 1975 Annual Handbook for Group Facilitators.* San Francisco: Jossey-Bass/Pfeiffer, 1975; R. L. Bunning, "The Delphi Technique: A Projection Tool for Serious Inquiry." In J. E. Jones and J. W. Pfeiffer (eds.), *The 1979 Annual Handbook for Group Facilitators.* San Francisco: Jossey-Bass/Pfeiffer, 1979.

Chapter Nine

1. B. Tuckman, "Developmental Sequence in Small Groups. *Psychological Bulletin,* 1965, *63,* 384–399; B. Tuckman and M.A.C. Jensen, "Stages of Small Group Development Revisited." *Group and Organizational Studies,* 1977, *2,* 419–427.
2. J. E. McGrath, "Time Matters in Teams." In Galegher, Kraut, and Egido, *Intellectual Teamwork.*
3. Ibid.
4. Ibid.
5. C.J.G. Gersick, "Time and Transition in Work Teams: Toward a New Model of Group Development." *Academy of Management Journal,* 1988, *31,* 9–41.
6. P. Calderfer and K. K. Smith, "Studying Intergroup Relations Embedded in Organizations." *Administrative Science Quarterly,* 1982, *27,* 35–65.
7. K. K. Kraemer and A. Pinsonneault, "Technology and Groups: Assessment of the Empirical Research." In Galegher, Kraut, and Egido, *Intellectual Teamwork.*
8. Ibid.
9. C.J.G. Gersick and R. J. Hackman, "Habitual Routines in Task Performing Groups." *Organizational Behavior and Human Decision-Making Processes,* 1990, *47,* 65–97.
10. D. Dougherty, *Interpretive Barriers to Successful Product Innovation.* Cambridge, Mass.: Marketing Science Institute, 1989.
11. O'Hara-Devereaux and Johansen, *Globalwork.*
12. T. Connolly, "Behavioral Decision Theory and Group Support Systems." In Jessup and Valacich, *Group Support Systems;* A. R. Dennis and J. S. Valacich, "Computer Brainstorms: More Heads Are Better Than One." *Journal of Applied Psychology,* 1993, *78,* 531–537.
13. See J. R. Hackman (ed.), *Groups That Work (and Those That Don't): Creating Conditions for Effective Teamwork.* San Francisco: Jossey-Bass, 1990.
14. W. Bridges, *Transitions: Making Sense of Life's Changes.* Boston: Addison-Wesley, 1980.

Chapter Ten

1. A. Lightman, *Einstein's Dreams.* New York: Warner Books, 1993, p. 31.
2. R. A. Heifetz and D. L. Laurie, "The Work of Leadership." *Harvard Business Review,* January-February 1997, pp. 124–134.
3. J. C. Collins and J. I. Porras, "Building Your Company's Vision." *Harvard Business Review,* September-October 1996, pp. 63–79.
4. Lightman, *Einstein's Dreams,* pp. 40–41.

FURTHER READING

"Act Locally, Think Virtually." *BizEd,* Sept.-Oct. 2005, p. 50.

Alvesson, M. *Understanding Organizational Culture.* Thousand Oaks, Calif.: Sage, 2002.

Ancona, D. "X-Teams: Teams Get Extroverted." June 2005 [http://mitsloan.mit.edu/newsroom/news-briefs-0605-ancona.php].

Anderson, A. H., Carletta, J., and McEwan, R. "The Effects of Multimedia Communication Technology on Non-Collocated Teams: A Case Study." *Ergonomics,* August 2000, pp. 1237–1251.

Beyerlein, M., McGee, C., Klein, G., and Nemiro, J. (eds.). *The Collaborative Work Systems Field Book: Strategies, Tools, and Techniques.* San Francisco: Jossey-Bass/Pfeiffer, 2003.

Birkinshaw, J., and Gibson, C. *Building Ambidexterity in an Organization.* Boston: Harvard Business School Press, 2004.

Branson, D., Martin, L., Richards, L., and Thompson, S. D. "Assessing Critical Thinking and Problem Solving Using a Web-Based Curriculum for Students." *Internet and Higher Education,* June 2003, p. 185.

Cameron, K. S., and Quinn, R. E. *Diagnosing and Changing Organizational Culture Based on the Competing Values Framework.* San Francisco: Jossey-Bass, 2005.

Crossman, A., and Lee-Kelly, L. "Trust, Commitment, and Team Working: The Paradox of Virtual Organizations." *Global Networks,* Oct. 2004, pp. 375–390.

Emelo, R., and Francis, L. M. "Virtual Team Interaction." *T+D,* Oct. 2002, pp. 17–20.

Fisher, K., and Fisher, M. *The Distance Manager: A Hands-On Guide to Managing Off-Site Employees and Virtual Teams.* New York: McGraw-Hill, 2000.

Gibson, C., and Cohen, S. *Virtual Teams That Work: Creating Conditions for Virtual Team Effectiveness.* San Francisco: Jossey-Bass, 2003.

Hakkinen, P., Javela, S., and Leinonen, P. "Conceptualizing the Awareness of Collaboration: A Qualitative Study of a Global Virtual Team." *Journal of Collaborative Computing,* Aug. 2005, pp. 301–322.

Heifetz, R. A., and Linsky, M. *Leadership on the Line.* Boston: Harvard Business School Press, 2002.

Kaplan-Leiserson, E. "Virtual Work: It's Not Just for Members of the Jedi Council." *T+D,* Aug. 2005, pp. 12–13.

Katzenbach, J. R., and Smith, D. K. "The Discipline of Virtual Teams." *Leader to Leader,* Fall 2001, pp. 16–25.

Malone, T. W., Laubacher, R., and Scott Morton, M. S. *Inventing the Organizations of the 21st Century.* Cambridge, Mass.: MIT Press, 2003.

Prencipe, L. W. "Do You Know the Rules and Manners of an Effective Virtual Meeting?" *Infoworld,* Apr. 2001, p. 46.

Rosen, R., Digh, P., Singer, M., and Phillips, C. *Global Literacies: Lessons on Business Leadership and National Cultures.* New York: Simon & Schuster, 2000.

Sarker, S., Sarker, S., Nicholson, D. B., and Joshi, K. D. "Knowledge Transfer in Virtual Systems Development Teams: An Exploratory Study of Four Key Enablers." *IEEE Transactions on Professional Communication,* June 2005, pp. 201–218.

Seeley, C. P. "Setting Up Effective Knowledge-Sharing Teams." *Knowledge Management Review,* July-Aug. 2001, p. 5.

Solomon, C. M. "Managing Virtual Teams." *Workforce,* June 2001, pp. 60–65.

Thomas, D., and Inkson, K. *Cultural Intelligence: People Skills for Global Business.* San Francisco: Berrett-Koehler, 2004.

Tovey, J., Southard, S., and Bates, C. "Building Trust in Virtual Teams." *Technical Communication,* Feb. 2005, pp. 103–103.

Wilfred, D. H., and Van Velsor, E. "Issues and Observations: Changing the Conversation About Leadership." *Leadership in Action,* July-Aug. 2005, pp. 21–22.

Zweifel, T. D. *Culture Clash: Managing the Global High-Performance Team.* New York.: First Books, 2003.

INDEX

A

Abandonment of plans and agendas, 196

Acausal world, 224

Accountability: and communication plans, 114; definition of, variation in, 130; discussing the meaning of, importance of, 130; making changes in, to meet shifting task goals, 134; mapping, during orientation sessions, 105; negotiating, 77; of owners and facilitators, distinguishing between, importance of, 167; for the work of the team, 76, 218

Accounting culture, 64, *65*

Action teams: analyzing competence gaps in, *92, 142*; and building trust, 145; described, 7–8, *9*; matching technology to, 80; and sponsors, 96; as startup teams, 95

Actions and words, ensuring consistency between, as an element of trust, 147, *152*

Ad hoc meetings versus facilitated meetings, 165

Adaptability: balancing structure with, 87, 88; of team members, 134

Adaptation, encouraging, importance of, *13*, 17

Adaptive challenge, identifying the, principle of, *214*, 215–216, 222

Adaptive environments: and team dynamics, 187, 190, 198, 199; versus technical environments, 187, 212

Adaptive or technical problems, identifying, 215–216

Adaptive team leaders, actions of, 213–219

Adaptive work: and the acausal world, 224; defined, 219; principles of, 213–219, 222–223; simulated exercise in, 219–223; virtual experiences in, 223–224

Adhocracy culture, 63

Adjournment dynamics, 209–210

Advanced launch vehicle (ALV) virtual team, case study involving, 48, 50

Advocate role, 84

African countries, 58, 117

Agendas: abandonment of plans and, 196; for orientation sessions, 105–117; targeted, and maintaining disciplined attention, 217; for team member role assessment, *129*; for team processes, 119; for validation sessions, *101. See also* Meeting agendas

Agreements, new, on the ultimate team direction, 196

Air time, use of, 204

Ambassadorial behaviors, 112–113, 114, 128, 129

Ancillary team members, 100, 102

Annotating, 35

Anonymity, 161, 175, 176, 177, 180, 182, 199, 201

Answers, continual search for, 216, 217

Arab countries, 57

Argentina, 68

Asian countries, 58, 75, 117. *See also specific countries*

HOW TO USE THE ACCOMPANYING CD-ROM

System Requirements

PC with Microsoft Windows 98SE or later
Mac with Apple OS version 8.6 or later

Using the CD with Windows

To view the items located on the CD, follow these steps:

1. Insert the CD into your computer's CD-ROM drive.
2. A window appears with the following options:

   Contents: Allows you to view the files included on the CD-ROM.

   Software: Allows you to install useful software from the CD-ROM.

   Links: Displays a hyperlinked page of Web sites.

   Author: Displays a page with information about the author(s).

   Help: Displays a page with information on using the CD.

   Exit: Closes the interface window.

If you do not have autorun enabled, or if the autorun window does not appear, follow these steps to access the CD:

1. Click Start -> Run.
2. In the dialog box that appears, type d:<\\>start.exe, where d is the letter of your CD-ROM drive. This brings up the autorun window described in the preceding set of steps.
3. Choose the desired option from the menu. (See step 2 in the preceding list for a description of these options.)

Using the CD with a Mac

1. Insert the CD into your computer's CD-ROM drive.
2. The CD-ROM icon appears on your desktop; double-click the icon.
3. Double-click the Start icon.
4. A window appears with the following options:

    Contents: Allows you to view the files included on the CD-ROM.

    Software: Allows you to install useful software from the CD-ROM.

    Links: Displays a hyperlinked page of Web sites.

    Author: Displays a page with information about the author(s).

    Contact Us: Displays a page with information on contacting the publisher or author.

    Help: Displays a page with information on using the CD.

    Exit: Closes the interface window.

To Download Documents

The documents on this disk are Microsoft Word files. To download a document, first open it. For Windows users, under the File pull-down menu, choose Save As, and save the document to your hard drive. You can also click on your CD drive in Windows Explorer and select a document to copy to your hard drive.

In Case of Trouble

If you experience difficulty using the CD-ROM, please follow these steps:

1. Make sure your hardware and systems configurations conform to the system requirements noted under "System Requirements" above.
2. Review the installation procedure for your type of hardware and operating system.

It is possible to reinstall the software if necessary.

To speak with someone in Product Technical Support, call 800-762-2974 or 317-572-3994 M–F 8:30 a.m. – 5:00 p.m. EST. You can also get support and contact Product Technical Support at http://www.wiley.com/techsupport.

Before calling or writing, please have the following information available:

- Type of computer and operating system
- Any error messages displayed
- Complete description of the problem

It is best if you are sitting at your computer when making the call.

mastering
VIRTUAL
TEAMS

THIRD EDITION

STRATEGIES, TOOLS, AND TECHNIQUES THAT SUCCEED

Deborah L. Duarte
Nancy Tennant Snyder

JOSSEY-BASS
A Wiley Imprint
989 Market Street
San Francisco, CA 94103-1741

www.josseybass.com

See end of *Mastering Virtual Teams*
for CD-ROM information

CPSIA information can be obtained
at www.ICGtesting.com
Printed in the USA
BVHW020838070223
657577BV00032B/26

9 780787 982805